BLOODY KNIFE:
CUSTER'S FAVORITE SCOUT

Bloody Knife: Custer's Favorite Scout
By Ben Innis
Edited by Richard E. Collin
Revised Edition ©1994 by Smoky Water Press
P.O. Box 2322, Bismarck, ND 58502-2322 USA

Printed in the United States of America

1 2 3 4 5 6 7 8 9 10 11 12 13

ISBN 0-9644389-0-9
Library of Congress Catalog Card Number: 94-69457

Cover photo courtesy
Little Bighorn Battlefield National Monument

BLOODY KNIFE:
CUSTER'S FAVORITE SCOUT

BY BEN INNIS

EDITED BY RICHARD E. COLLIN

Smoky Water Press
Bismarck, North Dakota
USA

Contents

Maps

Introduction to Revised Edition

More than 20 years have passed since *Bloody Knife: Custer's Favorite Scout,* by the late Ben Innis, first appeared. To date, it remains the only full length biography of the Arikara scout who died at the Battle of the Little Bighorn in 1876.

The story of Bloody Knife is a remarkable one. The mixed blood son of an Arikara mother and Hunkpapa Sioux father, he symbolized the dilemma faced by many Native Americans in the 19th Century, as they struggled to remain true to their heritage, yet tried to accommodate the encroaching white man as well.

Brutally treated at the hands of the Hunkpapas while growing up in a camp with future war chief Gall, Bloody Knife ultimately allied himself with the white man, serving several tours of duty as a scout for the U.S. Army. It was in this capacity that he came to know and form a friendship with Lieutenant Colonel George A. Custer, the flamboyant field commander of the 7th Cavalry. Like the story of Custer, the story of Bloody Knife transcends the man and has come to symbolize the times in which both men thrived and died.

Born about 1840, he became a scout, mail carrier and runner for the white traders at Fort Berthold in the early 1860s. He began the first of his 11 hitches as an enlisted scout at Fort Stevenson in present day central North Dakota on May 1, 1868.

The next nine, mostly continuous, were served at Fort Buford near what is now Williston, North Dakota. There he was promoted to lance corporal in 1872.

In 1873, he was assigned to scout for General David S. Stanley's Yellowstone Expedition, which was undertaken to protect surveyors with the Northern Pacific Railroad. It was on this expedition that Custer came to know Bloody Knife. The Arikara scout served the 7th Cavalry so well during the campaign that Custer persuaded him to transfer to his own command at Fort Abraham Lincoln near Bismarck, Dakota Territory. On the Black Hills Expedition of 1874, he was one of the chief scouts, serving as Corporal of Indian Scouts. That was his final enlistment. Custer would hire him as a civilian scout and guide for the Bighorn-Yellowstone Expedition two years later against the recalcitrant Sioux, Cheyenne and Arapaho. It meant a big jump in pay for the Arikara warrior, from the $13 a year he had earned as an enlisted scout to $50 a year.

At the Battle of the Little Bighorn on June 25, 1876, Bloody Knife was shot in the head and killed as he sat on his horse near Major Marcus A. Reno during the fight at the southern end of the huge Indian village camped along the banks of the Little Bighorn River, Montana Territory.

Despite Hollywood's and television's best efforts to simplify, there was much confusion between the Indian and white cultures as they clashed in the 19th Century. Bloody Knife's decision to cast his lot with the U.S. Army is evidence of this struggle to maintain cultural identity, yet also do what was perceived as necessary in order to survive and triumph over the common enemy, the Sioux. This clash of cultural views surfaces again and again in *Bloody Knife: Custer's Favorite Scout*, as the whites' Old World and Christian perspectives play a fundamental role in forming their attitudes and actions toward the Indians.

In light of the increased cultural sensitivities that have evolved since the first publication of *Bloody Knife* in 1973, I have made some changes in the text of this revised edition. While they do not alter the fascinating story Ben Innis told of Bloody Knife and his times, they do represent a greater degree of sensitivity to the Indian point of view. I made these changes with great care, always keeping in mind the story that Ben was telling. Indeed, I found two other works by him to be most helpful in the preparation of this work. His *Sagas of the Smoky Water* is a rich resource for stories of the Yellowstone-Missouri Confluence Region from 1805-1910, and there were several occasions I pulled information from that book to complement this text.

He also compiled a 720-page manuscript, entitled *The Great Buffalo Country Dictionary, Calendar and Atlas of Historical Events from 1670-1971,* that proved most helpful in providing me with additional background for several of the events and people he writes about in *Bloody Knife.* This unpublished text is a remarkable achievement of research. Divided into several sections, it focuses on the fur trade and Plains Indians Wars and includes several maps Ben drew of the frontier West. I drew heavily from this manuscript when compiling the Appendix detailing the many battles, fights and skirmishes mentioned in this book.

Ben Innis was a prodigious researcher, and his detailed use of such sources as journals, letters and Government documents and publications help greatly in telling the story of Bloody Knife. It is a story that took Ben 12 years to compile, and, as he points out in his Preface, he originally did not plan to do a biography of Bloody Knife. It was a byproduct of his research to write the histories of Fort Union and Fort Buford.

This book is not so much a traditional biography that provides great detail about Bloody Knife as it is an accounting of his times and the people around him. This was noted by reviewers of the first edition, more than one expressing surprise there was enough information available about the Arikara warrior to justify a book-length study.

"A biography of Bloody Knife would seem to be a difficult assignment, and yet there are records of a long scouting career, beginning in 1865 with the Sully Expedition," wrote Don Russell, Custer scholar and author of the definitive biography of Buffalo Bill Cody, in a February 1974 review in the *Westerners Brand Book.* Russell noted that "the story is filled out with much detail about the Indian scouts, who were regularly enlisted after 1868 ... (the book) is an interesting addition to the vast Custer literature."

Ben wrote in his Preface that he constructed this biography "from the few bits and pieces of information available" about Bloody Knife, and he wove the careers of such characters as Gall, Frederick Gerard and Billy Jackson throughout the text to provide a better perspective of the Arikara scout. In an August 1972 correspondence, Innis pointed out that, in addition to telling what he knew of Bloody Knife's life, the book "contains much on the life of Indian scouts, frontier military posts, Bloody Knife's Indian and white contemporaries, and the military expeditions on the Northern Plains ..."

Bloody Knife was an intriguing frontier personality who had a knack for being at important places at important times, from the early days of Forts Stevenson, Buford and Lincoln to the last days of George Armstrong Custer. That quality makes his story much more than just an accounting of his own life -- it demands an accounting of other lives as well, and Ben Innis accomplished that with this work.

He tells a fascinating story of the Arikara warrior, in a style that brings to life Custer's favorite scout. His passages from such works as *William Jackson, Indian Scout,* by James Willard Schultz and Joseph Henry Taylor's *Frontier and Indian Life and Kaleidoscopic Lives* add a melodramatic flair to the narrative. His account of Reno's fight at the Little Bighorn is as gripping an account of that tragedy as any of the scores I have read. Ben brings you to the heart of that action, and does a fine job of providing the perspective of the Indian Scouts who were with Reno.

Ben had a flair for language, referring to whiskey as the "Great Father's Milk" and Fort Laramie as the white man's big "War House," to cite two examples in this book. I have not been able to substantiate these terms anywhere else; however, I chose to leave them in because they help define the writing style of the author.

A couple of words of note here — Ben refers to the Arikaras as Rees, and vice versa. Both references are to the same Indian nation. He also used the term "Dakota" in many of his references to the Sioux in the first edition. I have chosen to identify all bands of the Sioux nation simply as Sioux in this revised edition.

I have also added Sioux descriptions for the months that Ben listed in Arikara. This was done in recognition of Bloody Knife's Sioux heritage. I also vary slightly the Arikara and Sioux spellings of Bloody Knife from what appeared in the first edition. His Arikara version was *Nes I Ri Pat;* mine is *nee si RA pat.* The *RA* is capitalized because in the Arikara language capitalized letters are phonetically silent. Bloody Knife's name in Arikara is pronounced phonetically as "Nay-seer-bud." I take this new spelling from Melvina Everett, an Arikara elder and language expert with the Sahnish Culture Society of White Shield, North Dakota. The Sioux spelling in the first edition was *Tamena Way Way;* I have altered it slightly to *Tamina Wewe,* based on a translation given me by Dr. David Rood, professor of linguistics at the University of Colorado-Boulder and an expert in the Souian dialect.

Also added are several new photographs, including three of illustrations from a war robe owned by Bloody Knife. This was a special garment made of several bison hides sewn together and covered with drawings detailing his exploits. The robe presented 24 different battle scenes, similar in concept to the campaign ribbons and medals worn by servicemen and women worldwide. The robe is part of the ancient Plains Indian tradition of hide painting, from elaborately decorated tipis to beautifully decorated pouches and moccasins.

An amateur scientist, Philetus W. Norris, asked Bloody Knife in about 1875 if he could purchase the robe. Through an interpreter and fellow scout, Charley Reynolds, Bloody Knife refused to sell it, but did allow Norris to draw copies of the robe's illustrations. Most of the scenes show Bloody Knife fighting Sioux, Cheyenne or Crow warriors. Only one does not. It shows, according to Norris's notes, Bloody Knife in combat with a cavalry officer, the only white man Bloody Knife claimed to have killed. His motive was to gain revenge for the officer's alleged sexual liaison with She Owl, Bloody Knife's wife.

Norris went on to become the Superintendent of Yellowstone National Park and later worked for the Smithsonian Institution. What happened to the robe is uncertain. Norris believed the Sioux might have taken it in the aftermath of the Little Bighorn Fight, although there are no known records indicating that Bloody Knife had it with him that day.[1]

The drawings and Norris's handwritten notes of Bloody Knife's explanations of some of the illustrations have survived. The credit for their discovery in the Smithsonian's National Anthropological Archives belongs to Dr. J. Daniel Rogers, a curator of anthropology at the Smithsonian's National Museum of Natural History.

Other photographs not in the first edition include three of Bloody Knife in his Indian Scout uniform. They were taken by photographer William R. Pywell during the 1873 Yellowstone Expedition. There is an interesting story as to how these remarkable photographs came to be identified as those of Bloody Knife. Until 1981, one of them was believed to be that of a Coyotero Apache scout from the Wheeler Survey of the 1870s (the other two remained unidentified in a separate collection stored deep in the National Archives). In the summer of 1981, Jonathan Heller, a research specialist with the National Archives, visited E. Marshall Pywell, a descendent of William R. Pywell, at his home in Washington, D.C. The purpose of the visit was to examine photographs taken by William Pywell's brother-in-law, Timothy O'Sullivan, who had been a photographer on the Wheeler Survey, a government expedition which surveyed the Southwest territories from 1871-74. Among the photographs Heller saw were four identified as being from the Yellowstone Expedition, which O'Sullivan did not accompany. Heller recognized these four as also being part of a set of unidentified 84 stereo glass negatives that could not be matched with collections in either the National Archives or the Library of Congress. A search through War Department and U.S. Army Corps of Engineer files confirmed that the set of 84 negatives actually were taken by William R. Pywell on the Yellowstone Expedition of 1873. One of the four photographs showed an Indian scout kneeling with his rifle amidst a grove of trees. Following some additional photographic research, Heller positively identified this scout as Bloody Knife. The other two identifications of Bloody Knife photographs on that expedition quickly followed. These three photographs of Bloody Knife are included in this book.

Introduction to Revised Edition   vii

Also included are several photographs from the private collection of Chester E. Nelson, Jr., of Bismarck, North Dakota, a longtime highly respected fiscal analyst for the state. I am honored that he agreed to allow 16 of his photographs, many of them previously unpublished or rare, to appear in this edition. One of the five previously unpublished photographs shows Custer and Frederic Calhoun in 1875 wrapped in buffalo robes, with the sisters, Emma and Nellie Wadsworth, friends of the Custers. Custer tried to have Frederic Calhoun reassigned to the 7th Cavalry from the 14th Infantry in March 1876, but his request was denied. Calhoun left the Army as a first lieutenant in 1890, and died in 1904 at the age of 56. He was the younger brother of First Lieutenant James Calhoun, who died with Custer the year after this picture was taken.

Another of the previously unpublished photographs is that of Charles L. Gurley, a junior officer when he was assigned the onerous duty of notifying the widows at Fort Lincoln, including Libbie Custer, of their husbands deaths' at the Battle of the Little Bighorn.

The remaining three photographs previously unpublished are all mysterious. I have been unable to locate any information about the Arikara scout, Black Buffalo; the identification of the Mandan chief is based on a remarkably similar photograph taken by Stanley J. Morrow and included in *Frontier Photographer*, by Wesley R. Hurt and William E. Lass; and the Indian holding the revolver across his lap remains unidentified. These three photographs are among six included here from Chester Nelson that were found in one of Custer's footlockers stored in the attic of the Custer Family farmhouse, located about two miles west of Monroe, Michigan. Another photograph provided by Chet is a rare image of Custer, taken on January 2, 1865 when he was a brevet major general in the Civil War. It is an especially striking image of the "boy general," taken shortly after he turned 25. Another image from Nelson's collection included here adds a bit of levity to the photograph gallery. It shows the Wadsworth sisters, dressed in the uniforms of their boyfriends, William W. Cooke and Thomas W. Custer, saluting in mock seriousness. It is a wonderful glimpse of the lighter side of life at Fort Lincoln; on Emma's uniform are the two Congressional Medals of Honor Tom Custer won in the waning days of the Civil War. It is the highest military award for bravery bestowed by the Government, and Custer was the only soldier in that war to win *two* of them. He also is one of only five soldiers in the history of the United States to do so. It was a source of some jealousy on the part of his brother, George, who sometimes referred to them as "baubles." The two brothers perished together in battle 11 years after Tom was honored for his singular accomplishment.

Unfortunately, Ben Innis gives credence to one of the more outlandish myths surrounding the Battle of the Little Bighorn. He embraces the tale that Custer sought a big victory over the Indians in the summer of 1876 in order to capture the Democratic Presidential nomination. The Arikara scout, Red Star, is the sole source for this story. In 1912 he told Orin G. Libby, Secretary of the State Historical Society of North Dakota from 1905-45, that Custer had told him that a victory, no matter how small, would make him President. In such a case, said Red Star, Custer would take Bloody Knife with him to Washington. Libby reprinted the tale in *The Arikara Narrative of the Campaign Against the Hostile Dakotas, June 1876.*

The historical records show that Custer's name was never mentioned at the Democratic convention, or even floated by the national press as a dark horse candidate.[2] The convention which met in St. Louis June 27-29, 1876 nominated Governor Samuel J. Tilden of New York on the second ballot on June 28. Custer struck at the Little Bighorn the afternoon of June 25, but not before seriously considering waiting until the morning of June 26 to launch his attack. A fear that the Indians were fleeing forced his hand, not some notion that he should move up his timetable in order to get news of a victory over the telegraph wires to the convention in St. Louis. His initial inclination to strike on the morning of the 26th is hardly the action of a man anxious to get word of a victory to delegates in enough time to create the needed momentum to secure a presidential nomination.

Noted frontier historian Robert M. Utley offers a more reasonable explanation of what drove Custer so hard that last summer of his life. In his 1988 classic *Cavalier in Buckskin: George Armstrong Custer and the Western Military Frontier*, Utley speculates that it was more plausible, given reasonable expectations and Custer's natural ambition, that what Custer was really after was the star of a brigadier general. In the summer of 1876, the Democrats were in a very strong position to retake the White House after eight years of a scandal-scarred Republican Administration under Ulysses S. Grant. Custer had many friends in Democratic circles, and certainly made no effort to conceal his political affiliations with that party. Utley, in *Cavalier in Buckskin*, offers this passage from a letter written in April 1876 by longtime Custer friend Lieutenant Colonel James Forsyth to Secretary of War William Belknap to indicate what was really on Custer's mind: "The fact of the matter is that both Hazen (Colonel William B., commander of Fort Buford) and Custer are now working to make capital with the Democratic Party — they want stars."[3]

Innis was certainly not the first historian to entertain the notion that Custer was striving to become the 19th President of the United States. Others, from David Humphreys Miller in *Custer's Fall* to Mari Sandoz in *The Battle of the Little Bighorn* have done likewise. You still hear the talk today. It *is* a wonderful tale, but that is all it is.

I will not attempt to refight the Battle of the Little Bighorn here, tempting as it might be for this 30-year student of the event. Suffice it to say that any judgement of how Custer performed that bloody Sunday 120 years ago must be made on the basis of what he knew that day, and not what was known later.

He was certainly foolish not to have reconnoitered the huge Indian village his scouts warned was ahead of him. He is also open to criticism for dividing his small regiment into four columns, without knowing the size of the warrior force he was about to engage in battle. However, this questionable strategy had paid off handsomely for Custer eight years earlier, when he won a headline-grabbing victory over the Southern Cheyenne at the Battle of the Washita in what is now western Oklahoma. Why not try it again?

The strategy was based on the assumption that the Indians would flee instead of stand their ground and fight. Indeed, Custer thought that was happening when his scouts reported some warriors fleeing as the 7th Cavalry approached their village. To avoid the humiliation in professional Army circles, as well as before the general public, that would have come if he allowed the large Indian village to slip away, Custer changed his planned time of attack from dawn of June 26 — the time of day he had attacked at the Washita — to mid-afternoon on the 25th. It was a fatal miscalculation.

One of Custer's fellow officers who deserves much criticism for his conduct during the 1876 campaign against the Sioux, yet has largely escaped it, is General George Crook. His 1200-man army fought many of the same warriors eight days earlier, in a clash along the banks of the Rosebud, only 40 miles south of where Custer fell. Crook was part of the same military expedition as Custer, searching for those Indians who had refused to come into the reservations. Yet he did nothing to inform Custer or the campaign's other commanding officers that he had met the Indians in battle. He claimed afterwards that he was unable to get couriers through because of the size of the Indian force in front of him. This failure to provide Custer and the others robbed them of the crucial intelligence that, unlike so often in the past, the Indians were now standing and fighting, using tactics much like a regular army.

Had Custer known this, perhaps his strategy, based on the notion that the Indians were fleeing, would have been quite different as he approached the massive village, with an estimated population of 12-15,000 Indians, camped three miles along the banks of the Little Bighorn. By withdrawing from the field of operations after the Rosebud Fight until early August 1876, Crook inalterably changed the outcome of the campaign. His withdrawal removed a major threat to the Sioux, Cheyenne and Arapaho alliance, allowing them to turn their full fury against Custer's 7th Cavalry. Had Crook continued to push north with his large command, as part of the planned pincer movement against the Indian confederacy, events involving Custer and the rest of the military expedition would certainly have played out much differently.

I first met Ben Innis in the fall of 1982, when I began working as news director at KGCX Radio in Williston, North Dakota. Ben was my counterpart at Williston's KEYZ Radio. His deep love of the history of the Old West, particularly the Yellowstone-Missouri Confluence region, was infectious. I often listened to him, fascinated, as he weaved the history-rich stories of the trans-Mississippi West in that magnificent baritone voice of his. Even the business card he distributed, replete with an image of a peace pipe, was indicative of the man's enthusiasm for history. It read: *Sitting Bull Trading Post, Ben Innis, Bourgeois, Historical Publications and Collectibles, Lodge: 601 First Avenue East, Williston, Dakota Territory.*

We met at a time when the sun was setting on his career, while mine, as a 27-year-old, was still in its early phase. Over the next two and half years, I visited Ben many times in his home, always coming away excited about the rich resource material he was quick to share.

There was something uniquely remarkable about the man. He had a way of bringing the history he so loved back to life, to make it move and breathe for the listener. It was no small talent, and this contagious enthusiasm helps in large measure to explain his influence on the writers and researchers who remember him fondly to this day.

This love for living history led Ben to found the Fort Buford 6th Infantry Regiment Association in 1962. He led the Indian Wars re-enactment unit, as the official North Dakota delegation designated by Governor William Guy, to the New York World's Fair in 1964. He later organized the Fort Union-Fort Buford Council, and led successful efforts to place Fort Union Trading Post in the National Park System in 1966.

The Fort Buford 6th Infantry continues to play a vital role in the living history movement of the Northern Plains. More than 32 years after its founding by Ben, the group remains active in its promotion of the military post that stood near the confluence of the Yellowstone and Missouri rivers from 1866 to 1895, two miles downstream from the abandoned fur trading post, Fort Union.

Ben's enthusiasm was contagious about the need to reconstruct Fort Union so contemporary visitors could appreciate what had stood at the Confluence from 1829 to 1867. "Fort Union is the only place in the West which can fully and correctly interpret the meaning of the Western fur trade to American expansion," he said in 1977 while serving as President of the Fort Union-Fort Buford Council. "There's nothing like it within a thousand miles. The only other two national sites where major rivers meet as a confluence have already vanished into urbanism — the meeting of the Alleghany and Monongahela rivers, where they form the Ohio River at Pittsburgh, and the junction of the Minnesota and Mississippi rivers at St. Paul-Minneapolis. Let's not let that happen here." He certainly did not. His efforts and the efforts of many other dedicated supporters over several struggling years eventually led to the reconstruction of the post. Tens of thousands of tourists each year now visit the restored National Historic Site 25 miles southwest of Williston, North Dakota. Many of them also stop at Fort Buford, which has also undergone a series of improvements in recent years under the management of the State Historical Society of North Dakota.

Shortly before he died in April 1985, Ben told me he would give anything to be able to stand in the courtyard of a reconstructed Fort Union in order to gain a sense of what it must have been like for those who had been there 150 years before. When the dedication of the reconstructed fort took place in August 1989, many of us attending took time to remember Ben and the major role he had played in helping bring that day about.

As this book again enters the marketplace 21 years after its initial appearance, those of us who had the privilege of knowing and working with Ben carry a deep sense of satisfaction in sharing with a new generation of frontier history students, as well as those already familiar with the subject, a fascinating and complex chapter in Native American history.

Despite the many barriers still existing, the past 20 years have been significant in many ways in fostering a new respect between Native Americans and their fellow citizens. By telling this story again, and with it the cultural conflict Bloody Knife experienced, I hope in a humble way to move this encouraging development even further along.

The story of Bloody Knife is the story of a Native American who performed admirably, even heroically, in his chosen profession while remaining true to his heritage. It was a remarkable achievement by a fascinating and formidable warrior of the Old West.

Richard E. Collin
November 1, 1994
Bismarck, North Dakota

Notes

1. J. Daniel Rogers, "Bloody Knife's Last Stand," *Natural History,* June 1992, pp. 39-42.
2. Paul Andrew Hutton, edited by, *The Custer Reader.* University of Nebraska Press, 1992, p. 236.
3. Robert M. Utley, *Cavalier in Buckskin: George Armstrong Custer and the Western Military Frontier.* University of Oklahoma Press, 1988, p. 164.

Richard E. Collin was born in Minneapolis, Minnesota in 1955. He lived in LaPorte, Texas from 1960-61 before moving to the Washington, D.C. suburb of Hillcrest Heights, Maryland. He earned a bachelor of arts degree in American history from the University of Maryland at College Park in 1977, a diploma from the Brown Institute of Radio and Television Broadcasting in Minneapolis in 1982 and a master of science degree in Space Studies from the University of North Dakota at Grand Forks in 1991. He has been Communications Director for Governor Edward T. Schafer of North Dakota since November 1993.

Collin worked as a radio news reporter and media relations coordinator for 10 years in North Dakota, at stations KGCX and KEYZ in Williston and KFYR in Bismarck, and at the University of North Dakota's Energy and Environmental Research Center in Grand Forks.

In the 1980s, he was active in the successful efforts to restore Fort Union Trading Post National Historic Site near Williston. He was chairman of the Friends of Fort Union in 1985-86 and a member of the Fort Buford 6th Infantry Regiment Association, a U.S. Army re-enactment unit of the 1870s that promotes the history of the Missouri-Yellowstone Confluence region.

He lived in Stillwater, Oklahoma, in the early 1990s, where he worked as coordinating producer for the National Aeronautics and Space Administration's education videoconference series, "Update for Teachers," broadcast live from Oklahoma State University.

A U.S. Army veteran, Collin was stationed in Erlangen, West Germany from 1979-81, serving as a telecommunications specialist with an armored brigade. He also worked as a reporter with the New Ulm Daily Journal in Minnesota.

Collin is married to Andrea Winkjer Collin, a native of Williston, North Dakota. They have twin daughters, Sonja and Elizabeth, who are four years old.

Acknowledgments

Working on this revised edition of *Bloody Knife: Custer's Favorite Scout* was a labor of love, pure and simple. I was able to pursue my passionate interest in the history of the Old West, as well as revive an important work by a talented biographer and old friend.

Many individuals and organizations were extremely helpful in making this edition a reality. First and foremost, I am most grateful to the widow of Ben Innis. Without the support and encouragement of Jane, this republication of *Bloody Knife* could not have taken place.

I also want to thank the following for their many services and kindnesses: the Sahnish Culture Society of White Shield, North Dakota, for taking the time to meet with us this summer and for their ensuing valuable contributions to the text. Organized in 1992, this group deserves great credit for its preservation and promotion of the Arikara history and heritage. I want to specifically thank those who attended the meeting in White Shield on July 30, 1994 that marked the beginning of our work together on this edition: Greta White Calfe, Melvina Everett, Yvonne Fox, Elaine Incognito, Lena Malnourie, Rhoda Star, and Dorreen Yellow Bird. A special thanks goes to Dorreen Yellow Bird for her insightful suggestions and inspiring Preface to this revised edition, as well as allowing the use of a photograph of a discharge paper of the Arikara scout, Sioux Stand. Deborah Painte, Executive Director of the North Dakota Indian Affairs Commission, also a member of the Sahnish Culture Society, was helpful throughout with my many questions about Bloody Knife and the Arikara culture.

Chester E. Nelson, Jr., Bismarck, North Dakota, was most gracious with his photographic contributions, as well as his perceptive advice, all of it most appreciated by this kindred spirit. Other thanks go to the State Historical Society of North Dakota, Bismarck, including Walt Bailey for his early guidance on how to approach this project, and Todd Strand for his extraordinary help in accommodating my numerous requests and inquiries regarding photographs; the staff of the Smithsonian Institution's National Anthropological Archives, Washington, D.C., for their aid in cutting through the federal bureaucracy to secure the images from Bloody Knife's war robe that appear in this book; Dr. J. Daniel Rogers, a curator of anthropology at the Smithsonian's National Museum of Natural History, Washington, D.C., for his suggestions and help in making these war robe illustrations part of this book; the National Archives Still Picture Branch, College Park, Maryland, especially Ouida Brown, who gracefully and patiently fielded my many telephone calls designed to speed up delivery of the three remarkable Bloody Knife photographs from the 1873 Yellowstone Expedition that appear here, and Jonathan Heller, who explained in fascinating detail how he determined one of these three photographs had been misidentified as that of an Apache scout from the Wheeler Survey of the same era, a determination that quickly led to the correct identification of the other two photographs as well; Staff members John A. Doerner, Douglas C. McChristian and Kitty Deernose of the Little Bighorn Battlefield National Monument, Crow Agency, Montana — John for his help in informing me about these three Bloody Knife photographs, as well as his overall cooperation throughout; Doug for his discussion of where the remains of Bloody Knife might be located; and to Kitty, an extra thanks for the quick turnaround and patience with my many requests and questions involving photographs from the impressive Battlefield archives.

I owe a special debt of gratitude to Paul L. Hedren, Superintendent of Fort Union Trading Post, Williston, North Dakota, who I have known as a friend and respected as an author since 1984, for his perceptive suggestions on how to enhance the text, his enthusiastic support of this republication effort, and his donation of the photograph of Lieutenant Mott Hooton. Others who have also helped include Paul A. Hutton with the University of New Mexico at Albuquerque and Robert M. Utley of Moose, Wyoming, frontier historians *extraordinaire,* whose encouragement of this effort, as well as inspiration over the years, helped me forge ahead with this project; my good friend and retired Oklahoma State University speech professor Fred Kolch, Stillwater, Oklahoma, who shares with me a love of history, especially the Civil War era; Stephen Schilling, a history and political science instructor at the University of Mary, Bismarck, for his review and proofreading of the text; Dr. David Rood, professor of linguistics at the University of Colorado at Boulder, who provided a Sioux translation for the months of the year, based on the 1992 calendar published by St. Joseph's Indian School in Chamberlain, South Dakota; Pastor Robert Nordvall, Charity Lutheran Church, Bismarck, North Dakota, for inspiring me with God's words, as well as his own; Kevin Cramer, Director, North Dakota Department of Tourism, Bismarck, for his steady support and encouragement; Don Schwarck, South Lyon, Michigan, editor of the Little Big Horn Associates newsletter, who helped provide background information for some of the photographs, as well as earned my everlasting gratitude for his aid above and beyond the call of duty; Michael J. Koury, whose Old Army Press published the 1973 edition of *Bloody Knife* and who was most cooperative in this republication effort; Robert Barr, Mandan, grandson of Orin G. Libby and a longtime member of the Old Scouts Society who showed Chester Nelson the break-through photograph from the Smithsonian's Bureau of Ethnology that provided the positive identification for the photograph of the Arikara scout, Black Buffalo, that appears here; and the Fort Buford 6th Infantry Regiment Association and Fort Union Muzzleloaders, for preserving the heritage of these two posts at the confluence of the mighty Yellowstone and Missouri rivers through their active promotional efforts and willingness to literally travel the extra mile to achieve that end.

Finally, I want to give special thanks to the various mem-bers of my family: J.B. "Cub" Lyon, Jr., Williston, North Dakota, for his many kindnesses over the years in giving me numerous books and other items relating to the history of the Old West; Betty and Dean Winkjer, Williston, North Dakota -- Betty was always there for us with a helping hand, and Dean's work as Ben's lawyer on the original edition, as well as this republication, was most generous and helpful — I am indeed fortunate to call them my mother- and father-in-law; my brother, Thomas J. Collin, Cleveland, Ohio, for his ability to always provide the quality legal advice we sought, as well as his encouragement to see this project through; my other siblings, Carol A. Kendrick, Columbia, Maryland, Mary L. McCormack, Arlington, Texas, and Daniel D. Collin, Windom, Minnesota, who, like brother Tom, have always stood behind me, providing invaluable support and advice over the many years as I have traveled the interesting road that brought me to this project; and my parents, Genevieve and Everett E. Collin, Windom, Minnesota, a remarkable couple whose strength and wisdom are a source of great inspiration to their five children. An extra bow to my mother, for combing the Cottonwood County Library for valuable information on the last clash of the Indian Wars, the Battle of Sugar Point, near Leech Lake, Minnesota in October 1898.

Most of all, credit for the achievement of this revised edition of *Bloody Knife* belongs to my wife, Andrea. Her unique combination of wisdom, grace, kindness and tenacity provided the inspirational fuel that I needed to begin and complete this work. More than once, when I was certain we would not have the time, energy or resources to meet our deadlines, Andrea counseled otherwise. Our twin daughters, Sonja and Elizabeth, deserve special praise for being as patient as three-year-olds can be with their parents during these past several months. Yes, girls, there is life after *Bloody Knife,* and your mother and father look forward to sharing more of it with you!

Preface to Revised Edition

Bloody Knife was the uncle of my great grandfather, Little Sioux. Both of these Sahnish (Arikara) men fought in the Battle of the Little Bighorn, lived at Like-A-Fishhook Village, and were scouts for the United States military.

This book about Bloody Knife, written by Ben Innis, is now revised and edited for republication. I was asked to write a Preface to it because of my relationship to Bloody Knife and because I am currently working on a history of the Sahnish people.

It is with a sense of awe that I write of Bloody Knife and the Sahnish people, perhaps because the haunting spirit of these people watch over my shoulder.

This revision of *Bloody Knife: Custer's Favorite Scout* is in itself historical because many writers of history are blind to anything but that written in historic journals or documents. They rarely ask for the perspective or listen to the oral history of the people about whom they write. I say this because I have read materials written by contemporary writers that have twisted historic information so that it bends the truth.

When Rick and Andrea Collin decided to edit Ben Innis's book on Bloody Knife, they contacted the people from the White Shield, North Dakota area and the Sahnish Culture Society to provide insight and another perspective on the lives of our people.

In the initial printing, Innis wove such a narrow theme that, in some of the cases, his point appeared to be an obsession. He projected his perspectives, religious beliefs, and philosophy into a distorted picture of the Sahnish people and Bloody Knife. For example, in most of the first edition of the book, Innis referred to Indian people as savages and portrayed them as soulless creatures. The Collins have edited the book to something more palatable and truthful.

The Collins arduously searched the Smithsonian and other historical institutions, as well as through dusty records of the tribe for additional information. They also found new photographs that they added to the book.

One of the photographs the Collins included in this book continues to haunt me. The photograph, taken at Fort Lincoln in 1875, shows Bloody Knife standing hard against a post, an Indian blanket pulled tightly around him. He is visibly removed and isolated from George Armstrong Custer, Custer's wife, Libbie, and other military officers, who are casually seated on stairs in front of a house in this picture. So foreign and so cold is the environment to this warrior that the photograph cries out alienation and pain.

This photograph evokes a universal image of the pain of all Indian people as they began the metamorphoses into the white culture. These are people and lifestyles so foreign to the Indian that their struggle is evident even in this old picture. This alienation of the Indian people is evident in this book.

The Sahnish nation, at one time, was so large and fearsome that when the bands moved they left a broad swath and a storm of dust. It is said that other tribes moved out of their way when they moved across the prairie. These were a proud and fierce people whose ceremonial powers were well known by many of the tribes of the Upper Missouri. Even the white men who saw their powers acknowledged it but could not understand it. They could only describe these ceremonies as "magic or sleight of hand."

At first contact, many tribes openly welcomed the white men and accepted their trinkets and gifts as symbols of friendship. However, this relationship between Indians and whites gradually deteriorated, turning the white nations into greedy landlords and the tribes into scattered defenders of their homeland. The Sahnish nation is one of a few tribes with little written about them because they were so openly hostile to the whites.

The result of the volatile relationship between the Sahnish and the white men caused the whites to blame raids, attacks, and killings on the Sahnish. Many of the incidents, however, were attributable to them. The Sahnish returned hate with a vengeance, trying to wipe all white men from their homeland. They had a reputation for being the most hostile tribe in the Upper Missouri River area. George Catlin, who recorded the history of tribal nations with his water colors and brush, only viewed the Sahnish from a boat in the middle of the Missouri. He was afraid, as were most explorers, to come ashore for fear of the Sahnish.

The Sahnish were Davids against a gluttonous Goliath who would soon consume them. However, the greed for the land of the Indian nations was insignificant when compared to the devastation wreaked by the smallpox virus. The Sahnish were struck by wave after wave of diseases, including cholera, measles and tuberculosis, for which they had no immunity.

The most devastating was smallpox. When it infected the Indians, it nearly destroyed whole tribes. Historic journals tell of the vast numbers of bodies of dying and dead people that covered the prairies. Villages were silenced, with only the frail wailing of women and last cries of children heard as they succumbed to the horrid disease. The virus cut into their numbers, killing band after band until only three villages of the once powerful Sahnish nation were left. Ceremonies, governments and their strength dwindled, as the disease ate into the very heart and soul of the people.

It was during this time (the middle 1800s) that the Sahnish were most at risk. They were living near the Hidatsa (Gros Ventres) and the few remaining Mandans. These three tribes agreed to live together for mutual protection against marauding tribes. These marauders had escaped most of the devastation of the virus and began to attack these now vulnerable tribes, stealing their food, horses and trade goods.

To make matters worse, the treaties that the Sahnish signed with the Government took away their weapons. The Government, in turn, promised to provide food, protection and a chance to once again grow crops and hunt in peace. However, the agents of the Government stole the food from the mouths of the people. Many children and women starved under the very protection of the white men with whom they signed peace treaties.

It is this time of great stress that I see in my dreams. I see the Sahnish warriors and leaders weeping for their people. For as much skill as these brave men possessed, they could do little to protect their people.

It was also during this era that the military recruited scouts from among the Sahnish, Mandan, and Hidatsa. The Sahnish readily enlisted. This offer from the Government gave the Sahnish an opportunity for the freedom to hunt and move out into the prairie without fear of being attacked and killed by other tribes. The majority of the Indian scouts recruited from Fort Berthold by the Government came from the Sahnish, rightly so because the Sahnish had a reputation for being fierce warriors even at that time. Bloody Knife was not unlike many of the Sahnish warriors, or Ree Scouts, as they were commonly referred to during that time. The majority of the Ree scouts were, however, more distant to the white military.

Bloody Knife was of Sahnish and Lakota Sioux blood, but he claimed his Sahnish blood. Innis implied his "savage nature" was something he learned or inherited from his Sioux heritage. Untrue; his nature was a deeply protective one and in character with his Sahnish people. He lived among his people where death was a constant companion, his nature reflecting a world so extremely hostile that in order to survive, he had to maintain superior warrior skills. And so he did. Bloody Knife saw his brothers viciously murdered and mutilated by other tribes. He felt the bind and chaff of the reservation that put him in a walless jail, with no access to free living, and he longed for freedom.

Bloody Knife studied, learned, and became very skilled in the military world that George Armstrong Custer admired. Custer was the leader of the 7th Cavalry, the military unit for which Bloody Knife provided scouting services. Bloody Knife's hunting skills were particularly exemplified when the Army needed to take extra wagons along to bring back all the game he brought down. A photograph of Custer crouching near a large grizzly bear, claiming it as his kill also depicts Bloody Knife kneeling beside the downed animal. Of course, the kill was Bloody Knife's, but he gave Custer the honor.

Custer knew and understood the skills of "his favorite scout." He saw Bloody Knife as a man with finely honed warrior skills, and he found himself befriending the man. It is noted in sources that Custer would send Bloody Knife into a camp and he would single-handedly subdue it. Custer and Bloody Knife had a special bond, each respected the skills of the other. Bloody Knife was the Rambo of his time. This fictional Hollywood character of the 1980s, portrayed by Sylvester Stallone, is admired for his killing skills and considered a hero. Yet this same kind of skill is interpreted by Innis in his original edition of this book as savagery.

Custer's and Bloody Knife's careers ended at Greasy Grass in Montana Territory on June 25, 1876 during the Battle of the Little Bighorn. Bloody Knife knew by prophecy he would die in that battle and he accepted his death, a death that was the result of the miscalculations of his leader and friend, George Armstrong Custer.

This infamous battle has been the subject of countless books, journals and articles because the military strategies of the Sioux made an arrogant military stop and take notice.

Unfortunately, the battle did little to keep back the waves of white people and only angered the Government, who gathered more military troops that poured into Dakota Territory and forced the Sioux onto reservations.

The Ree scouts who survived the battle returned home to Like-A-Fishhook Village, where their lives began to change. The Battle of the Little Bighorn was the event that marked the beginning of the assimilation by the whites which would change the lives of Indian people forever.

The Sahnish people honor Bloody Knife and the Ree scouts who fought at the Battle of the Little Bighorn. They honor them with songs and dances on Memorial Day each year, but they also honor Custer with a song, because as the words of the song indicate, he was a brave and respected man -- albeit foolhardy.

It is told by the Sahnish that a horse returned to Like-A-Fishhook Village from the Battle of the Little Bighorn. It is thought by the people that the horse belonged to Bobtailed Bull, one of the Ree scouts who died in the battle. The people believe the horse was the embodied spirits of the brave men who died at Greasy Grass, and it came home to tell of those brave deeds.

Dorreen Yellow Bird
Medicine Rattler Woman
October 31, 1994
Grand Forks, North Dakota

Dorreen Yellow Bird is from the Three Affiliated Tribes in central North Dakota, and is currently development director for the Center for American Indian Legal Programs and Resources at the University of North Dakota in Grand Forks. She holds a bachelor of arts degree in education from Western Oregon State College and a master of education degree from Oregon State University.

She was a manager for the Siletz tribes in Oregon, and a national program coordinator for the National Health Screening Council and the National Congress of American Indians in Washington, D.C. In 1984, she returned home to Fort Berthold to manage the tribal radio station, KMHA. In 1989, she added a tribal newspaper, The Mandan, Hidatsa, Arickara Times, to the tribes' communications enterprise.

She is active in the Sahnish Culture Society, which is dedicated to promoting and maintaining the history and heritage of the Arikara people.

Her family includes two daughters, one son and three grandchildren.

Preface

Bloody Knife. A resounding name. A name which inspires fear. A name ringing with full, round tones that fill the ear and mind, a name which conjures nightmarish visions.

Regardless of all the years he spent among the whites, Bloody Knife never lost the basic instinct of survival characteristic of his people. He knew how to work with those with enough power to benefit him, yet he always returned full value for their efforts on his behalf. Among his white acquaintances there were few, if any, complaints about his honesty, his efficiency, or his trustworthiness. A brash, bold brevet major general of cavalry, George Armstrong Custer, called him his favorite scout. His Arikara relatives were still quite reticent about him as late as 1912, which makes it rather difficult to assess the Rees' opinion of their famous fellow tribesman.

Nevertheless, from the few bits and pieces of information and reports available, a heretofore relatively obscure Bloody Knife emerges as quite a man, one whom a western frontier, replete with the brave, the great, the cowardly, the odd, the strange and the terrible, should welcome and enfold as one of its own.

****

The idea of some sort of a publication on Bloody Knife began several years ago in the process of transcribing microfilmed records at Fort Buford, Dakota Territory, from the National Archives, in preparation for histories of Fort Union and Fort Buford. The Buford records contained rather frequent references to the Indian scout. Not necessarily being a Custer buff, I marked the passages for later study. However, a later conversation with Michael J. Koury, Editor of The Old Army Press, convinced me that the story should be done now. So, in a sense, this biography of Bloody Knife is a by-product.

I believe the Arikara history is a necessary part of the narrative; some of the reasons why Bloody Knife decided to throw in his lot with the white man should be apparent, given the history. The same principle applies to the Indian scout background at the military posts. The careers of Gall, Frederick F. Gerard and Billy Jackson are lightly interwoven with the same idea in mind — to keep the story of Bloody Knife in perspective.

No attempt has been made to interpret any of the battles or campaigns or their affects on United States history. Others have covered the subject thoroughly. In most cases, only the portions of the incidents in which Bloody Knife was involved are related.

Much of the official correspondence is reproduced verbatim in its entirety simply because I thoroughly enjoy the odd turns of phrase those people came up with a hundred years ago.

There are no informational footnotes, just references. I dislike the interruption of a narrative when I am reading, so every effort was made to provide explanations within the text. Amateur's license was taken only in punctuation in the speech and in the writings of the characters used. No word changes were made.

Some clarifications are necessary:

● Since the American Fur Company was almost universally known by that name during all of its history, I have not seen fit to change the allusion to it with every change of ownership and management.

● There is a question whether the incident of the mutilation of the young Sioux warrior at Fort Buford took place in 1869 or 1870. I have chosen to adopt Joseph Henry Taylor's date of 1869.

● The same problem appeared in a couple of minor incidents involving Gall. I have been arbitrary in choosing the date which seemed more reasonable.

● Civilians in those days were referred to as "citizens."

● An asterisk indicates that the preceding parentheses are mine.

● The Indian interpretations of the months of the year are Arikara.

● It is argued in some historical circles that casualty figures of the Indian Wars are suspect. I have printed what I found, for what they are worth.

● Then we come to the Hidatsas. Actually, they were better known as the Gros Ventres, or Minetarees, by the fur traders and the military. These were the people classified by the fur trade as the Gros Ventres of the Missouri. Perhaps my use of the term, "Hidatsa," is just a wishful attempt at effecting an educational revolution.

● It will be seen that the Sioux were bent on wiping out some of the small Missouri River tribes.

****

A first fling at a publication has been most rewarding for this amateur. The simplest appeal for help and information brought immediate cooperation in every case. These are the people and places who aid unselfishly in making the job of a researcher so much easier, not necessarily listed in order of importance of their contributions: the Nebraska Historical Society; Donald F. Danker of Washburn University; the South Dakota State Historical Society; Ray H. Mattison, Historical Consultant; Michael J. Koury, Editor, The Old Army Press, for editing the book; Cynthia Schaff, Librarian, James Memorial Library, Williston, North Dakota; William Howard, Williston businessman, for the use of personal articles; Williston attorney, Arley R. Bjella, for the unrestricted use of his private library and papers; J.B. Lyon, Jr., of Williston, for the gifts of books and articles; Boyd Nelson, Williston, for the gifts of books; Frank Vyzralek and Liess Vantine, research and archive friends at the State Historical Society of North Dakota; Elmer O. Parker, a correspondent of long standing at the National Archives in Washington, D.C.; and Dr. John S. Gray, Wilmette, Illinois, Indian Scout researcher extraordinaire. What would I have done without him!

Ben H. Innis
January 1972
Williston, North Dakota

For Janie

> *Chapter 1* ◄

The Heritage
of Bloody Knife

Every man is the sum of the people who have gone before him. From the North American Native nations which we call the Arikaras and the Sioux came a warrior named Bloody Knife. The history of his father's people, the Sioux, has been extensively documented, but now in order to understand the character of this man — *nee si RA pat,* as he was called by the Arikaras, or *Tamina Wewe,* as he was known by the Sioux — we must also know the history of his mother's people, the Arikaras.

****

Striking boldly northward into a vast unknown from their base at the French settlements on the Mississippi in the winter of 1738-39, the Mallet brothers, Peter and Paul, were probably the first white men to visit the Arikara villages, at that time located in the country above the Niobrara River in what is now northern Nebraska. The brothers were searching for furs. The Arikaras — or Rees, as they were also commonly known — were of Caddoan linguistic stock, the most northerly situated of that Indian family.[1] They were permanent earth lodge village people and agriculturists; their towns were fortified with stockades of upright log pickets fronted with moats, surrounded by their crudely cultivated fields of beans, corn, pumpkins, squashes and tobacco.[2] At first, they were friendly to most white men. Sensing they were in country unfrequented by white men, the brothers Mallet took the opportunity to name the Platte River. By early spring, they were in Santa Fe.

Papa Verendrye, or Pierre Gaultier de Varennes Sieur de la Verendrye, of Fort La Reine, Manitoba, Canada was too sick in the year 1742 to follow up his 1738 expedition into what is now North Dakota, so he sent sons Francois and Louis in his stead.[3] As a fur trader governed by Montreal financial power and the French competitor to the British-held Hudson's Bay Company, La Verendrye was anxious to expand into the untouched beaver country to the south before the English got to it. After wandering southwestward almost to the Rockies, then bearing to the east where the historically-oriented sons buried their lead plate near present-day Pierre, South Dakota, the young men returned in July 1743. They were able to tell their father that, among other new nations, they had met the Arikaras and that those Indians already had horses.

Like the Mandans he had seen in 1738, Les Ris, or "the Rees" in French, lived in earth lodge villages, engaged in the rite of the Sun Dance and other ceremonies, and were traders of a sort. Middlemen, or wholesalers, would actually be a better description of their status. They were pottery makers and they were hunters, with each family owning in addition to its home lodge, a buffalo hide tipi for use when the tribes took to the Plains for their semi-annual buffalo hunts. And they were fighters. The fighting spirit of their warriors and their numbers enabled them to hold their own among the violent nations of the Great Plains. They were not much inclined to trapping as a means of income for themselves, reported the dutiful sons. But their trading contacts with some of the Teton

Sioux, the Cheyennes and other more southerly Indians, such as the Arapahoes, Kiowas and Comanches, made them good people to know and do business with. From the Indian viewpoint, Les Ris lived well and enjoyed the trade goods which passed through their hands.

Their earth lodges were large, inverted bowl-shaped dwellings that resembled great mounds rising out of the ground. They were built of timber and willow thatch, covered overall with a foot or so of dirt, and measured 30 to 60 feet in diameter and up to 18 feet high, with a hole in the roof for smoke to escape.

Interiors were divided into apartments by robes or skins hung from the ceiling. Cool in summer and comfortable in the winter, the lodges were an architectural masterpiece. An average of 10 people, usually members of two or more related families, lived in each lodge. In good weather, the men of the villages sat around on the roofs of their houses, smoking and talking, while the women worked in the fields or at their household tasks.

They called themselves Sahnish. Sioux and Cheyennes, with whom they were seasonally friendly, called them Corn Eaters. The Mandans came closest to their true origin by addressing them as Panis, but it was the Pawnees who gave them the name that stuck — Arikaras, or Antlers, or Horns, referring to an old custom of forming their hair around two pieces of bone to stand erect on the head like horns.[4]

La Verendrye died in 1749. By that time, he was in disfavor at Montreal, so his ambitions and recommendations were buried with him.

About 1770, later French traders, now operating under the British flag, established themselves among the Rees when the tribes had relocated at a site on the Missouri below the mouth of the Cheyenne River.[5] Trading proceeded on a mutually profitable basis until 1781, when tragedy struck. Smallpox killed off so many Arikaras that their power for sustained warfare was permanently broken. Afterward, they were no longer a deterrent to the expansion of the Sioux.

Until the smallpox epidemic, the Arikaras had been uniformly friendly to whites. They knew the source of the horrible disease was white men, and they blamed them for it. But it was not until 1793, when Joseph Garreau arrived to live with them, then treated them with violence and dishonesty, that the seeds of hatred were sown. A year earlier, they had allowed the French trader, Jacques d'Eglise, to pass their villages on his way to the Mandans.[6] In 1793, they stopped him. Besides the sickness and mistreatment they had endured, white traders were encroaching on their trading territory.

The next year, they moved north to the vicinity of the Mandans and Hidatsas, where they were joined by trader Jean Baptiste Truteau.[7] Truteau found himself undersold by his combined hosts and competitors and could not compete with them. Another trader, John Evans, on his way to the Mandans in 1796, was stopped and forced to leave most of his goods with the Rees, being allowed to proceed with only a small part of his outfit. Trading may not have been that important to Evans. A Welshman, he was looking for the legendary Welsh Indians and he was sure he would find them in the Mandans. That was another dream of discovery that died hard.[8]

Truteau wrote that the Rees, at first friendly and gentle, had turned against whites because of bad treatment and disease. They told him that three smallpox epidemics before 1795 had reduced the number of their villages from 32 to three, and that they could currently muster at the most 500 fighting men. However, they still enjoyed the economic role of important middlemen in the Plains trading pattern, selling their agricultural products and horses to the Sioux and Cheyennes in exchange for dried meat, skins, guns and ammunition. Intermarriages with the Sioux were fairly common. But much of the time, when the tribes were not trading, they were at war with each other.

Human nature being what it is, the Indian was no better and no worse than the white man. His social structure centered on warfare. One way in which an Indian male could advance in his tribe socially, politically and materially was through success on the warpath. With few exceptions, Indians did not consider or attempt alliances to drive out their common enemy, the white man, but continued to fight among themselves, even though faced with this most dangerous threat to their way of life in their history.

Meanwhile, another white man's curse, venereal disease, had reached them, and it was widespread. The French termed it, "King's Evil."

In 1799, they returned to a site near the mouth of the Grand River in present day northwestern South Dakota, which was a better trading location, even though the stronger Teton Sioux were now bullying and exploiting them. Crows and Cheyennes brought them mules, horses, meat, furs, women captives and leather goods for their corn, beans and tobacco. The horses, corn and beans the Rees traded to the Tetons, the dominant Sioux paying for the merchandise in any amount they chose to give. Trading middlemen of a sort themselves, the Sioux were ambitious to take over that portion of the Great Plains trade enjoyed by the Rees, and they were attempting to force the weaker nation into trading through them.

Thus far the Arikaras, unlike other Indians, had not succumbed to liquor. This circumstance surprised Lewis and Clark, who got to their towns on October 8, 1804.[9] Clark described the people as " ... Durtey, pore & extravigent," probably because they treated the explorers very well, in contrast to their tormenting of Canadian trader Pierre Tabeau, who had come among them in the preceding May. Lewis thought they were " ... the best looking, most cleanly, most friendly and industrious Indians I saw anywhere on the voyage." The leaders estimated the population of the three towns at 2600.

An unforeseen incident contributed heavily toward the Ree distrust of white men. Lewis and Clark had arranged for the Arikara chief, Ankedoucharo, to visit Washington, D.C., leaving his country for the east with an interpreter in the spring of 1805. Unfortunately, the chief died in Washington in April 1806. The news of his death did not reach the tribes until a year later, after the exploration party had passed their villages on the return down river trip. Naturally, the white men were scapegoats for Ankedoucharo's death. It was the beginning of real Ree hostility toward whites, strengthened perhaps by the British, who were pressing strongly from the north. In 1807, they did let Manuel Lisa pass after they fired in front of his keelboat and stopped him with every intention of robbing him of his goods and killing his men. The unshakeable Lisa understood Indians. He smoked with them and listened to their grievances, then at an opportune moment showed them his cannon and his armed men zeroed in on their village. He was allowed to proceed unmolested onward to the Yellowstone River.

Outright war now opened on the Upper Missouri with all the fur trading companies, both English and American, currying favor with each of the Indian nations, setting them to robbing and killing their white competitors and to fighting each other. In the midst of the confusion, a military escort of 95 whites, under the command of Ensign Nathaniel Pryor, attempted to pass and was attacked on September 9, 1807. Pryor, formerly a sergeant with Lewis and Clark, was on his way to the Mandan country to return

Shahaka, a Mandan chief, to his people after a visit to Washington. The Rees, already at war with the Mandans and others, killed four of the escort and wounded 10, sending the survivors fleeing downriver.[10] Lewis and Clark had taken Shahaka to St. Louis with them on their way home in 1806, from where he had traveled east to visit the Great Father. It would be another two years before he got home.

By now, British influence was strong in the upper country, and it was disturbing to the Indians caught in the vise of appeasement between two separate white nationalities. Here and there an expatriate white man or mixed blood made his lot with the Indians. Thus it was that Alexander Henry, visiting the Arikaras in 1809, discovered in their midst a riverman by the name of Edward Rose, who would become well known throughout the region for his scouting and trading skills.

The same year, the U.S. government contracted with Lisa's Missouri Fur Company to again attempt to return Shahaka to the Mandans. The fee was to be $7000 in cash, plus a pledge that no other American trading licenses would be issued for the region north of the Platte River. Lisa and Pierre Chouteau set out upriver in 10 boats, carrying 160 men. The appearance of this strong force before the Arikara villages on September 12 alarmed the Indians, who protested that the 1807 ambush was a misunderstanding. Unperturbed, Lisa distributed presents and whiskey, which the Rees accepted, but whether for trading stock or personal use was not clear. Mollified, they dropped the price of their robes and agreed to allow a small trading post to be established there.[11] The important thing was that they were at peace with the Mandans, and Shahaka was delivered home safely within a few days. When the expedition returned, though, the Rees proved unpredictable, blaming the Americans for the killing of some of their tribesmen, who had actually been killed by the Sioux.

The International Naturalistic Year was in 1811, or so it seemed on the Upper Missouri. Two Englishmen, Henry Brackenridge and Thomas Nuttall, and a Scotsman, John Bradbury, found their way into the Indian Country with Lisa's fur brigade and Wilson Price Hunt's overland Astorians.[12] There the visiting naturalists explored, dug, shot, picked, collected, pruned, sketched and wrote of their findings. Unpredictably, the Rees were friendly. Lisa again left a trading outfit there and the Astorians purchased horses. Hunt met Edward Rose and hired the mixed blood as guide, interpreter and hunter.

As weak as the Arikaras had grown through a series of disastrous wars and diseases, by 1812 they were still holding a precarious balance of power with the Sioux by means of their continued status of trading middlemen. This provided the stronger nation with goods it could not get elsewhere. They strongly protested when Lisa moved his trading post 12 miles from their towns. They wanted the post near them in order to get white traders' goods to sell to other tribes. The move meant that Lisa would be in competition with them. Together with the efforts of the Sioux to unseat them in their merchandising operations, the pressure was steadily increasing.

By 1813, they were definitely hostile, and moreover, were joined in their resistance to the encroaching white Americans by the Sioux and Mandans. Lisa was forced out of his trading house at Fort Manuel. They remained violent and hostile for the next decade, robbing traders and trading posts and killing traders wherever they found them, with the exception of Edward Rose. After leaving the Astorians and living for a period with the Crows, he was back with his friends, the Arikaras. In 1822, they drove James Kipp out of a Columbia Fur Company post on the Knife River.

Kipp sought and got sanctuary with the Mandans.

Again living up to their reputation for unpredictability, the Rees welcomed William Ashley when that fur trader's brigade arrived at their towns on September 8, 1822. Quite peaceably, they traded with him for horses, and Ashley left for the mouth of the Yellowstone.

► *Chapter 2* ◄

The Arikara War of 1823

The year 1823 is entered in the Cranbrook Dakota Winter Count as The Year a Large Quantity of Corn was Captured.[13] Although they lost their village too, the corn was a small enough price to pay for the damage the Rees did to the American fur trade and the expense and trouble they caused the U.S. Army. On the first day of June, the second Ashley-Henry party, on its way up the Missouri, encamped at the main Arikara village to rest and trade. Some of the men pitched camp on a strip of sandy beach; others slept aboard their boat. At first light, the Rees greeted the trappers with a blast of gunfire and a shower of arrows.[14] In the brief fight that followed, before the brigade could regroup and retreat, 14 of the 90 whites were killed and 10 wounded against a possible Indian loss of eight warriors. Then the attackers appropriated most of the company's goods, property and horses. It had not gone unnoticed by the Rees that Edward Rose, who had left them recently, was now with the white men.

Stunned and furious, Ashley fled downstream to the mouth of the Teton, from where he sent frantic expresses for help, one to Major Benjamin O'Fallon, Indian Agent at Council Bluffs, and another to Colonel Henry Leavenworth at Fort Atkinson.

Leavenworth responded by moving north on June 22, 1823 with six companies of the 6th U.S. Infantry, forming the nucleus for an army which grew more motley as it beat its way northward. At points upriver, it was joined by Joshua Pilcher and 60 men of the Missouri Fur Company, hardheaded competitors but eager to aid against the common foe. Ashley's survivors were picked up and about 750 vengeful Sioux came along in the hope of a great victory, many coups, many horses, many scalps. Leavenworth saw fit to bestow a label upon his oddly assorted command — the Missouri Legion. At the same time, he loosely issued quasi-official commissions to the leaders of the trapping brigades and to some of their men, including an appointment as ensign to Edward Rose.

At dawn on August 9, the Army attacked the main Arikara village, with the Sioux doing most of the actual fighting in the open, away from the town, losing two killed and seven wounded to the 10 or 15 Rees dead. When the troops and trappers eventually were ordered to advance, the defenders broke and retreated behind their stockade. The next morning, Leavenworth opened with artillery fire. His first round killed the chief, Grey Eyes. After a sustained pounding, which caused little damage, the Rees sued for peace and Leavenworth granted it.[15] They told him that 30 of their people had been killed. Two soldiers were wounded.

A peace treaty was negotiated on August 11. However, the wary Rees abandoned their villages the following night. The 750-odd Sioux warriors, disgusted with the ineptitude of American troops, raided the village cornfields, then carried off corn by the bushel and struck out for their camps. Ashley and Pilcher, especially Pilcher, were incensed with Leavenworth's failure to destroy the village. The two traders felt that large numbers of the Rees should have been killed as punishment and to teach them a lesson. They found it impossible to be civil to the colonel. Bitter, recriminating letters were exchanged for months on the debacle. However, as the Army was leaving on August 15, the town was seen to be burning. The rumor that Pilcher's men were the arsonists was most likely true.

As a result of the Arikara War, as it was henceforth called, American prestige sank to an all-time low among the Indians of the Upper Missouri. It would not be regained for decades.

In the months following the fight, the Arikaras scattered in different directions, some as far south as the Platte country, where they killed and scalped trappers with impunity. Andrew Henry, leading the Ashley-Henry remnants overland to the Yellowstone, lost six more men in two scrapes with Indians that he strongly suspected were Rees. Even more important to the fur trade, the great highway of the Missouri was abandoned to the Indians for years, Ashley turning to the much safer overland route.

The campaign as a whole, though, was invaluable experience for men who were about to become the backbone of the American fur trade — men like Louis Vasquez, Jim Bridger, Bill Sublette, Hugh Glass, Edward Rose, Tom Fitzpatrick, Jedediah Smith and many more. The Arikaras gained the distinction of being the objective of the first campaign of the United States Army against a Plains Indian nation.

Chapter 3

The Rees in Transition

The Rees did not rest. Several weeks later, they killed a party of trappers near the Mandan villages, then continued to harass any whites in the country.

It was July 1825, the month the Arikara call the Hot Middle Moon, and the Sioux call Moon of the Red Choke Cherries, when General Henry Atkinson and Indian Agent O'Fallon landed their Yellowstone Expedition flotilla of nine keelboats and 500 men at the Rees' new home area in an abandoned Mandan village in present day North Dakota.[16] Edward Rose was the whites' interpreter. There was no trouble. For three days, the peace commissioners counciled and made treaties with their hosts and with a band of Hunkpapa Sioux, temporarily friendly while trading. They passed out presents to the Sioux with a lavish hand, but reprimanded the Rees for their conduct in 1823 by cutting them off with only a few hundred carrots of tobacco. Not that the slight made any difference. The Rees continued to attack travelers. As far as results with them were concerned, the expedition's cost of $20,000 was a complete loss.

During the next few years, most of the small Arikara tribes wandered from the Missouri into the central and western Plains, taking a toll of whites as they moved, their great trading center gone, their usefulness as middlemen usurped by white traders. Slowly, over a period of years, they gravitated back toward the upper country. In 1830, a Mandan sub-agent wrote that they had killed about 30 whites on the Missouri alone in seven years and that " ... nothing but a good and sound flogging can or will put a stop to their murder and robberies ..." On one occasion, three traders were murdered and then robbed of their outfit by Arikaras who smoked with them and professed friendship. A short time afterward, they plundered the goods of a party transporting Fort Union material for Kenneth McKenzie.

In the spring of 1831, the American Fur Company's James Kipp established Fort Clark eight miles below the mouth of the Knife River on the Missouri for the Mandan, Hidatsa and Arikara trade.[17] The Rees traded for the things the white men had taught them they could not do without. The arrival of the first steamboat, the *Yellow Stone*, in the summer of 1832, frightened them until they were shown it would not harm them. Artist George Catlin painted portraits of members of the three tribes, along with members of a visiting band of Crows.

In the dead of that winter, Indian moccasin telegraph brought news from out of the west, long before white men knew of it, that was pleasing to tell around the lodge fires. Edward Rose — known to them as Five Scalps because he once killed five Blackfeet warriors in a fight — Hugh Glass, and a companero had been caught out on the ice of the frozen Yellowstone near Fort Cass in faraway Montana Territory by one of their own war parties and had been killed and scalped.[18] They had almost killed Glass several times before, and as for Five Scalps, he was considered a traitor for accompanying the soldiers in 1823 and 1825. They were now rid of two of their old enemies. Portions of the scalps of the three slain trappers were left decorating poles stuck into the riverbank at the scene of the killings, the mutilated bodies left to freeze.

By 1833, in spite of their pitifully inadequate warrior force, the Arikaras were estranged from most other tribes, including the Hidatsas and Mandans, who were friendly to the whites, and the Sioux, who opposed them all.

Meanwhile, the Arikaras continued to make war on the hated whites. Their war parties were constantly depredating on the Plains to the west and south. This circumstance caused Nathaniel Wyeth, when he heard of it, to change his route to the States from the previously safe overland route to the water journey by way of the Yellowstone and Missouri. When Alexander Philip Maximilian, Prince of Wied-Neuwied of Germany, passed their villages near the mouth of the Grand River in the middle of June 1833, he noted that they were abandoned.

Maximilian retraced his trail in the early part of November as far as Fort Clark, where he wintered and made studies of the neighboring tribes.[19] There, he narrowly escaped death from scurvy. He wrote, "The Arikaras are tall, robust, well-made men, some of them nearly six feet ... in height ... their women are said to be the handsomest on the Missouri, but also the most licentious." Of their warlike demeanor he wrote, "No tribe has killed so many white men as the Arikaras." Like many other travelers, the Prince specifically mentioned the expert sleight of hand magic tricks performed by the sorcerers of the tribe. And he was another white man who noted that the Rees did not seem to care for liquor.

For a brief period, the Rees lived in the Black Hills, then again trekked northward to visit the Mandans and Hidatsas.

► *Chapter 4* ◄

Smallpox Disaster

Tragic decimation struck all of the nations of the Upper Missouri shortly after the Arikaras moved their 250 lodges into an abandoned village and built new dwellings near Fort Clark in April 1837. In June, the deadliest cargo ever to enter the Indian Country was unloaded onto the tribes gathered at the fort by passengers aboard the white man's Fire Canoe, the steamboat, *St. Peter's*. Smallpox had returned, the dreaded disease of the white man, and again the Indians were completely helpless before it. The sickness swept the Plains, raging all through the summer and into the autumn. Countless thousands of Indians and numerous white men and mixed bloods died. Most of the dead were left unburied.

Fear of the disease was so great nobody wanted to touch the dead. Despair was everywhere. Many Indians committed suicide. Artist George Catlin said the methods of self-destruction were many:

> They destroyed themselves with their knives, with their guns, and by dashing their brains out by leaping headforemost from a 30-foot ledge of rocks in front of their village.[20]

Some tribes scattered their people in all directions in an

effort to escape; some went into hiding. But the Rees remained huddled in their village, not knowing whether to brave the open country and the ever watchful Sioux or to let the smallpox run its course. By September 30, Francois Chardon at Fort Clark estimated that half of the Arikaras and Hidatsas were dead and that the Mandans had lost seven-eighths of their number.[21]

A witness noted:

> Many of the handsome Arikaras who had recovered, seeing the disfiguration of their features, committed suicide; some by throwing themselves from rocks, others by stabbing and shooting. The prairie had become a graveyard; its wild flowers bloom over the sepulchres of Indians.

Quite properly, the whites were blamed for the ravages of the disease. If there was any thought of redress in the minds of the Indians, it was postponed until families, tribes and nations could dare to gather, count and mourn their dead and attempt to re-establish their blood lines.

The damage to the fur trade approached ruin. Few of the Indians working at gathering furs were left. In fact, few Indians were to be found anywhere near a white establishment. Most of the Indian agencies quit operating early in 1838 and were not re-opened until 1842. And over the whole country, the smell of death lay like a pall.

The Commissioner of Indian Affairs reported that of the six Missouri River tribes most affected by the smallpox epidemic, at least 17,200 died. Those tribes were the Mandans, Arikaras, Hidatsas, Sioux, Assiniboins and Blackfeet. This number is guesswork at best, with the total derived from information provided by traders and Indian agents. There was no census of the tribes.[22]

The epidemic greatly weakened most tribes and broke forever the power of the Mandans, Hidatsas and Arikaras. In contrast, the Sioux, who did not suffer such terrible losses, were stronger than ever. Never again did the Plains and Mountain tribes approach their pre-epidemic populations. When the military conquest of the West took place, it was not the prolonged holocaust it would have been if it had been undertaken two or three decades earlier.

On March 20, 1838, a few bands of the Arikaras quietly took over the old, abandoned Mandan village near Fort Clark and built new lodges, where they at least had the protection of the traders they had so despised in the past. They were to live there until 1861.

****

An interesting speculation arises out of an entry in Chardon's *Journal at Fort Clark* in February 1835, where an account is listed under the name of an Arikara by the name of Bloody Knife.[23] Four years later, in January and May 1839, Chardon is again visited by the Ree. Since it was Indian custom to pass respected family names down through generations, it would be worth a guess that the man may have been an uncle of the future Indian scout. Because his father was Sioux and his mother an Arikara, it could be the only relationship possible, other than the chance that he was named for a close family friend, or that the identical names are a case of sheer coincidence.

➤ *Chapter 5* ◄

Bloody Knife and Gall: The Early Years

Somewhere in the Dakotas in the 1830s, an Indian rite of marriage took place between a Hunkpapa Sioux warrior and an Arikara woman.

Bloody Knife, born about 1840 in a Sioux village somewhere in Dakota Territory, was one of at least four children — three sons and a daughter — born to the couple. Although historically enemies, marriages between the Sioux and Arikaras did occur, usually in a time of peace. Most likely it was during such a time that Bloody Knife's parents were married.[24] He would be known by the Arikara as *nee si RA pat* and the Sioux as *Tamina Wewe*. Some sources state that he was related to Sitting Bull. Be that as it may, in future years Bloody Knife would pay a terrible price at the hands of the Sioux for his mixed ancestry. He was the product of two divergent Indian cultures — one, the warrior and hunter class, the other, warrior turning agriculturist and tradesman, both interrupted by the degrading influence of the white man.

In approximately the same year in present day South Dakota, near a waterway now known as the Moreau River, another child was born. His existence would exert a profound influence on the life of Bloody Knife. Gall, or *Pizi*, as the new arrival was to be called by his Hunkpapa people, lost his father at an early age. It was then that Sitting Bull came forward and adopted the fatherless boy as his younger brother. Under the tutelage of the war chief and medicine man, Gall was to pursue a bright future.

A strong possibility exists that the two boys were born in the same camp since, as the youngsters grew older, they became acquaintances. The paths of *nee si RA pat* and *Pizi* were to cross frequently with unfortunate consequences for both.

Not long after the smallpox epidemic subsided, the remnants of the utterly defenseless Mandans joined the powerless Hidatsas. In 1844, the united tribes settled at a bend on the east bank of the Missouri, just below the mouth of the Little Missouri River, where they established a permanent Indian town to be called Like-A-Fishhook Village, from the appearance of the river bend at the site.[25] The next spring, at the urgent request of those tribes, the American Fur Company moved its trading post from Fort Clark to the neighborhood of the town, where the traders, with the assistance of Indian women, built Fort Berthold.[26] Left without a trader, the Arikaras protested so loudly and vigorously that Fort Clark was soon reopened for their convenience, although their trade was not considered as worth much.

Superintendent of Indian Affairs Thomas A. Harvey reported to the Commissioner of Indian Affairs in September 1846 that the Arikaras had measles, another curse of the white man, and that there were many deaths. He warned that they were still treacherous and still ridiculing the prowess of American troops in the Arikara War of 1823.[27]

In 1847, the Upper Missouri Indian Agent, G.C. Matlock, undertook an estimated census of the tribes under his charge. He reported the Arikara population at 1800 people; the regional Sioux at 19,960; at Like-A-Fishhook Village, there were 1350 Hidatsas, and just 350 Mandans.[28] His unsolicited opinion was that the Arikaras were far better Indians than their reputation warranted, better by far than the Blackfeet and Assiniboins. His report echoed rather hollowly, however, in July 1848, when some Rees, defiant even in their weakness, fired into the American Fur Company steamboat, *Martha,* below Fort Berthold, killing a man.[29]

The year 1849 brought a new trader to Fort Clark, Frederick F. Gerard, who was destined to spend more than 40 years on the Upper Missouri.[30] A Frenchman, born in St. Louis in 1829, Gerard came with brief previous experience from Fort Pierre. A smart trader as well as a sharp dealer, Gerard took pains to learn the Arikara language and made it a habit to winter with his customers in the deep, sheltered coulees along the Missouri for many years.

But Gerard had his troubles with the stubborn Indians, as did other traders. In one escapade, they practically kidnapped and held for ransom the general supervisor for the American Fur Company posts on the Upper Missouri, Alexander Culbertson. An Arikara chief had taken a trip on a company steamboat from Fort Clark to Council Bluffs, where he was attacked and killed by what was thought to be Pawnees. Since the chief had traveled on their boat, the company was responsible for his safety, reasoned the Rees. Culbertson was ordered to produce indemnity for the death. Two horses was the price, or possibly he would pay the supreme penalty himself. He paid. Not that he gave in from fear; Culbertson was too old a hand with Indians for that. He believed it was simply good business for the American Fur Company to settle for the horses and keep the customers happy.

The next year, Culbertson brought with him on his annual inspection tour his younger brother, Thaddeus, an enthusiastic fossil collector and interested observer.[31] At Fort Clark, after the Rees had been feasted and presents distributed, young Culbertson related in his journal what he had been told of them and what he had seen. "(They)* ... are said to be great thieves, pilfering anything they lay their hands on — they are also great beggars like all other tribes. If a feast and some presents are not given to them, they injure the boat, and perhaps would take the lives of some of the traders in the winter season."

Culbertson thought their lodges were not as bad as he had been led to believe. "Many persons in the States live in much more filth and in less comfort."

****

In the Hunkpapa camp, Bloody Knife and Gall were now 10 years old. The mixed blood Ree-Sioux began to be subjected to all sorts of humiliations. He was taunted, bullied and tormented by the other boys of the camp under the eager leadership of Gall, according to an account by Joseph Henry Taylor, a longtime hunter, trapper and newspaper editor in the Painted Woods area near what is now Washburn, North Dakota.[32] It was common practice for Indian war parties to bring captured enemy children back to their camps when they had the time and opportunity, adopting them and raising them as full tribal members in order to renew the strength of the tribe. But for some reason, the boys refused to accept Bloody Knife. Perhaps it was a personal difference between the two youngsters, with Gall dominating Bloody Knife, supported by the prestige of his adopted elder brother, Sitting Bull. And would not Sitting Bull have intervened had he been related to the outcast? Blood ties were strong among Indians. Trifling with Indians was a family affair. Bloody Knife's attitude toward Gall, Sitting Bull and their cohorts hardened as time went on. However, for the time being, he had no choice but to endure their insults and embarrassments.

Bloody Knife was learning the things an Indian boy was required to know, things which would enable him to survive when he reached manhood. As the nomadic Hunkpapas traveled, Bloody Knife's powerful memory stored away the sights and scenes of hundreds of geographical landmarks, from the Bighorn Mountains to the Black Hills, from the Iron Line that was called Canada to the Platte River. He was taught the name and location of every stream, hill and mountain he saw. Long talks around the glowing lodge fires instructed him in travel routes, the availability of game, water and wood. The basic arts of survival, tracking and trailing all became a part of his formal education.

The years passed.

► *Chapter 6* ◄

Grounds for Revenge

It must have seemed to the Rees in the terrible summer of 1851 that white men were continually devising new ways and means of reducing their strength and number. Cholera came and with it the old hatreds which erupted into violence and death. The sickness began in the summer and by fall, 300 Arikaras as well as thousands from other tribes had died of it. Father Jean Pierre De Smet, on one of his periodic trips to visit the Indians, on July 7 baptized 186 Arikara children, many of whom he knew would not be alive in another month with the epidemic raging. This time the tribe scattered out on the prairie to escape the deadly, unseen menace.

From Fort Union, Swiss artist and American Fur Company clerk Rudolph Friederich Kurz wrote on October 8, 1851: "Arikaras are still dying ... like flies under frost. The survivors are in a fury; have razed the blockhouses of the opposition and stolen their goods."[33] By "opposition," Kurz meant the St. Louis Fur Company. The company was also named Harvey, Primeau and Company, after its founders, who left the American Fur Company to compete against it. Again, the whites, the Rees felt, had contrived to pare down their population through the medium of their loathsome disease.

The observant Kurz had a good word for them, though, and for their friends, the Hidatsas. He wrote that the Rees and Hidatsas were clean and bathed in the river " ... once, if possible, twice a day."

Early in the year, messages had come from the Indian Agent, on behalf of President Millard Fillmore, issuing invitations to all tribes to attend the greatest peace council ever held at the white man's big War House, Fort Laramie. The council was to take place in September 1851, or what the Arikara call the time of the Harvesting Moon and the Sioux the Moon When Wild Rice is Stored. In spite of the threat of cholera at home then just beginning, the Arikaras sent their delegation off in August.[34] Their portion of the treaty, in conjunction with the Hidatsas and Mandans, amounted to the grant of a triangle of land east of the Yellowstone River, most of which they already regarded as their territory. They also were promised supplies of annuities for 50 years. True to tradition, however, the United States Senate, when ratifying the treaty, reduced the annuities portion to such an extent as to render it almost unrecognizable. Faith again was not kept.

Annuity payments became a source of questioning, wonder and frustration. Indians looked on in astonishment and disbelief, for instance, when they saw the hundreds of sacks of corn delivered to them. They already annually raised more of the grain than they needed for their own use in order to turn the surplus into a trade commodity.

****

After six years at Fort Clark, Fred Gerard was transferred to Fort Berthold in 1855. His yearly salary of $500 indicated that he held the position of chief clerk.[35] Temporarily, the Rees lost one of the few traders with whom they had a rapport and with whom

The Upper Missouri in the 1850s

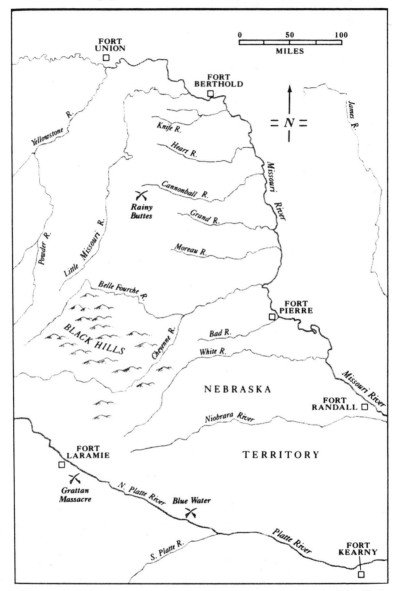

From *The Lance and the Shield: The Life and Times of Sitting Bull* by Robert M. Utley. Map by Jeffrey L. Ward. ©1993 by Jeffrey L. Ward. Reprinted by permission of Henry Holt and Co., Inc.

Bloody Knife: Custer's Favorite Scout

they could communicate.

****

In the Hunkpapa camp, Bloody Knife's life was a continual torment. Stoically, he endured the insults and torments and abuse heaped upon him by Gall and his followers. Through it all, he was being watched and when it was seen that the boy's courage and fortitude would keep him going, those who understood his predicament came to him as friends.[36]

Sometime in the early 1850s, Bloody Knife's mother came to a decision to leave her husband and return to her own people. She took the children with her, the sons now nearing warrior age. Bloody Knife's life underwent a complete change. He soon doubted that it was for the better. For one thing, 63 of the Arikaras died in 1856 of another outbreak of smallpox.

****

At Fort Berthold in 1857, Fred Gerard was promoted to bourgeois and began to collect his now princely salary of $1200 annually.

****

On September 19, Indian Commissioner Alexander H. Redfield visited Fort Clark, where he found 600 lodges of the Sioux trading and dictating to him what they wanted from the government. They were " ... very independent," he said, "and asserted all

Grounds for Revenge   27

they wanted was to have access to traders and wanted neither annuities or soldiers."[37]

Henry A. Boller, clerk for a new opposition outfit known as Frost, Todd and Company, quickly experienced Ree hostility in 1858 shortly after his arrival at the new post, Fort Atkinson, built by the competitor near Like-A-Fishhook Village. On June 19, Agent Redfield sought to deliver the annuities from the steamer, *Twilight*. But the enraged Indians, loudly complaining that the goods from the 1851 treaty were inadequate, fired guns into the ground at his feet, some of the muzzle blasts close enough to leave powder burns on his clothes. A young Ree took a pot shot at a passenger and missed. " ... one fellow coolly proposed a general scalping of all the whites," reported Boller. The Indians accepted the goods after five hours of wrangling.

Relations between the Sioux and the Arikaras were again becoming strained. Agent Redfield, recognizing the danger of the weaker nation being wiped out, recommended the establishment of a military post at some upriver location in the heart of Sioux country as protection for all three tribes, the Arikara, Mandan and Hidatsa.

For years, the Sioux had been intermittently raiding them, which led Boller to believe that all Indians were troublesome. "They all want a good whaleing by Uncle Sam's troops," he wrote. An indication of Sioux intentions came on July 21, 1859, when a buffalo hunting party of Arikaras was attacked near Fort Berthold by a war party of 600 Minniconjou, Sans Arc, Two Kettle, Cut Head and Santee Sioux.[38] The fight swayed back and forth for hours in the peculiar style of individual Indian combat, with the outcome in doubt. When darkness set in, the attackers withdrew, leaving 33 of their dead on the prairie. Arikara losses were 10 killed and 34 wounded.

Bloody Knife must have thought the future looked bleak, with only continual harassment by the enemies of his youth, a life of stagnation behind walls, and the loss of the freedom of the open Plains enjoyed by the young men of the stronger tribes. Somewhere, there had to be an escape.

Early in 1860, Frost, Todd and Company, facing financial ruin as a result of fierce competition from the American Fur Company, decided to consolidate with the American Fur Company. It was only a matter of months, however, before new competition developed, organized by the old veteran of the Upper Missouri, Charles Larpenteur.[39] He formed a partnership with traders that included Boller. Larpenteur's responsibility was operating a trading house at Poplar River on the Missouri. The new firm barely survived two years, and Larpenteur and Boller parted enemies.[40]

****

Captain William F. Raynolds paused at Fort Clark on the inbound trip of his surveying expedition in August 1860 and described the people as " ... the degraded remnant of a once powerful nation." The Arikara chief told him that his young men could not go out to hunt because the Sioux were always setting ambushes for them, and even in the cornfields women were shot and scalped.[41]

This was also the year that Bloody Knife made an unwise decision to visit the camp of his youth. The wish to see his father, his relatives and friends was overpowering; the freedom of the wide Plains beckoned. So he made the long journey to the Hunkpapa camp at the mouth of the Rosebud River alone, a hazardous undertaking since he could expect no mercy if he encountered any of the Sioux out in the open country. He got safely to the camp, where ordinarily a visitor could claim protection, food and shelter. In defiance of the ancient code, though, and disregarding his previous habitation among them, a soldier band of Hunkpapas numbering some his old enemies took him prisoner. Gall was the instigator. First, they humiliated him by stripping him; they cursed, reviled and insulted him and spit upon him; then they beat him with musket ramrods and coup sticks until he was raw and bleeding. The punishment ended with a threat to Bloody Knife that he get out of camp or be killed.[42] Somehow, he made it back to Fort Clark, consumed with hatred.

➤ *Chapter 7* ◄

Skirmishes With the Sioux

White men, or *Wasichus,* as the Sioux called them. There was something darkly sinister about the manner in which the white men kept coming in ever-increasing numbers. No matter how many were killed, there were always that many more to take their places.

Even though the intellectuals of the Sioux had realized for years that they were in danger of being overrun or destroyed by the creeping tentacles of the white man, they now understood that to stop the white flood, to roll it back, to destroy it, was perhaps beyond the power of their nation alone. And so, cautiously at first, they began testing other nations and tribes, friends and enemies, seeking alliances, one great alliance to end the threat of white encroachment for all time.

Gall and Sitting Bull, meanwhile, were blooding themselves at the expense of a perennial enemy, the Crows. At Rainy Buttes, in the spring of 1859, in what is now western North Dakota, a war party of Crows, raiding far from their homeland, had the audacity to assault the moving Hunkpapa camp in bright daylight. In a wild, running fight, many Crows and some of the Sioux were killed. Sitting Bull lost his father. But Gall and his adopted elder brother collected many coups.[43]

Fort Clark burned down in 1861. Their agent strongly urged the Arikaras to move upriver as soon as possible.[44] They accepted his advice and relocated in a timbered bend above Fort Berthold. In March 1862, the Arikaras began construction of a new earth lodge village on the Missouri, just opposite the site called Star Village, named after the chief's band. A census taken that year showed 392 males and 588 females at the new earth lodge village.

The always-present danger of the Arikara, Mandan, Hidatsa and their traders being massacred by the Sioux led the latter to appeal to Captain James L. Fisk to recommend to the War Department the establishment of a military post nearby.[45] Fisk, who was sheperding the first of his four wagon trains from Minnesota to the Montana Territory over the Northern Emigrant Route, agreed and penned an eminently satisfactory recommendation. The pleas were repeated in a barrage lasting for years when the captain's opinion produced no results.

The request marked a complete turnabout for the traders. During the heyday of the fur trade, the last thing they wanted was governmental supervision and the scrutiny it would bring to their operations. But now that fear had replaced greed, they were the first to bellow for help.

****

Another competitor went under that year, and Fort Atkinson, located near Fort Berthold, fell within the American Fur Company fold.[46]

****

On August 3, 1862, the Sioux attacked the uncompleted

Arikara village. That was enough. Shortly thereafter, the majority of the Arikara tribe moved across the river and built their village near what was left of the Mandans and Hidatsas for common protection at Like-A-Fishhook Village.[47] However, several Arikara bands chose to stay behind because of sacred tribal traditions which compelled them to remain on the river's west side.

This joining of forces by the Arikara, Mandan and Hidatsa nations in the late summer of 1862 marked the beginning of an alliance which has resulted in an often-shared cultural, economic and political history to this day. However, each nation has maintained its independent tribal identity through language, customs and beliefs.[48] The alliance was formalized in 1936, when representatives of the Mandan, Hidatsa and Arikara signed an agreement designating them as the Three Affiliated Tribes.[49]

The Sioux struck again in the autumn, not at the village, but out on the buffalo hunting range. It brought Bloody Knife a severe personal loss and cost the Three Tribes the lives of two of their warriors. A war party, led by Gall, surprised the two brothers of Bloody Knife as they were hunting in the Badlands. The war party killed, scalped, and mutilated them, then left their remains for the wolves or the elements. Bloody Knife was stunned.[50]

It was Christmas Eve morning when the Sioux made one of their most determined attempts to wipe out the Indian village and the traders at Fort Berthold, at a time when the Three Tribes were in winter quarters a few miles away. Six hundred of them attacked at nine o'clock and despite a heroic defense put up by the 17 traders, succeeded in setting fire to the fort and the village. At their winter camp, the Berthold Indians saw the smoke and guessed the source of it. They returned in strength, drove off the assailants, and chased them for 20 miles. By four o'clock the battle was over, but most of the fort and a large part of the village was gone. Forty of the Sioux were reported killed and 100 wounded.

Fred Gerard and Pierre Garreau distinguished themselves in the fight. After that, Gerard was known to the Berthold Indians as Seven Yanktons, in recognition of the number of warriors of that tribe he had assisted on the journey to the Great Beyond.[51]

Chapter 8

War Breaks Out

Since the outbreak of the Civil War, all of the Plains tribes had been restive. This offered a good excuse for the British trading posts in Canada, or what the Sioux called Grandmother's Land, to attract the Indian trade to their houses. They promised them future supplies of arms, followed by aid, in expelling the Long Knives that was the U.S. Army from the Indian Country. Hence, Sioux hearts were strong and they raided whenever an occasion arose. It was the beginning of irregular but more frequent raids, which reduced the Berthold people to an impoverished and starving condition. The Cranbrook Dakota Winter Count showed that the Sioux killed 20 Mandans that winter.

Not that the Sioux were entirely responsible for the plight of the Three Tribes. The villagers were also the victims of incredible corruption and mismanagement of the affairs of their agency. For example, when steamboats discharged their annuity goods, people were forced to await distribution for some days while the agents opened the boxes and barrels and bales in the privacy of the warehouses — goods were removed to be put out for sale through the post trader and not replaced, condemned flour from the traders' current stock was substituted for fresh flour.[52] It was a cozy and highly profitable arrangement for the clique of agents and traders. And Fred Gerard was a trader.

At one time, the venerable Arikara chief, White Shield, refused to sign an annuity receipt for Agent Mahlon Wilkinson. The agent was infuriated. He deposed White Shield as chief, deprived him of his personal annuity, and shouted at him that age was troubling his brain. Whereupon White Shield replied, "I am old, it is true; but not so old as not to see things as they are. And even if as you say, I were only an old fool, I would prefer a hundred times to be an honest red fool than a stealing white rascal like you!"[53]

Those were indeed frustrating years for a warrior the caliber of Bloody Knife. Not much could be done in the matter of reprisal against his sworn enemies. Even to leave the village to hunt was to court sudden capture, torture and death. And to hole up in the village was to grow weak from near starvation. In common with his tribesmen, he bided his time, sometimes joining the infrequent war parties sent out. Living conditions were intolerable.

Sioux hearts swelled with pride in the late summer of 1862 in response to exciting words from their cousins, the Santees, living toward the rising sun in Minnesota. There, in August, or what the Arikara know as the Hot, Mature Moon and the Sioux the Moon When All Things Ripen, their destitute relations had risen against their white oppressors. A small band of half-starved Santees revolted against their corrupt agents and killed five white settlers. Immediately, all of the Sioux tribes of the Upper Missouri took to the war path against the whites. By the time the Minnesota Uprising was over in late September 1862, more than 400 whites had lost their lives and an uncounted number of Indians were dead.[54]

Ponderously, the huge Plains armies of Generals Henry H. Sibley and Alfred Sully, the largest white forces the West ever saw, swept across what is now eastern and central North Dakota in the summer of 1863, meeting and beating the truculent Sioux in five engagements.[55] Gall was present at the Big Mound Battle and it is quite probable that he was fighting in some of the others. Inkpaduta, a Sioux leader of the Minnesota Uprising who also later fought with Gall at the Battle of the Little Bighorn, got in on all of them.

Sully came back in 1864, and destroyed a large Sioux camp at Killdeer Mountain in July, then inflicted severe casualties on the Indians in a three-day battle in the Badlands in August.[56]

In at least some of the contests, Gall rode at the head of his warrior band. Although the two campaigns resulted in six of the biggest Indian fights in the west and the Sioux came off second best in all of them, their strength remained relatively undiminished.

Nagging worry was the constant companion of the fur trade in those troublous days. Enraged as the Indians were, the traders feared they would be engulfed and wiped out of existence. This prompted La Barge, Harkness and Company in January 1862 to petition the Government for troops, pointing out that an 1800 mile stretch of the Missouri from Fort Randall to Fort Benton was entirely without a soldier, a civil officer or a government.[57]

Cautiously, in the summer of 1862, a party of Minnesota Sioux approached Fort Berthold and called for a parley with its Indian inhabitants. A council was organized at a coulee about three miles from the post, during which the Sioux pressed for an alliance with the Three Tribes to fight the whites. Apparently, the refusal of the Berthold people was not expressed in the best of Indian diplomatic terms, because a fight started in which two Hidatsas and nine Sioux were killed.[58]

Fred Gerard's close personal involvement with the Indians paid off handsomely in August. A mackinaw load of 20 miners stopped at Berthold, where the travelers showed him their hidden cache of gold dust estimated to be worth about $100,000. He advised them to wait to go on until the Sioux had left for the west, but he was ignored and the miners embarked downriver. Within a matter of hours, they were ambushed from the riverbank and every one of them was slain. Some Rees heard the firing and told Gerard. The trader was sure he knew what had happened. He sent two Rees, Soldier and Howling Bear, to look for the gold, a part of which they found strewn about on a sand bar. Filling a good-sized sack, they brought it to Gerard, who rewarded them with liberal trading privileges.[59]

That autumn, Henry Boller almost lost his life to the angry Rees, who were demanding better trading prices. Bullets sang around him and one warrior was only stopped from tomahawking him by the interference of one of the Indian party. Hours of talk ensued, with neither side satisfied. Bad interpreting, a bane of the frontier, was responsible for a good deal of the misunderstanding.

****

By the next year, the Berthold Indians were not only asking for troops, they wanted guns with which to defend themselves. They produced a startling statistic to prove their need — every one of the Three Tribes' signers of the 1851 Laramie Treaty was dead, killed by the Sioux. But their hopes were soon dashed, when Department Commander General John Pope ruled that no guns were to be given to friendly Indians.[60] It was an empty consolation that at the same time he ordered all Sioux annuities cancelled. The only Sioux affected were the peaceful bands on the reservations.

Father De Smet appeared at Fort Berthold on June 9, 1863, appointed by the Commissioner of Indian Affairs to embark upon a peace-making mission with the Sioux.

Through the happenstance of a Sioux raid on July 13, this Jesuit priest from Belgium was able to see first hand the dire necessity for protection of some sort. It moved him to write in behalf of the Three Tribes:

> They were told at the Laramie Treaty to bury the war club. They have buried it, and have never since waged war. They have been promised protection against their enemies at the treaty, but no protection has ever been given. They have suffered much from the Sioux. Many of their people have been killed by them. The (Rees)* were robbed by them, since the treaty, of over 1500 horses; the Gros Ventres have been robbed of over a thousand horses. Their fields of corn, their last support for their children and little ones, have been repeatedly destroyed by the Sioux and reduced them to starvation. The Sioux keep driving them from their hunting grounds; they have taken forcible possession of all their lands from the Cheyenne to the Yellowstone River. They have been compelled to unite in one single village the remnants of their once-powerful tribes. They are now, as it were, penned in and surrounded by their reckless foe — overpowered by numbers. They hardly dare leave their village in quest of food. They now look forward towards utter extermination, unless their Great Father takes pity on them, and takes them under his powerful protection.[61]

De Smet, also known as Black Robe to the Sioux, then held two councils with them near the post, preaching peace. The very bands he consulted with were there only to again attempt to induce the Three Tribes to join in the war to exterminate the whites. Two of the chiefs did admit they would like to prevent their young men from going to war. Encouraged, De Smet left Fort Berthold. On his trip down the Missouri, however, he met contingents of Sully's troops on a mission to destroy the Sioux. He knew then his peace overtures were a failure.

****

On August 29, 1864, Sully dragged his battle-weary army into Fort Berthold for a couple of days of badly needed rest. [62] They had chased the Sioux into what is now western North Dakota, fighting the Killdeer Mountain and Badlands battles, handling the Indians roughly in both instances, but not destroying or subduing them. In addition, they had fought thirst and starvation. So the troops relaxed and frolicked with the Indians at horse racing, playing cards and trading. But the Indians put up a howl when they caught the light-fingered soldiery in their vegetable patches. Sully ordered a guard put over the plots. Noticing his men unerringly finding their surreptitious ways to certain hovels in the Indian village, the general was moved to include in a report written later that the morals of the Arikaras were in a " ... terrible state ... as bad as it is possible for a human being to be."[63]

Detaching Company G, 6th Iowa Cavalry, as a garrison for the fort, Sully picked up his army and departed southward on September 1, charging the small force left behind with protecting the Indians and keeping the river open to traffic. Few though they were, at last the Three Tribes had their troops.[64]

****

Somewhere among the free-roving Hunkpapas in 1864 was war chief Gall, now a band chief of half a dozen lodges, a matter of pride for one so young. He was filled with a plentiful supply of the personal trait which his name implied and blessed with unbounded courage. His mistake was in not taking care that he was so often identified in his depredations around Fort Berthold, where he kept whites and Indians alike in a state of terror with his horse stealing and killing.

At the fort, the young warrior Bloody Knife studied the ways of the traders and soldiers intently. Slowly and tenaciously he ingratiated himself with the whites, gaining their confidence and respect. His first reward came when the fur company hired him as its hunter. He was a good one. His prowess with the gun and bow often required two wagons to haul in the game he killed. It was not long before his employers found out that he was fluent in both Sioux and Arikara and in the sign language, skills most members of his tribe had. After that, his duties were enlarged, with his linguistic talents leading to an appointment as an emissary, a "runner," as the job was called, to the non-reservation camps to urge them to bring their hides, robes and furs into the company store at the fort.[65]

With the presence of the soldiers at the fort, the Sioux were reluctant to come in. Being a runner was highly dangerous work and it took unlimited nerve to brave the enemy on his own grounds and in his camp as a representative of the hated whites. But he not only escaped getting into trouble, he was successful in bringing the sought-after trade in to his employers. The garrison too came to regard him as trustworthy enough to engage him as a guide for hunting parties and to carry military mail. As a sideline, he hunted for meat that he sold to the troops.

Bloody Knife was described in those years of the early to middle 1860s as dependable and loyal, skillful, knowledgeable and efficient in his work, and courageous in a time of danger. To his credit, he was never overawed by officialdom, citizen or military. It was true that he was on occasion hot-tempered and moody, but

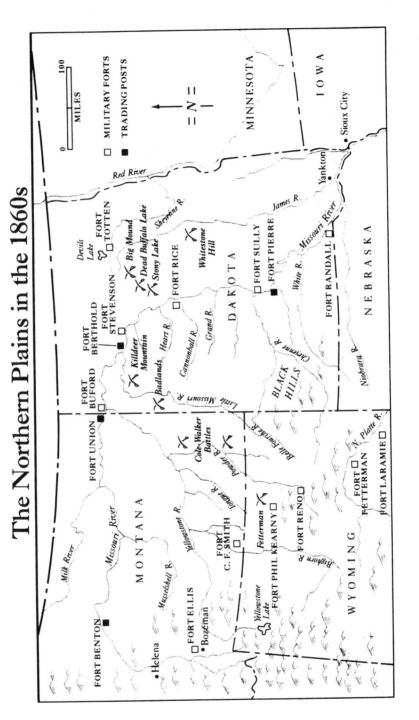

The Northern Plains in the 1860s

MILES

MILITARY FORTS
TRADING POSTS

From *The Lance and the Shield: The Life and Times of Sitting Bull* by Robert M. Utley. Map by Jeffrey L. Ward. ©1993

Bloody Knife: Custer's Favorite Scout

those characteristics were seldom revealed to whites. He did have a taste for quantities of the Great Father's Milk, the execrable trade whiskey. Certainly, the Rees could take it or leave it. If Bloody Knife's failing was the bottle, he was no more at fault than a goodly percentage of Army officers and enlisted men as well as Indians. In all other respects the warrior *nee si RA pat* was a rugged individualist, able to get along under any conditions.

****

Company G of the 6th Iowa Cavalry, a volunteer outfit, was due to go home. They had battled bedbugs, fleas and scurvy all winter. On May 14, 1865, they were relieved at Fort Berthold by Company K of the 1st Volunteer Infantry, better known in the Civil War soldiering trade as Galvanized Yankees, one of the units recruited from among Confederate prisoners of war.[66]

President Lincoln authorized the action on September 1, 1864 that allowed the creation of the Galvanized Yankee units. Also called Whitewashed Rebs, these men were recruited into the Union Army from Northern prison camps, preferring to serve in the West rather than languish in captivity. Six regiments and one independent company, a total of about 6000 men, were brought into the Union ranks. The bulk of the forces were stationed in the West for almost two years.

The men were required to take the oath of allegiance to the United States Government for their term of service. Those who witnessed their actions in garrison and campaigning on the Plains judged them to be an excellent class of soldier, brave and well disciplined. Their desertion rate was slightly higher than that of the Regular Army. The outfits saw quite a bit of action in the course of their duty, which included such tasks as guarding the Overland

Trail and stagecoach routes, patrolling and repairing telegraph lines, escorting Union Pacific Railroad survey parties, and actively campaigning with the Powder River Expedition of 1865. They garrisoned such far-flung posts as Fort Douglas in Utah Territory; Virginia City and Fort Benton in Montana Territory; Fort Union in Dakota Territory; and Santa Fe in New Mexico Territory. The last of them were mustered out at Fort Leavenworth, Kansas on November 13, 1866.[67]

Chapter 9

A Measure of Revenge

The Northwestern Indian Expedition of 1865 was a miserable failure. Sully marched his army over a good portion of the real estate of present day North Dakota without finding an Indian to shoot at. To the southwest, the troops of General Patrick Connor's Powder River Expedition were absorbing a beating from the allied Sioux, Cheyennes and Arapahoes, as well as the weather. On his homeward march, Sully again stopped at Fort Berthold on August 8. There, from Fort Rice, well-founded rumors reached him of an impending Sioux attack on the fort, which set the small garrison on edge. With the approach of Sully's force, however, the Sioux disappeared.

Here, Bloody Knife stepped into the picture. Someone was needed who was familiar with the country and courageous enough to travel the Indian territory and trail the retreating warriors, determine their immediate purpose and locate their main camp. That someone was Bloody Knife. General Sully described the spy's services in his report: "A trusty Indian, half Arickaree and half Uncpapa, followed their trail across the bad lands, the Little Missouri, to Beaver Creek, which empties into the L. Mo. and found their trail still going westward toward Powder River."[68]

Then Sully explained his failure to pursue the Sioux: "I could not follow for there are no means here of crossing the river."

****

In October, Company C, 4th U.S. Volunteer Infantry, another Whitewashed Reb outfit, Captain Adams Bassett commanding, relieved Company K of the 1st at Fort Berthold.[69]

****

It was a frosted day in November 1865 when Bloody Knife, home again and partially unemployed with the troops inactive, watched from a corn guarding scaffold as a small band of Hunkpapas raised their lodges on a willow bar south of Fort Berthold. He watched as his lifelong enemy, arrived for trade or diplomacy, or both. Without losing a moment, the mixed blood hurried for the soldiers' camp, determined that his old nemesis should not be alive to see another sunrise. Gaining an audience with Captain Bassett, Bloody Knife asked the officer if he wanted " ... the bad Sioux who has been killing these white men found dead and scalped in lonely places along the river?"[70] Bassett replied that he did. The warrior pointed out the Hunkpapa lodges to the southwest of the village. Calling in a lieutenant, Bassett ordered him to take a platoon and arrest Gall. If the chief would not submit, then Bassett ordered the lieutenant to kill him and any others attempting to resist or make trouble.

That evening, Bloody Knife led the soldiers to the small campsite where they surrounded Gall's small tipi. A surprised Gall emerged from the skin doorway, then reacted immediately when he saw Bloody Knife and realized the intent of the troops. He tried to get away, but in the confused struggle, he was bayoneted and knocked to the ground. Twice more the slender, vicious, triangular blade pierced his body. Blood gushed from his mouth and nostrils. The lieutenant bent over the fallen chief, examined him perfunctorily and pronounced him dead. But the avenging Bloody Knife was not satisfied. His simmering hatred exploded. Stepping up to the prostrate form, he stuck the barrel of his buckshot loaded gun within inches of the blood-welling face. Just as he did, the officer, with a sweep of his arm, struck the barrel and knocked the gun aside. The murderous charge tore a smoking hole in the earth next to Gall's head. Hot words were exchanged between Bloody Knife and the white officer, while the stinking white cloud of powder smoke drifted off. Filled with rage and frustration, Bloody Knife stamped off to the Arikara quarter of the village, where he tried to enlist reinforcements to finish the job in spite of the soldiers. Older heads prevailed, however, and his last chance for his long awaited revenge was gone.

The bluecoats left Gall's body on the frosted ground and marched away, convinced that the war chief had killed his last white man. But the members of Gall's band bound up his wounds, struck their lodges and departed in haste for a large Hunkpapa camp with their leader's body strapped on a travois. He recovered.

In 1868, he showed Father De Smet the scars of his wounds, two in the body and one in the neck. He boasted that within the next year, seven white men had paid with their lives for the incident on the willow bar at Fort Berthold. Significantly, the Cranbrook Dakota Winter Count identifies that Sioux winter as the year in which Chief Gall Stuck With Bayonet by Soldier.

****

A hard winter crept through anxious days at Fort Berthold. Smallpox, crop failure and famine reduced the Indians to beggars and scavengers. Fifty people died of starvation. A majority of children of tender ages did not live to see the spring. In the locked warehouses, the Indians were systematically robbed of their annuities by their agents and traders. A witness wrote:

> When the old women with their starving babies (went)* to the fort to scrounge for the filthy refuse thrown from the soldiers' kitchens, they were driven off with scalding water thrown upon their emaciated bodies, covered only with rags in the severest of cold weather.[71]

If the men left the fort to hunt, they were pounced on by the Sioux, who were ever waiting.

When spring broke and the short buffalo grass was exposed enough for pony feed, Gall again went on the offensive, attacking small parties and individuals around military posts and raiding settlements. He was pronounced an outlaw in military district orders and a price was put on his head.

June, the Moon of the Ripened Berries to the Sioux, and the Planting Moon to the Arikara, spread its soft warmth over the land and new soldiers came, Regular Army men, Company D of the 13th U.S. Infantry.[72] Other companies of the same regiment were on their way farther upstream. They were told they were to build forts at certain places in order to keep watch over the Sioux and to fight them whenever necessary. The Three Tribes were informed that the Sioux would not feel so free now to depredate in the future and the pressure on their poor village would be lessened.

****

Far to the east, the U.S. Congress, acting on an idea borrowed from British colonial experience, authorized a measure on June 26, 1866 which, in effect, furnished the American Frontier Army with eyes and ears it had never had before. The enlistment of Indian scouts into the Regular Army was now a reality.[73]

An Act of Congress, signed by President Andrew Johnson, provided for the Indian scouts, specifying that:

> The President is authorized to enlist a force of Indians not exceeding one thousand, who shall act as scouts in the Territories and the Indian country. They shall be discharged when the necessity for their services shall cease, or at the discretion of the Department Commander.[74]

They were enlisted as an official branch of the U.S. Army with the same pay and allowances of a white enlisted man. Some of their non-commissioned officers came out of their own ranks. They were commanded by white commissioned officers. They were not subject to military drill, and could be discharged when not needed, or at the discretion of the Department Commander.

Basically, the purpose of hiring Indian scouts was to aid white troops out of their element in Indian country. They were intended for scout and guide duty on campaigns, for pulling outpost duty at military posts, guard duty, carrying mail and herding livestock. Prior to the Recruiting Act of 1866, some Indians served as scouts with just the lure of booty and plunder in the form of horses, weapons and scalps. As enlisted U.S. Army scouts, they were paid at the same rate as Army privates, which was $16 a month, plus another $12 when they furnished their own horses. They were provided their own rations and quarters.

Term of enlistment was for six months. The Act was revised on August 12, 1876, and continued until 1914.[75]

****

At some time during the year of 1866, Bloody Knife married an Arikara woman. Her name was She Owl.[76]

Chapter 10

The Army Moves In

Another of the eternal peace commissions turned up in that summer of 1866, and on July 27 signed the Berthold Indians to a treaty ceding some of their land and allowing the whites to construct roads and telegraph lines. The commission recommended that the village be assigned a farmer and the necessary agricultural implements to teach the Indians farming. The population was now estimated at 1500 Arikaras.

Gall was with Red Cloud in the autumn at Fort Phil Kearny, building warrior strength for the coming contest there. Sitting Bull, by early winter, was besieging Fort Buford, at the mouth of the Yellowstone.

****

Agent Mahlon Wilkinson was pleading for the Fort Berthold Indians. He wrote his superiors that the Three Tribes must have help from the Government or perish from starvation and the Sioux. He continued by saying that the Sioux sought to attract them into an alliance against the whites, but they refused. And, like other whites on the Upper Missouri, Wilkinson denounced the policy which prevented friendly Indians from getting arms from their own traders with which to defend themselves, while the Sioux were able to obtain unlimited amounts of arms and ammunition from the Red River mixed bloods and from the British.

All this fell in line with the Government's plans for the Upper Missouri. On June 14, 1867, the company of infantry at Fort Berthold moved 17 miles to the east. Reinforced by other companies from the same outfit, the troops began construction of Fort Stevenson on the left bank of the Missouri. [77]

The Indians thought the 17 miles was too great a distance for the infantry to be of much help in an emergency. And there were many emergencies. Stevenson's site was chosen for a multiplicity of reasons — as protection for friendly Indians and local whites, to aid in keeping the river open to traffic, to keep the overland traffic moving on the Minnesota-Montana road, to assist other posts in controlling the Sioux, and to serve as a base of supplies for Fort Totten, another of the new posts scheduled for construction within a few days on the southern shore of Devils Lake. The Indians were not told of another reason for Stevenson's location — that military heads deemed it inadvisable to have the troops as close to the Indians as they had been at Berthold.

****

Far up the great Missouri River, which the Arikara know as the Mysterious River and a Sioux translation calls the Smoky Water, the post commander at Fort Buford was doing his best to recruit scouts from among reluctant Assiniboins. He was experiencing a notable lack of success. All the while, Sitting Bull's Sioux were staging a loose sort of siege before the fort. Captain William

Rankin advised headquarters for the Middle District of his problem by letter on August 8, 1866.[78] It would be months before he got his scouts, and then only through shrewd bargaining on the part of the Assiniboins. And by October 5, Colonel de Trobriand at Fort Stevenson was writing to Fort Wadsworth, in what is now South Dakota, for 15 Indian scouts. Warriors from the Three Tribes refused to enlist, saying they were afraid of weakening the defenses of their village and considered the scouting service too dangerous because they were at war with the Sioux.[79]

****

Fortunately, Fort Stevenson's baptism by the Sioux was not as severe as those suffered at Fort Rice and Fort Buford. Three nuisance raids mounted in July, August and October 1866 netted the attackers the life of a teamster and the wounding of another man.

At some undetermined date in early summer, Gall lost a fight. Sarah E. Canfield, an Army wife who later wrote an account of her experience on the frontier, witnessed on June 24 a scalp dance at Fort Berthold, " ... in honor of a victory over their enemy — Bad Gaul, an Unc-pa-pa chief of one of the most hostile of the hostile bands of Sioux." She described this rare event from the perspective of a white woman who had little, if any, understanding of the meaning of this sacred Indian ritual:

> The dance was the most rediculous sight I ever saw. Nearly 200 men, women and children almost naked, painted in the most hidious manner made up the company. Some wore buffalo horns and were painted to represent Scales like an alligator. One wore a white horse hair wig with a black streak

painted on it, with a bright red Streak where the hair was parted over the forehead, one had white streaks painted around their eyes making them look about five times their usual size, and one warrior had long bear claws for fingernails (I wonder how they were fastened on).[80]

Bloody Knife was now in his element. His reputation as an able and trustworthy Indian had preceded him to Fort Stevenson and finding employment was easy. He carried mail, hunted for the fort and guided hunting parties. Government contractors supplying the place with hay, lumber, fuel and subsistence also hired his services as hunter, courier, guide and scout. In a slack season he returned to being a runner for the Fort Berthold traders.

In common with countless other nimrods, Bloody Knife's hunting luck did not always hold up. In February 1868, he led three officers on a hunt out of the fort, but he was the only one fortunate enough to shoot a deer. Another hunt in early March was even worse. No game was found.

Not all was sweetness and light, however. A case of murder found Bloody Knife suspect, although no evidence is known to exist that substantiates the allegation. Joseph Henry Taylor, the longtime frontier hunter, trapper and newspaper man, told the story:

> Late in the spring of 1868, in connection with an Aricaree known among the traders as Red Legs, Bloody Knife was accused of the murder of an old trapper named La France, for his peltries. The trapper was found by a party of Gros Ventres on a creek near the mouth of the Little Missouri. He was lying dead, face downward, with a bullet hole through the back of his head. An unsprung trap was lying by his side, and was evidently a clear case of a trapper trapped.[81]

Bloody Knife certainly had the skills as a warrior to commit the deed, whether he did so or not. There must have been a complete lack of evidence or charges would definitely have been pressed. The death of a lone white man in that rough, lawless country never failed to rouse a cry against "murdering Indians!" Given the same circumstances, the death of a lone Indian would cause no more than a ripple of casual interest among the whites.

➤ *Chapter 11* ◄

The Indian Scouts

Toward the latter part of April 1868, Fred Gerard was asked by the Fort Stevenson post commander, Colonel Philippe R. de Trobriand, to contact the Berthold Indians with the intent of enlisting some of them as scouts.[82] With the nuisance the Sioux were making of themselves, de Trobriand was also falling back on the Old World colonial tradition that the most effective way to defeat an enemy was with others of the same tribe or nation.

Furthermore, the Indian Scout Enlistment Act of 1866 gave him the power to do so, although thus far he had met with no success. Gerard naturally talked with his friends and customers the Rees, who by now were willing to listen. The enlistment preliminaries dictated the usual ceremonies of smoking, feasting and talking in order to win the consensus of the tribal leaders, while the duties of the proferred employment were detailed. Fringe benefits included care in case of wounds or injury and replacement of ponies lost or killed, an important consideration since each scout was expected to furnish his own horse, for which he was paid the animal's subsistence allowance of 40 cents a day.

Three days later, on May 1, 1868, ten Arikara young men presented themselves at the office of the Fort Stevenson post surgeon for a medical examination. Bloody Knife was among them, signing up for his first of 11 hitches as an enlisted scout.

Bloody Knife: Custer's Favorite Scout

His enlistment papers described him as five feet, seven inches in height, brown-eyed, black-haired, and with a copper complexion.[83] Inspection completed, the fledgling scouts were shunted along to the enlisting officer, Lieutenant Phillip H. Ellis, where they were shown how to "touch the pen." Their marks were made, witnessed for them, and they were sworn in. Next came the trip to the quartermaster storehouse, where they drew their uniforms, then to the Ordnance Sergeant, where each of them was issued a breech-loading, single shot Springfield 50/70-caliber Army rifle with its accouterments.

But it was at the quartermaster storehouse where the unscheduled entertainment took place, with the young Rees having the stage all to themselves, exuberantly and boyishly unaware of an audience that was, to say the least, aghast. They were given their clothing with the assumption that they would take it to their tents to change at their leisure. De Trobriand had a first row seat and he described the scene from the perspective of a white man, not considering the centuries-old Native American tradition of being unashamed of the naked human body:

> The joy of getting a uniform, trousers and a hat with a black feather fastened up to one side by the American eagle and bearing in the front two crossed sabers above the yellow cord of the cavalry — the joy was too much to brook the slightest delay. Scarcely were they out of the store, when right in the middle of the parade ground, they threw off the buffalo robe or blanket, old shirts and leggins, and in flash appeared in *naturalibus*, to put on the uniform of the *Isatankos*. Some women were looking through their windows or were in front of their doors, hardly expecting such a surprise. You can figure out for yourself whether they hurried to close the curtains or dash into the house.[84]

The Indian Scouts

The colonel had observed earlier that through habit, the scouts continued to wear their moccasins, if nothing else.

Within a short time, a change in scouts' armament occurred. The clumsy Springfields, awkward to handle on horseback, were replaced by the stubby Spencer 50-caliber, seven-shot, lever-action repeating carbines.

As the new enlistees soon perceived, scouting was a full time job. They considered the more entertaining assignments to be carrying mail, performing courier service, and guiding and leading search parties after deserters. Onerous duties were herding livestock and mounting post guard at fixed picket stations.

The very existence of the scout force proved to be a deterrent to desertions. A trooper considering the move gave considerable thought to being pursued and caught by an Indian who knew the land and regarded the chase as a game, trailing the deserter the length of the river.

In all probability, an overriding inducement to becoming a scout was the precious freedom enjoyed after suffering years of ignominy cooped up behind the picketed palisade of the Indian village. And to collect payment for being freed from what amounted to a prison sentence was too good to be true.

Action came sooner than expected. A dozen or so Hunkpapas ran off a few Arikara horses and tried to stampede Gerard's herd on May 17, 1868, but they were driven off by the fire of the Indian guards. Pursued by a platoon of 25 soldiers and the Ree scouts, the Sioux wheeled about for a brief flurry of fighting and chased their harassers back, unhorsing one of the scouts, stripping and disarming him, but unexplainably leaving him otherwise unscalped and unharmed with the exception of a few bruises.

On the same day, two white mail carriers set out for Fort

Bloody Knife: Custer's Favorite Scout

Totten and were never heard from again. A week later, two other white mail carriers left Fort Stevenson for Totten, but had the hard luck to be waylaid by a war party under Sitting Bull. They were stripped, disarmed, their horses taken, and were held captive for several hours. They got back to the post in an exhausted condition. On August 3, a military mail party was attacked at a point between the two forts and three of the men were killed.

The few mail parties accompanied by scouts did not run into trouble. The landing of a steamboat at Fort Stevenson on August 11, with its attendant crowd of noisy welcomers, attracted the fire of a hidden band of Sioux from across the river. One Indian was wounded. A small measure of retribution was exacted by warriors of the Three Tribes on September 4, when they stormed out of their Berthold village after seven Sioux fired on them from across the Missouri, in the mistaken belief that the water obstacle gave them safety. It did for all but one of them. The hapless one was killed and scalped, his feet and hands severed and borne noisily to the village. De Trobriand predicted, "There will be dances and rejoicing at Berthold for a week."

****

After 1864, when the American Fur Company sold out to the Northwestern Fur Company, there had been a rash of changes in the post traderships along the river. Fred Gerard ventured into an independent trader's status, with the Arikaras as his special customers. The time came when Gerard, not entirely innocent himself in the past, reported to Washington the Indian claims that their annuities were being stolen. In retaliation, Agent Mahlon Wilkinson refused to sign his license renewal and Gerard was forced out of business.[85] Such was the power of the Indian Bureau that appeals got nowhere. He next tried a store at Fort Stevenson and then opened another at Fort Buford.

Spring brought to Fort Berthold one of those self-reliant characters who seemed to appear in troubled times on the frontier, when their talents were most needed. The newcomer was a white man, a former soldier, school teacher, trapper and hunter by the name of Luther S. Kelly.[86] Fate decreed that his moccasin tracks would soon merge with those of Bloody Knife. His exploits to the west in succeeding years would earn him the sobriquet, "Yellowstone."

The Arikaras did not attend the Fort Laramie Peace Council that summer of 1868. Neither did the Hunkpapa Sioux, although all other Sioux branches did. Father De Smet found the Hunkpapas on the Powder River in the latter part of June. He was warmly welcomed but got nowhere, as usual, with the Sioux bands.

Going back to Fort Rice, the priest was accompanied by Sitting Bull's trusted lieutenant, Gall, sent along to hear the words of the white peace commissioners who had come to find the Sioux, since the Sioux would not go to meet them. As always, the officials wanted more Indian land. Gall, when it was his turn to speak, tolled the long roll of Indian grievances against their white usurpers, taking the Plains Indians' own time about it, waxing lengthily eloquent, ending with a dramatic gesture: "You ask (me) where are your lands? I answer you. Our lands are wherever our dead are buried."[87]

Opinions differ on Gall's role in the negotiations, but evidence indicates that he signed the treaty whereby the Sioux were given the country between the North Platte and Yellowstone rivers.

****

It was September 30, 1868 when Bloody Knife elected to take "French leave," or "the grand bounce," as the bluecoats liked to term desertion.[88] The scout's action at this period of his life seems to be somewhat out of character. Over the years, he had concentrated on building a steadfast reputation for trustworthiness, loyalty and acceptance of responsibility. Then, in a moment's weakness, he tossed it aside. His reason must have been a strong one.

Military authorities could not have made much of an issue of his disappearance, for four months later he was sharing the comfort of a fire and the shelter of a hunting lodge with Yellowstone Kelly, who was on his way back to Fort Buford from taking the mail from that point to Fort Stevenson.

The next morning, February 4, 1869, Kelly, the loner, proceeded on his way westward over the frozen landscape. A few miles along the trail, he unexpectedly ran into two Sioux. As surprised as the mailman, the Sioux tried to set an ambush a little late. In the sniping duel which followed, both Indians forfeited their lives.[89] Kelly immediately got out of the vicinity, fearful that the two were scouts or stragglers from a war party. He returned to the hunting camp where he had spent the night. Not long after, Bloody Knife and his hunting party appeared and were told of the fight. All of them vaulted onto their ponies and galloped off for the battleground, where they scalped the two dead Sioux, mutilated the bodies, and rode back to the camp, waving their trophies in triumph. The first three or four men to touch the bodies were awarded coups in a descending order of importance. Bloody Knife led the triumphant party to Fort Berthold, where they effected a dramatic victory entrance. The celebration went on for days.

Chapter 12

Scouting at Fort Buford

At Fort Buford, across from the mouth of the Yellowstone on the Missouri, the little garrison of one company had been hard pressed to hold the place over the first winter of 1866-67, due to a constant siege by Sioux of all branches under the general leadership of Sitting Bull. Had it not been for the concentration of warriors at Fort Phil Kearny in northern Wyoming Territory, the understrength post might well have faced real trouble. It was near Fort Phil Kearny on December 21, 1866 that Captain William J. Fetterman's entire command of 81 men was destroyed by an estimated 1500-2000 Sioux, Cheyenne and Arapaho warriors after being lured into an ambush by a decoy party led by Crazy Horse.[90]

In the summer of 1867, Fort Buford was reinforced with four more companies of infantry, which did not seem to make the least bit of difference to the besiegers watching from the clay buttes and willow thickets of the river bottoms, attacking anyone who chanced to step from the protection of the palisade. The tenacity of the Sioux before Fort Buford was probably an important factor when the Assiniboins closed their ears to the entreaties of the officer from the fort trying to attract the young men into the scouting ranks. They wanted to stay as far away as possible from their estranged cousins, the Sioux. Somebody, though, eventually got to them, and on February 17, 1869, Post Surgeon James P. Kimball noted in his Medical Record that "eight (8) Indians, Assiniboines, were today enlisted in the U.S. service as scouts."[91] Two more enlisted in March.

Kimball's entry for May 18 recorded the loss of the first scout:

> A war party of Tetons, Santees and Yanktonnais numbering from 60 to 75 attacked the guard over the herd this AM about one mile east of the fort. Through the vigilance of our Indian scouts the attacking party was discovered before they made their charge or 'rush' and when they came on they were repulsed and driven back across the Missouri with a loss of one killed and several wounded. We lost one killed, an Assiniboine named Blue Horn.[92]

Two days later, Kimball reported that the scouts had again seen warriors sneaking around the herd in time to prevent a stampede. One of the reasons for the scouts' alertness was Fort Buford's geophysical position, situated as it was with high bluffs and hills beginning half a mile to a mile north where some of the scouts stood outpost guard, equipped with field glasses. It was a lonely, hazardous job.

Fred Gerard's private commercial venture was little better at Fort Buford than it had been at Berthold. His store at Buford, trustingly turned over to the management of his brother, J.B. Gerard, was closed by the post commander in February, when J.B. was charged with violation of the "Intercourse Law," which was not as seductive a statute as it would appear. He was, in addition, accused of conspiring with certain soldiers to secure government grain for illegal sale. Officially, the Indian Trade and Intercourse Regulations of June 30, 1834, stipulated, among other provisions, that no liquor could be manufactured or sold in the Indian Country, that is, with the exception of the traders' private stock. And J.B. Gerard had been caught selling liquor to Indians. There was no appeal. He was banished from the post and the military reservation and allowed two hours to get out.[93]

Ordinarily, he might have gotten off with a warning. But they threw the book at him because he had earlier been found guilty of selling illegal liquor to soldiers at Fort Stevenson, then drinking with them when Fred Gerard had temporarily entrusted him with the store there. For that offense, he was evicted from the post and Fred was excused when he pleaded that he had not been personally involved. Now, at Buford, Fred was lucky enough to persuade the commanding officer into allowing him to continue in business — again since he was not personally involved.

****

First Lieutenant Mott Hooton of the 22nd Infantry presided over the swearing-in ceremonies when Bloody Knife enlisted for his second hitch in the scouts on May 21, 1869, this time at Fort Buford. Previously, requests had been made of the Indian Agent at Berthold by Buford's commanding officer to recruit scouts from among his people.

Word was received about the middle of June that the Sioux had absorbed what could be construed in the Indian mind as a disastrous defeat at Fort Berthold on June 8. Five hundred of them attacked at the Four Bears coulee near the fort with 100 women following after them to mop up the field and pack the plunder. But brave old White Shield brought his warriors plunging into the overconfident invaders, and in a three-hour fight killed and wounded

40 of them, with a loss to the Three Tribes of about half that number.

August, and the Sioux did not let the blasting heat of summer interfere with their designs on the bluecoats at Fort Buford. On Tuesday, August 10, 1869, they came at the haying party at work below the post and simultaneously attacked a party of four white citizens who had just left the fort. The haying party drove off its assailants and found much evidence of killed or wounded Indians. The four citizens were killed to a man.[94]

In their retreat, the warriors were chased by a group of scouts, a handful of soldiers, and a band of Assiniboins which just happened to be at Buford collecting their annuities. Bloody Knife was probably in the forefront, since he seems to have been the pursuer who discovered the wounded young Sioux warrior on the riverbank, shot through the thigh, his longing eyes watching his red brothers make their way to safety across the Missouri. Apparently, the young man had lost his weapons, for Joseph Henry Taylor's lurid, melodramatic description of the incident has Bloody Knife advancing from the cover of some willows without haste, savoring his advantage over the Sioux youth. First, he went for the scalp and as his fingers locked in the hair and the scraping knife point encircled the crown, the boy, who seemed to know him, pleaded despairingly, "Bloody Knife, have pity. I am only a boy as you may see — and this was my first trip to war."

Mercilessly, the scout tore off the scalp. It made a popping sound. Blood streamed down the Indian's face and head. "Bloody Knife will take care that you will not make that mistake again," he intoned. Then he reached down and clasped the youth's hand and with the keen knife blade cut into the victim's wrist, circling it and breaking down the bone joints. Now, blood spurted.

"You will kill me, Bloody Knife," pleaded the young Sioux

again. "Bloody Knife prepares his enemy for the Happy Hunting Ground before starting him on his long journey," said the scout with unfeeling sarcasm. He treated the youth's other hand in the same manner, but by that time, it didn't matter. Suffering from pain and loss of blood, the youth became unconscious and died shortly thereafter.[95]

But the score was not quite even that day. Surgeon N.H. Marselis, acting in place of the absent Kimball, reported in the case of the four slaughtered citizens: "I extracted from one man Thirteen arrows, the others were almost as badly treated, being scalped and mutilated by the savages ..." One result of the fight was the hurried hiring of four additional scouts.

As a matter of fact, Bloody Knife was known to most of the Sioux. The first dozen or so years of his life spent with the Hunkpapas and his work as a runner for the Berthold traders had made his face a familiar one to many bands. Moreover, he still had friends and relatives with the tribes who often unwittingly volunteered information about the planned activities of Sitting Bull's people, which the scout duly reported to his post commander.

On August 17, 1869, the Post Adjutant, Lieutenant Thomas Newman, discharged Bloody Knife from one enlistment period and swore him into another, all within a matter of minutes.

On May 26 of the same year, the companies of the 22nd and 31st infantry regiments in garrison at Fort Buford were replaced by three companies of the 13th Infantry, commanded by Colonel Henry H. Morrow. That the new commandant was anxious to keep and reward his scouts was evident from the content of the first portion of a letter written by Morrow to the Department Adjutant at St. Paul on August 25:

... I am informed that the Major General Commanding, on his return to St. Paul, will ascertain whether
non-commissioned officers are allowed for Indian
Scouts and if so that he will appoint Bloody Knife
and the Lone Wanderer over the Scouts at Buford.
This would certainly be a move in the right direction. It would show the Indians that they were *trusted*
by the White man and that fidelity and courage on
their part would be rewarded. Lone Wanderer is now
out on the chase, but Bloody Knife is here, and well
merits any distinction that may be conferred upon
him.[96]

The effect of the request was less than immediate. It would
be 1872 before Bloody Knife would wear the chevrons of lance
corporal.

The major general referred to was Winfield S. Hancock,
Commander of the Department of Dakota, who, with the usual
official retinue, had passed through Fort Buford on a tour of inspection on July 16.[97]

Eleven years later, Hancock would come within 10,000
votes, out of almost nine million cast, of becoming the 20th President of the United States. His 1880 election loss to the Republican, James Garfield, was the narrowest popular vote margin in any
presidential election up to that time.[98]

The second portion of the same letter dealt with the problem of Blue Horn's widow. The Assiniboin scouts, like the Arikaras,
had not been informed of any provisions relating to the care of
their families in the event they were killed or died in service. Now
there was a test case. Morrow wrote:

... I invite attention to the fact that Blue Horn, a

Scout, was killed here last spring in the execution of his duty. He was on guard with the post herd when it was attacked by a band of Sioux, and he was killed while attempting to defend his charge. I respectfully inquire whether or not his widow is entitled to a pension. During the pending of this inquiry, I have given orders to the A.C.S. (Adjutant Commissary of Subsistence)* at this post to issue her rations. Such a course I deemed no less just than politic. When I made application to the (Assiniboin)* chiefs a few days since for Scouts the case of Blue Horn was referred to by them and inquiry was made whether government was going to take care of his widow or throw her upon the Charity of the tribe. I assured them that she should be fed and she has accordingly come to the Post now and lives with the families of the Scouts. Is my action approved?

With some trepidation, Morrow waited.

A heartening and well-founded rumor flew through the fort about the middle of September, confirming the troops' suspicions that they had hurt the Sioux in the August 10 fight. Morrow was able to report to St. Paul that 10 of the attackers had been killed and that their camp was a scene of deep mourning. He cited several sources for the story, which probably meant that Bloody Knife's informants had been in touch with the scout. Another source had to be someone in one of the several Yanktonnai bands at that time, visiting Buford and dickering with Morrow for the privilege of making a treaty with the United States in order to receive annuities.

By November 1, 1869, the Fort Buford post roster listed 29 Indian scouts currently serving. Several of them had been on the sick list during the year, but none had died. When Colonel Morrow paid the troops that day, the total amount of money delivered to the scouts was $511.44.[99]

For the Arikara scouts, the news from home was not pleasant. There had been a crop failure and game was scarce; people again were starving. The new agent, Captain Walter Clifford of the Army, a true humanitarian, was honestly trying to get something done about the plight of the Berthold Indians. He knew that the valley of the Yellowstone River was one of the world's finest game areas and virtually untouched, so in the late fall, he loaded most of the able bodied Indians aboard a steamboat and sent them to Fort Buford, where, after a brief reunion with the scouts and their families, the tribes undertook a long winter hunt in the territory of their enemies. Those Indians remaining at Berthold were fed daily.[100] It was an emergency measure, but it averted disaster for the village.

December 9 arrived and Morrow still had no reply to his August 25 inquiry about the future of Blue Horn's widow. He wrote again, repeating a portion of the story and asking, "Is this woman entitled to a pension? As no answer has been received to this communication, I renew the inquiry."

Then, trouble invaded the scout quarters in a fatal and rather intimate nature. Post Surgeon Kimball's report:

> To-kah-A-ten, or He That Kills His Enemies, an Indian scout in a quarrel with a fellow scout on the 5th inst. received a penetrating arrow wound of the pelvis and abdomen. The arrow entered midway between the right ischium and the anus. The shaft of the arrow having been withdrawn before he came under surgical observation, the exact direction of the arrow could not be determined, but as the blood marked on the shaft showed that it had penetrated about twelve inches and the arrow head would make at least three inches more. It is supposed that the arrow had passed up through the pelvis into the abdomen ... He appeared to progress favorably for

several days when symptoms of peritonitis appeared and death occurred January 18th. An autopsy could not be obtained owing to the feelings and (objections)* of the relatives.[101]

The diagnosis would indicate that the warrior with the assertive name had to be, at the moment he was shot, half prostrate in the classic pose of mortal fear. He must have been on his knees, head to the floor covered with his hands, and with breech-clothed rear aimed into the air and toward his opponent, who had no other target. A medical dictionary describes the ischium as "the bone upon which one places his weight when sitting." If Surgeon Kimball settled back in his office chair in wonder and ruminated that now he had seen everything, he could hardly be blamed. Poor *To-Kah-A-Ten* was most likely an Assiniboin. His murderer remains unidentified.

****

The New Year was still young when Colonel Morrow's conscience was cleared. A communication from Department Headquarters enlightened him:

> ... The Acting Commissioner of Pensions is of the opinion that if an Indian Scout is serving with a regular organized Military force of the U.S. and is killed while in the performance of duty, his widow will be entitled to the same benefit of the Pension Laws, as the widow of any other Enlisted man ...[102]

Nobody along the line, it would seem, had wanted to make

the decision, but had boosted the inquiry all the way back to Washington. General William T. Sherman had earlier granted grudging permission to feed the woman, but not beyond the opening of the spring of 1870.

Most frontier military posts kept stock of condemned Army food on hand which could be doled out to Indian bands and tribes when they visited the posts. In some cases, the food issue was all that kept destitute bands from starving on the move from one location to another. Colonel Morrow had second thoughts in February 1870 about his use of "Indian Stores." He wrote the Acting Adjutant General at St. Paul advising that officer that the pay of an Indian scout was not sufficient to support his family and unless the man had assurance that rations would be issued to his family, he would not enlist. Morrow said that he had been in the habit of issuing rations to the families from Indian Stores, but he was afraid the day would come when they would no longer be available. Then he got to the heart of the matter, requesting an opinion whether the stores should be issued to families. In true Army fashion, he was covering his actions.

****

On the 18th of February 1870, Bloody Knife re-enlisted.

****

Authorities at Fort Buford had not seen fit to erect buildings specifically for the housing of scouts, preferring at first that the Indians camp outside the stockade in tipis. In the spring, a few of them were assigned new quarters in a citizen's vacant house near the Post Trader's store a few rods to the southeast and off the post grounds.

Charles Larpenteur, now trading independently at Buford, hired a new employee in the spring and Bloody Knife made some new friends. Thomas Jackson, a white man married to a woman of mixed white and Blackfeet blood, had brought his family from Fort Benton. Of Jackson's two young sons, Robert, age 16, and Billy, age 14, the latter is the source for the statement that the first friend the boys made was Bloody Knife.[103]

What Jackson did not mention was that being a family of mixed bloods, they were not welcome in the makeshift salons of the fort's white social set. They found they were outcasts from the Yanktonnai Sioux camped around the fort at that time, too, as a result of a run-in with some of that tribe on the journey from Benton to Buford in which a Sioux was wounded. A close acquaintance must have blossomed, though, for the Jackson brothers and the Ree scout traveled paths which often paralleled in the next few years. It may have been empathy, seasoned with a bit of compassion, which formed the bonds between them. At any rate, the two youngsters made acquaintances of all the Ree scouts and began to learn the language.

Ambush was once again the order of the day when a large Sioux war party dashed at four men in the employ of the wood contractor three miles from the fort, at nine a.m. on June 13, 1870. The official report read:

> The affray was seen by one of the scouts of the Post who at once brought in the news, wherefore Lieuts. E. H. Townsend and Thos. Newman 13th Infantry with 17 Indian Scouts and about 20 men were at once dispatched to the scene of action and arrived

in time to save the wood cutters from death, although not until they were all wounded, two slightly and two severely. The Indians were closely followed and one Indian killed by Lieut. Townsend. It is thought that several others were killed or wounded.[104]

Visiting photographer Stanley J. Morrow, however, had a different version of the fight, in which the scouts did not come off so well:

A party of men ... eight in number ... about three miles from the Fort ... were set upon by a party of about three hundred Indians. They ... fought the Indians for about an hour. It appears there were a few Indian scouts in the rear of the party who made good time to the Fort and gave the alarm. General Morrow at once dispatched Lieut. Townsend with a squad of men in a mule team, and although one of the wheels of the wagon came nearly off twice, they arrived in time to save the men ...[105]

But Morrow was not an eyewitness to the fight, which could account for a garbled version.

To make the situation even more confusing, the raid took place precisely at the time the 13th Infantry was being relieved as post garrison by the 7th Infantry, commanded by Colonel Charles C. Gilbert. Because Colonel Morrow was still in command, he ordered out his people in defense and he made that distinction in his report.

****

Scouting at Fort Buford

Gilbert, being new to the post, needed information. He wrote St. Paul asking how many Indian scouts were authorized and some related questions. His three companies of the 7th were only slightly below the average strength of the post complement for the past several months. It had ranged as high as five companies. The point, as he saw it, was that he was short of manpower. His reaction can be guessed at when the reply informed him that previously he had been authorized 10 scouts, that he was now authorized 20 more. But, Gilbert's Post Returns showed that he was already carrying 20, two of whom were sick in the hospital.

From August 2 the scouts were busier than usual. On that date, Captain Charles C. Rawn took 25 men of his I Company to Fort Stevenson to bring the beef herd to Fort Buford. On the 12th, a survey of the 30-mile square military reservation was commenced. Rawn brought the herd in on the 21st. On the 22nd, Captain Alonzo A. Cole with Company F started out for Fort Peck, while at the same time Lieutenant William Henry Nelson led a detachment of infantry and mounted infantry into the Yellowstone Valley as escort to a "Board" examining the region for the possibilities of a railroad. That scout was a portent of events to come. On the 28th, Captain Richard Comba rounded up an escort to take no less a VIP than the Assistant Quartermaster of the U.S. Army over to Fort Stevenson. And all those jobs required scouts. Their ranks were spread thin.

A hit and run strike by some Yanktonnais on the log camp six miles up the Yellowstone in September left a citizen dead. A mixed force of 20 soldiers and scouts went up the rescue but the hostiles had faded into the Badlands.

Bloody Knife missed most of those tiresome scouts and patrols. He was discharged on August 18, 1870 and did not re-enlist until September 30. When he did, it was under the new, reduced pay scale of $13 a month for the private soldier. He was at the fort, however, on September 9 when he and a brother scout, Lean Bear, were unexpected witnesses to the killing of a Mandan Indian, Going Eagle. An unofficial military version is in the Medical Records:

> A difficulty occurred this evening between Mr. Farwell of the firm of Durfee Peck Co. and some of the Indians encamped just below the Post. It seems that an old Mandan Indian had a horse belonging to Mr. Farwell taken from the latter's corral and removed to his camp in the willows. Mr. Farwell and a man in his employ went to the Indian camp to bring the horse back, and as he found it and was about to take it, an Indian (supposed to be Lean Bear a scout at the post) fired at Mr. Farwell wounding him in the back of the neck which caused him to fall from his horse at which moment the Mandan Indian rushed upon him with two bowie knives inflicting one serious and one slight wound in the right shoulder. Mr. Farwell rallied and shot the Mandan Indian through the head with a Navy revolver. His attendant commenced to empty his Henry rifle, shooting the Mandan Indian through the heart and Lean Bear through the right lung. The bullet entering between the 2nd and 3rd ribs in front and passed downward and made its exit between the 7th and 8th ribs posteriorly.

So much for the military version, flavored with professional medical diagnosis. Evidently, Lean Bear thought he was aiding a wronged Going Eagle, but in his deposition the convalescing scout did not state that he fired a shot. Bloody Knife's affidavit of the incident was not much more help, his unsatisfactory story showing a reluctance to inform on a brother Indian. He did not intend to displease the officers, either. Lieutenant William L. English, who was killed seven years later at the Battle of the Big Hole against the Nez Perces, extracted his account through an interpreter, Joseph Lambert:

> I was sitting at the front of my tent, rubbing some medicine on my arm, when I perceived Mr. Farwell riding down to the camp. I heard him say, 'Hold on, hold on,' in English. When I heard him use these words, I stood up and looked in that direction, and I saw the old Mandan, Going Eagle, coming towards Mr. Farwell with a knife. I seen him strike Mr. Farwell twice with the knife, and then Mr. Farwell shot, and he shot again and again, and then I saw Mr. Farwell coming out of the woods, coming away from there; at the same time there was a white man, the man who went down with Mr. Farwell, fired into the camp. I don't know whether he killed anybody or not. That is all I saw. I do not know for certain, but to the best of my knowledge it was the man who rode with Mr. Farwell that killed Going Eagle, the Mandan.[106]

It was a sad case of mistaken intention and injustice all around. Lean Bear and Abel Farwell recovered.

Billy Jackson said it was about this time that Bloody Knife received a visit from relatives who gave him two good horses which he in turn presented to the Jackson boys.

The Jacksons were ambitious to become scouts and wanted Bloody Knife to put in a good word for them. He could and he probably did. The boys presented themselves before Gilbert in December and asked that they be enlisted. It was hardly necessary for the colonel to ask them their ages, but he let them down gently and relented enough to grant them permission to ride with the scout detachment on occasion.

****

From the scout quarters on December 28 a keening from Indian women, abrasive to the eastern ear, drifted through the frigid air over the post grounds. A daughter of Bloody Knife lay dead, the victim of an unspecified disease. Post Surgeon Washington Matthews, a replacement for Kimball in November, and normally a recorder of every event, major or minor, did not consider the tragedy of sufficient importance to enter in his journal. Fort Buford cemetery records reveal only that the girl was buried in an unmarked grave.[107]

****

As 1871 dawned, it was obvious that politics was dipping its stained fingers ever deeper into the post trader mess. An order received in January relieved Buford's current traders of their licenses and informed the Post Commander and the traders that henceforth only one trader would be licensed for each post. Moreover, none of the present companies would be allowed to continue, meaning that Durfee and Peck, Larpenteur and Fred Gerard would have to close their doors. The new man would be Alvin C. Leighton of the firm of Leighton and Jordan. The order broke the spirit of Larpenteur; Gerard looked bewilderedly about for another enterprise. They did have a little time, but they must be off the post in June.[108]

****

A concerned Colonel Gilbert wrote St. Paul on January 16:

At a period last fall, when the Indian Scouts were going out of the service in considerable numbers and no Indians offering to replace them, certain frontier men presented themselves, who had served in the Detachment, producing their discharges and stating that there was authority from the Department Commander to enlist them to a limited number, though white men. I have caused the records of the office to be examined for the authority referred to, but do not find it — will you please state whether or not it exists and if not, I shall be obliged to you if you will ask the Major General Commanding to sanction such enlistments, as have been made by Lieut. Nelson, Commanding the Scouts. These men were greatly needed at the time as escorts and guards to Contractor's working parties and as escorts for parties seeking coal, limestone, sand and the like building material, in the neighborhood of the Post.[109]

Gilbert had reason to be concerned. His Indian scout force was down to six, with two of them in the hospital. On the 19th, most of those still able bodied were assigned to a party ordered to Fort Peck to investigate a report of renegade whiskey traders operating there. His request was approved.

By February, the month the Rees know as the Black, Storming Moon and the Sioux call the Moon of the Popping Trees, only four scouts were left on the roster. All of them were on the sick list, including Bloody Knife. Optimistically, though, Gilbert fired off another missive with an idea designed to improve the efficiency of his scout detachment, if and when he got them:

The Indian Scouts at this Post have hitherto been kept in a separate Detachment with an Officer in command. From my observation it appears to me that it would be better to have them distributed among the Companies for pay, clothing and subsistence, and service. The chief reason for the change

Bloody Knife: Custer's Favorite Scout

is that under the present arrangement, when a company or detachment goes out the soldiers and Indians are strangers to each other and in every case where it has not been practicable to send an interpreter, the scouts have been but little better than useless, whereas if by constant contact with the men, the scouts and soldiers had come to understand each other, the services of the Indians would be highly valuable. Please inform me as to the views of the Department Commander in this matter.[110]

The views of the Department Commander differed. Integration was denied.

On the 30th of March, Bloody Knife made what was getting to be a milk run to the Adjutant's office and the usual call on the Post Surgeon and was re-enlisted.

The fierce, deadly winters of the Upper Missouri may have had some bearing on the low enlistment rate. It was customary for Indian tribes and bands to hole up in the deep, timbered coulees through the cold months. Arikara scouts were wont to go home to Fort Berthold during this time, to live in their warm tipis or bark and log lodges and enjoy friendships around the perpetual lodge fires. Centuries of experience had taught them that it was impossible to heat the monstrous earth lodges adequately in the dead of winter.

March found Gilbert with seven scouts at work, and he must have felt sailor-rich in April when Lieutenant Nelson daily called roll on 30 of them. It was about time. Contractors were screaming for protection and they got it.

****

Down at Fort Rice, on the right bank of the Missouri in its

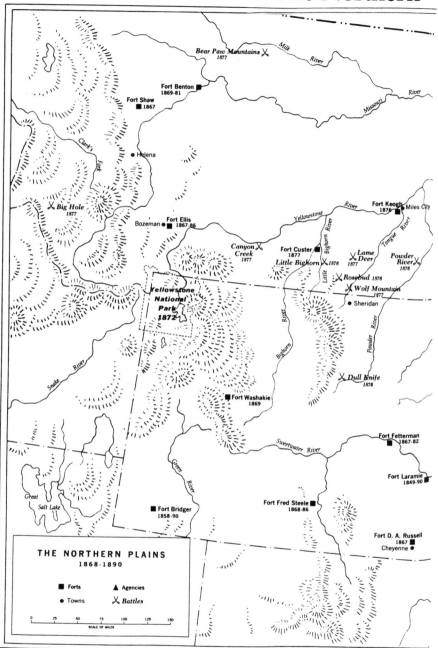

From *The Indian Frontier of the American West, 1846-1890* by Robert M. Utley (Albu-
University of New Mexico Press.

Bloody Knife: Custer's Favorite Scout

Plains, 1868-1890

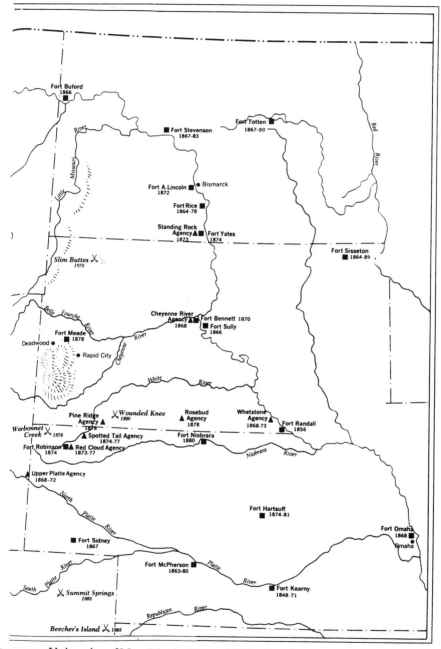

Fort Buford
1866

Fort Stevenson
1867-83

Fort Totten
1867-90

Red River

Missouri River

Little Missouri

Fort A. Lincoln
1872

Bismarck

Fort Rice
1864-78

Standing Rock Agency
1873

Fort Yates
1874

Fort Sisseton
1864-89

Slim Buttes
1876

Belle Fourche River

Cheyenne River Agency
1868

Fort Bennett 1870

Fort Sully
1866

Fort Meade
1878

Deadwood

Rapid City

Cheyenne River

White River

Pine Ridge Agency

Wounded Knee
1890

Rosebud Agency
1878

Whetstone Agency
1868-73

Fort Randall
1856

Warbonnet Creek 1876

Spotted Tail Agency
1874-77

Fort Niobrara
1880

Fort Robinson
1874

Red Cloud Agency
1873-77

Niobrara River

Upper Platte Agency
1868-72

North Platte River

Fort Hartsuff
1874-81

Fort Omaha
1868

Omaha

Fort Sidney
1867

Fort McPherson
1863-80

Platte River

Fort Kearny
1848-71

South Platte River

Summit Springs
1869

Republican River

Beecher's Island 1868

uerque: University of New Mexico Press, 1984). Reprinted by permission of the

Scouting at Fort Buford   81

reaches below the Great Bend, Doctor Benjamin Slaughter, irate at what he regarded as a perfect example of official stupidity, vented his wrath on his diary: "The Ree scouts have been discharged by the Commanding Officer! Bah! Had nothing else to do."[111]

A look at the record would have vindicated Slaughter in his temper tantrum. The previous year, all the Arikara scouts at Fort Rice had been discharged in favor of hiring Sioux from Standing Rock for a reason which at the time seemed perfectly sound — that the Sioux could make the mail and escort trips to and from Fort Sully in safety since they were traveling through a country populated by their own people.[112] Thirty days later, the scout recruiter was talking to Rees again and possibly to himself. It had taken the Sioux just 25 days to decide they wanted to go home — and they deserted wholesale.

****

Four hundred miles to the northwest, Gilbert may have talked to himself too. Of his 27 active scouts, two were sick and seven under arrest, most for drunkenness. With his known attraction to the keg, the chances are better than good that Bloody Knife was one of them.

Assiniboins had not been noted for quickly stepping forward to volunteer for the scouting rank and file. Ten of them were due to be discharged in the latter part of August and all had indicated that they did not intend to touch the pen again. Gilbert picked up his pen and asked the Indian Agent at Fort Berthold to notify his Indians that Fort Buford had scouting vacancies. After that, the scout roster showed little fluctuation for the rest of the year.

Then, one day, one of the detachment stopped a bullet with his number on it. There would be no bragging about the wound because it was accidental, and luckily, it was not fatal. The Post Surgeon made only a brief entry: "August 20: Whistling Elk, I. Scout, accidentally shot this P.M. while on Det. service as escort to Mr. Anderson's Hay party."

The Army took care of its own until September 4, when Matthews penned another entry: "Whistling Elk, Indian scout, recently wounded, was discharged the service today."[113]

The wounding of a man did not seem to affect recruiting. Six Indians were sworn in the next day, two Arikaras on October 24, and three mixed bloods enlisted on October 26.

Another knotty problem, embarrassing, and a sore point to officers at a strictly infantry post like Buford, arose and Gilbert on September 16 went to the top about it:

> During the last year the scouting and patroling of the country about the Post has fallen well nigh exclusively to one Officer, viz: to the Commanding Officer of the Detachment of Mounted Infantry and Indian Scouts. As at present situated, I am obliged to have each Officer go in his turn, and accordingly, respectfully request that the Government forage and shelter one private horse for every Company Officer pertaining to this Command. It is understood that these Officers either own a horse apiece or are willing to buy one if the animal can be kept in the public stables without too much expense to the owner. Whenever I have had Mounted Infantry at my post heretofore in some way or other the Officers liable to be called on to use this force have either had the advantage of constant practice on Government horses or have been able to keep private animals in the public stables at no great expense to themselves or the Government on their own responsibility — although from the remoteness of the Post and the difficulties which surround it I

had become impressed with a somewhat better idea. A public horse for the Officer Commanding the Indian Scouts and one for the Post Quarter-Master Sergeant is as many as can well be spared from the Mounted Detachment for constant use. The manifest hardships of requiring an Officer of Infantry to mount a strange animal on a sudden summons and fight as formidable wild horsemen as are to be found on the continent, will suggest that something be done in the matter being referred to.[114]

Gilbert was right, as he had been right about integrating the scouts with the troops, but nothing official was done.

Chapter 13

Scouts and Traders

Other events were beginning to build toward a climax on the Northern Plains. Sitting Bull, firmly rooted in power among his Hunkpapas and disaffected Indians from other Sioux tribes, began overtures to alien Indian nations in an effort to entice them into a great alliance reminiscent of the days of Tecumseh. From out of the awesome stretches of country along the Missouri, Yellowstone and Powder rivers disquieting rumors emerged. Sitting Bull was talking with Cheyennes and Assiniboins; Sitting Bull had been seen at the Arapaho villages; the Three Tribes were next to be approached about joining his confederation; the subtle mastermind had even said he would council with the Crows and Shoshones, long-time enemies of the Sioux. Yet it was true. The shrewd warrior and medicine man knew what most of his race did not or refused to realize — that the real enemy, the most deadly enemy, was the white man.

****

The restrictions of carrying on trading, not all of it legal, under several hundred pairs of watchful eyes evidently proved to be a bit binding on Leighton and Jordan. Bands of Sioux considered hostile came in to Fort Buford to trade, but never in small groups. They called in sufficient numbers to protect themselves in the event the fort's scouts chanced to be in a fighting mood or in case the Long Knives had gotten word of their latest depredations. Citizens and Indians were not always able to purchase certain articles much in demand, such as arms, ammunition and liquor, and thirsty soldiers all too often wound up in the guardhouse when they were picked up drunk in their own dooryards. It was a serious disadvantage to be 400 miles from the nearest town.

And so it happened that in November 1871, partner James Leighton of Leighton and Jordan, at the head of a small wagon train of goods, traveled south out of Fort Buford along the north bank of the Yellowstone to a point where he believed he had cleared the southern boundary of the military reservation. There he stopped and founded a trading post.[115] He was accompanied on the trip by the commanding officer of Fort Buford, Colonel Gilbert, and an escort of 50 scouts and soldiers. Leighton named his new prairie emporium Fort Gilbert. It was a bargain in exchange for a wink of the eye at the right time.

Having been involved in founding the trading post, Gilbert was now bound to protect it as part of his regional responsibility. He left a small detachment of Indian scouts to permanently guard his namesake. It was good duty for the scouts, not much to do, and they were probably living higher than their brothers at the home station. That is, it was good duty until they lost their horses. In the latter part of the next May, a small party of the accomplished Sioux horse thieves ran off the scouts' mounts. Had they all been personal horses, the matter would no doubt have been dropped after a tongue lashing, with the scouts forced to find replacements. But one of the animals was a public horse, a government horse, for which the Post Quartermaster was responsible. Under the command of a sergeant, a patrol was sent out to follow the marauders and, if possible, recover the pilfered livestock. Thirty miles up the Yellowstone, they ran across unmistakable signs of a large Indian encampment, and since it was known that no friendly Indians were in such strength in that part of the country, the patrol prudently withdrew to Fort Gilbert.

****

On January 1, 1872, First Lieutenant William Logan, 7th U.S. Infantry, was assigned to the command of the Indian scouts and mounted infantry detachment.

****

Gilbert, foreseeing more vacancies in the scout force, wrote in February to John Tappan, the Indian Agent at Fort Berthold. The colonel specified the rules under which a man could enlist, just so there were no misunderstandings:

> This is a proper time for asking you to notify the Indians pertaining to your Agency that there will be some vacancies in the spring in the Scouts and that I prefer yours to any others likely to offer. It is proper, however, that it should be understood that the Scouts will probably have to serve Weekly, semi-Monthly, or Monthly tours with detached commands, in camps or stockades at distances of one, two, three and perhaps five days march from the Post, also that a Scout's family will be limited to himself, wife, children and his infirm parents. Relations of wife will not be allowed excepting under special permit in each case. An earnest effort was made to have rations issued to Scout's families, but

the General of the Army objected and they cannot therefore expect rations. This should be understood.[116]

Lieutenant Logan did not need to request a professional appraisal of the condition of the Indian scouts' quarters in various unused buildings. It was all too obvious. On April 9, 1872, he ordered them out of the buildings and into Army tents at a location off the fort grounds. The very next day a blizzard struck, one of those unseasonal storms which are not unseasonal at all in North Dakota. Post Surgeon Washington Matthews' entry for the day was in a chiding vein when he wrote, "The scouts and their families who are living in common 'A' tents and without fires are suffering greatly."[117]

Presumably, they were furnished with some sort of warming equipment, but they stayed in the tents. In June they were moved to the neighborhood of the corral to the east of the post, where they could be near their horses.

That season, Agent Tappan was able to report to his superiors from Fort Berthold that 40 of his Indians were employed as scouts, serving at Fort Stevenson, Fort Buford, and at the new post downriver on the west bank of the Missouri, Fort McKeen.[118]

****

Perhaps trader James Leighton berated himself in June for his haste in the naming of his trading post when his close friend, Colonel Gilbert, departed with his 7th Infantry for Fort Shaw, Montana Territory. The troops were replaced by five companies of the trans-Mississippi veteran regiment, the 6th Infantry, under the command of a frontier-wise ramrod known as somewhat of a martinet, Colonel William B. Hazen.[119] If the desk jockeys at St. Paul and Washington imagined there would be a respite from the flood that was Gilbert's correspondence, they were doomed to an early disappointment, for Gilbert simply was not in the same penmanship league with Hazen.

****

Fresh from the states, 6th Infantry recruit Reed staggered into Fort Buford several days late in the care of an unnamed Arikara scout. Fifty miles downstream, Reed had become lost from his steamboat. He had about exhausted himself looking for help when the scout, traveling alone from Berthold to Buford, came upon him. To the raw recruit Reed, there was no such thing as a friendly Indian. Somehow, communication was established and the unnerved Reed was led safely to his company.

****

Scouts were included in the issuance of annuities at their home agencies, generally allocating their shares to their families. But when the annuity volume doubled in 1872 from previous years, there were a number of dissatisfied scouts at Buford. Unhappy because they had missed the windfall, they protested to the Post Commander, who wrote Tappan about the problem. Tappan replied that he had distributed the goods in good faith, reserving the portions intended for the scouts and presenting them to the families. He did not appreciate, he said, the applications for annuities by two unqualified men, one of them a Red River mixed blood not entitled to annuities there, and the other a Mexican not entitled to annuities anywhere. Among the names he listed as being present for the distribution was that of Bloody Knife.

During a respite from warrior raids, the scout detachment performed the duties expected of them. On June 28, 1872, an overland party proceeded westward to Big Muddy Creek as protection for a skiffload of soldiers on their way to pick up a misplaced pump; on July 4, others were assigned to the force sent to Fort Stevenson to bring in the cattle herd; four scouts were detailed on July 13 as escort to hay wagons; and another detail returned to Stevenson in August for more cattle. They lost one of their number on July 31, when *Ba Ki Na,* or Roulette, died of consumption. Matthews recorded on August 1 that the man was buried with full military honors.[120]

That same summer, Matthews received from Charles Larpenteur the diary the trader had kept during his four decades on the Upper Missouri. It may have been Matthews' intention to publish the story of his old friend, but it was not to be. The manuscript eventually ended up in the hands of Assistant Surgeon Elliot Coues, who edited and published it under the title *Forty Years a Fur Trader on the Upper Missouri.* It is one of the most valuable accounts of the Western fur trade ever written.[121]

Matthews is best remembered for his deeply researched articles on the manners and customs of the Hidatsas and Navajos, as well as a dictionary of the Hidatsa language.[122] Matthews constructed the dictionary entirely from memory after his research notes collected during six years of study among the Hidatsas were destroyed in a fire that broke out at Fort Buford the night of January 28, 1871.[123]

****

Bloody Knife sat out a part of the season after being discharged on April 2, 1872. He did not enlist again until October 2, this time as a lance corporal.

Bloody Knife: Custer's Favorite Scout

Chapter 14

White Men in Red Country

An event which was to make the Sioux extremely angry was afoot at Fort Rice. General David S. Stanley led a Plains Army of 1200 men out of the fort on July 25, 1872, escorting the surveying party of the Northern Pacific Railroad. His guides, a platoon of Arikara scouts recruited by Fred Gerard at Fort Berthold, roamed the flanks and provided the head of the column with far ranging eyes and ears. The previous year, the first of the surveying expeditions had penetrated deeply into Indian country along the Heart River.

Stanley's command in 1872 proceeded as far as the Powder River when the year's work was considered done, and they turned back for their station. Their western counterpart, surveying eastward from Fort Ellis under Major Eugene M. Baker, got to Pryor Creek on the Yellowstone River before they were struck on August 14 by a large war party of Sioux, Cheyennes and Arapahoes, resulting in the Pryor Creek Fight. Gall was there. The Indians were unable to make any headway against the troops.

Stanley's column fought a couple of skirmishes with Sitting Bull and Gall and their warriors. On August 18, Gall appeared across the Yellowstone and actually conversed with Stanley, threatening the general with many Indians and a big fight. In one of the small scale scraps, Gall rode dressed in a war bonnet and brilliant scarlet clothing, reaffirming another of his names, Walks in Red Clothing.

Some of the Indian bands harassed the column all the way back to Fort Rice. Just a matter of hours out of the post, they scored in an ambush led by Gall, killing two of the lieutenants and a servant. As a climax, the victorious Gall displayed the victims' scalps to the helpless troops from the top of a nearby hill.[124]

****

On July 6, 1872, Fred Gerard was hired as interpreter at Fort McKeen, a position he was to hold until 1882. Seven of the Arikaras he had recruited were killed in the hit-and-run raids of the Sioux around the post that season. The Post Surgeon there had high words of praise for them: "The Indian scouts in the several skirmishes with the Sioux in Oct. and Nov. exhibited instances of the greatest personal bravery and fearlessness."

****

One activity of interest to the scouts bestirred otherwise quiet days at Fort Buford. New quarters were being built for them.

When three prisoners escaped and deserted on October 7, it was probably with the collaboration of their guard, who took the "grand bounce" with them. The next day a lieutenant at the head of a group of scouts went after them, returning on the 10th empty handed. New information about the absconders was received on the 11th, and the Rees were off on the chase again under their commanding officer, Lieutenant Richard T. Jacob, Jr. Somebody, not the scouts, caught the guard and sent him back from Fort Stevenson by the 14th. It was not until the 27th that the Rees and Lieutenant Jacob filed back into Fort Buford, but they had with them the three cowed deserters.[125]

News of the re-election of President Grant was brought in by scouts from Fort Stevenson on November 21, 1872.

A directive of December 5 to the Adjutant Commissary of Subsistence from Lieutenant Colonel Daniel Huston, Jr., commanding in Hazen's absence, offered insights into the scouts' appetite:

> The Lieut. Col. cmdg. directs that hereafter the entrails of all beeves (beef)* killed be given to the scouts. He also directs that the brains, heart, kidneys, liver, tongue, sweet bread, shank and their bones be issued in turn to each officer desiring them.

To each his own.

****

Bloody Knife was accused of overstepping the bounds of his authority, judging from the content of a May 21, 1873 letter from Lieutenant Colonel Huston to Fort Berthold Indian Agent John Tappan:

> I have the honor to state in reply to your communication of April 25, 1873 that the scouts being enlisted now are subject to the same regulations as govern other enlisted men of the Army and of course are subject to confinement at hard labor in the Post Guard House for any violations of orders. The charges against Bloody Knife have been fully in-

quired into by me and found not true in any one particular. No Noncommissioned officer of Scouts has authority to inflict any punishment whatever on the men of the detachment. None but their commanding officer has that power and he to an extremely small extent. Gross breeches of military law and discipline are punished by the sentence of a Court Martial after a fair and impartial trial.[126]

It was not the first, nor would it be the last time that Bloody Knife's excesses would be officially overlooked.

Chapter 15

The Yellowstone Expedition of 1873

When the *Key West* sidled up to the Fort Buford pier at two o'clock on the morning of May 6, 1873, the scouts knew the talk they had heard the summer before about another expedition into the Yellowstone was true. On board the boat captained by Grant Marsh was Major George A. (Sandy) Forsyth, the respected hero of the September 1868 Battle of Beecher's Island in Colorado Territory, where his command of 50 frontiersmen had been besieged by several hundred Sioux, Cheyenne and Arapaho warriors for more than a week.

Major Forsyth was now in command of an exploratory expedition up the Elk River. He was to ascertain whether the stream was navigable as far as the mouth of the Powder River to enable the planners of the Yellowstone Expedition of 1873 to decide whether supplying the troops by steamboat was practicable. Hurriedly, two companies of the 6th Infantry were hustled aboard as escort. Calmly observing the activity was the expedition's guide, Yellowstone Kelly, recently picked up at the mouth of the Little Muddy, his long, snakeskin-covered Springfield rifle, "Old Sweetness," never far from his hand.[127] A handful of his old friends, the Ree scouts, also boarded.[128] Whether Bloody Knife was along was not recorded. Ten days later, the *Key West* was back at Buford carrying a favorable report.

Toward the end of the month, Bloody Knife and another scout, Fire Cloud, boarded a boat for Fort Abraham Lincoln and special duty with the Yellowstone Expedition.[129] She Owl and the children accompanied Bloody Knife as far as Fort Berthold, where they were to stay until the campaign was over.

The choice of Bloody Knife as scout and guide for the command was a logical and excellent one. He was thoroughly familiar with most of the country to be traversed, owing to the years he had spent living with the Hunkpapas.

From Fort Lincoln, the two Rees were sent on to Fort Rice, where they joined a contingent of their tribesmen waiting for the campaign to begin.

Billy Jackson, whose accounts are not always trustworthy, and yet who manages to evade building a hero's image for himself as so many of his class on the frontier were wont to do, wrote that Bloody Knife counciled with General Stanley, the expedition leader. He then reported to the assembled scouts that Sitting Bull was collecting an Indian army of Sioux, Cheyennes and Arapahoes with the intention of wiping out the soldiers and stopping the advance of the Iron Horse, the railroad. "My friends," Bloody Knife concluded, "maybe we are going to have soon one big fight."[130]

****

Lieutenant Colonel George A. Custer arrived a few days later. The Rees, Jackson noted, were impressed with the flamboyant officer's appearance in his fringed buckskin coat, fringed buckskin trousers, boots with red leather tops, and a wide-brimmed soft hat, instead of the regulation officer's uniform. Custer rode his spirited horse with grace and ease, his yellow curly hair hanging almost to his shoulders. Bloody Knife's reaction approached adulation, wrote Jackson, who reported the Arikara scout said, "That long, yellow-haired one, he is a real chief; of all white chiefs, the greatest chief!" This is doubtful. Bloody Knife was his own man, capable of respect for power, but he was not an idolator.[131] There was no way he could know that when he shook hands with Custer he had met his executioner.

Some months previously, the wife of Doctor Benjamin F. Slaughter, Army surgeon, was enjoying a horseback ride in the cool of the morning not far from Fort Lincoln. As she and her escort passed a dense growth of willows, an Indian rose out of concealment near them, upon which the lady's officer escort whipped their horses to a gallop, firing at the warrior with his revolver as they passed. The shot and the running horses brought rescuers on the run, but the Indian got away. Some time later, Isaiah Dorman, a black interpreter who would later be killed at the Little Bighorn, told Mrs. Slaughter that the warrior was a Sioux who had vowed at a scalp dance to one day wear her luxuriant tresses as an ornament.[132]

The end of the story came when one day a grinning Arikara scout presented himself at Mrs. Slaughter's door at Camp Hancock, held up a freshly taken scalp with an ear still attached, and proudly boasted that it was the hairpiece of the Sioux who had desired her scalp. An ill and shaken surgeon's wife gave the Ree the signed order for the 10 pounds of sugar he was asking for the prize and told him to begone.[133]

Billy Jackson wrote that Custer sent for Bloody Knife that first night and counciled long with him about the Sioux and their probable location in the Yellowstone country. Ever after, said Jackson, Bloody Knife was Custer's favorite scout.[134] Very quickly, Custer and Bloody Knife were *siinani* — Arikara for friend — to one another.

Holding Custer in varying degrees of reverence and awe and aware of the preferential treatment they were getting from him, the Ree scouts admiringly addressed him as Long Yellow Hair Chief. This was soon shortened to Long Hair. To Custer, it was immeasurably better than the pet nicknames of Hard Ass and Ringlets, which he knew his troops had pinned on him.

Separate units of the expedition began leaving Fort Lincoln and Fort Rice on June 20, with the remaining outfits departing on subsequent dates. Forty Arikara scouts had been hired, with Fred Gerard riding with them as their interpreter. Basil Clement was chief guide, along with Charley Reynolds.[135]

Besides the railroad surveying party of citizens, the command under General David S. Stanley consisted of 20 companies of the 6th, 8th, 9th, 17th and 22nd infantry regiments and 10 companies of the 7th Cavalry, a total of almost 1500 men. Thomas L. Rosser, former Confederate general and friend of Custer at West Point, was in charge of the survey crew numbering more than 350 people. Four of them were scientists and two others were independent travelers, members of British nobility. Two hundred and seventy-five wagons transported equipment, the noise of their movement drowned out by the bawls and squeals of the 2300 mules and horses and the 600 cattle in the beef herd. In addition, three steamboats — the *Key West*, the *Far West*, and the *Peninah* — belched their way upstream to rendezvous with the column at the mouth of Glendive Creek on the Yellowstone.

Bloody Knife and the Ree scouts rode far in advance and on the flanks, aiding the guides in locating the trail and choosing good camp sites. They were often accompanied by Custer.

Early in the campaign, Custer left the column on an unauthorized scout, found himself 15 miles out and cooly sent a message to General Stanley requesting forage and rations. They were not sent. He was ordered in and all of the 7th Cavalry was disciplined by being relegated to the rear of the line of march for a day. Long Hair was placed under arrest for a few days.[136]

The expedition reached the mouth of Glendive Creek on July 13, where they met the *Key West*, together with three companies of the 6th Infantry from Fort Buford under the command of Captain H.J. Hawkins. At a point eight miles above the mouth of the Glendive on the south bank of the Yellowstone, Stanley erected a stockade as his supply depot and named it after himself. Then the whole force rested.

Colonel William B. Hazen watched from his vantage point at Fort Buford, keeping in constant touch with the expedition by steamer and Ree scout shuttle mail service. He forwarded to St. Paul an excerpt from a letter received from Glendive Creek from an unidentified officer, presumably Captain Hawkins. The column had missed its objective through an error of the guide, the letter stated. This would have been Basil Clement's mistake. The informant also wrote that Custer had been arrested. The letter concluded: "There have been no incidents of note and monotony has tired out the whole expedition. I have no doubt when they cross the river they will welcome the vicinity of Indians as a relief to the everyday sameness."[137]

When survey work began, the country above the mouth of the Powder proved to be so rough that Stanley often ordered Custer to scout ahead to search out a road suitable for wagon travel. On the fourth day of August, Custer, with two companies of about 90 men and some scouts explored a route above the mouth of the Tongue River. It was a hot day and around noon, the men unsaddled, ate their midday meal, and rested under giant cottonwood trees. Suddenly, six Sioux swept boldly into the horse herd and attempted to stampede the animals out of the timber. But the Indians were driven off with the cavalrymen hastily saddling and galloping off in pursuit.

Custer halted his men as they approached a heavy growth of trees, and as he did so 300 mounted warriors exploded from the cover, screaming war cries. Gall was among them. Custer barked an order and the men dismounted to fight on foot. Later, he wrote, "The first Indian killed was shot from his pony by Bloody Knife, the Crow who acted as my guide and scout."[138] (His error of his scout's national origin must have been a slip of the pen).*

In the midst of the firing, the lofting arrows and the brave runs of their warriors, the Sioux tried to fire the grass and burn the troops out. But the wind was slight and the grass too green. Fighting continued until three o'clock in the afternoon. Seeing that an easy victory was not forthcoming, the Sioux wearied and drew off, whereupon the soldiers mounted and charged them, chasing them for three miles. Only one trooper was wounded. But when the fight was over, the bodies of two citizens were found, those of the 7th Cavalry veterinary surgeon, Dr. John Honzinger and the sutler, August Baliran. A private was missing. His body was found at the battlefield on the return trip a month later, obviously a victim of the Sioux. The troops thought they had killed four Indians.

Soon afterward, the scouts picked up the trail of a sizable Indian village of an estimated 80 lodges. Custer clung to it with the tenacity of a hunting hound for the next four days. Stanley turned him loose with four battalions of the 7th Cavalry, together with a complement of scouts, and Long Hair moved out that night.

On the morning of August 9, 1873, the scouts reported the retreating Indians had crossed the Yellowstone three miles below the mouth of the Bighorn. Here, Bloody Knife was convinced the Sioux village was close enough to attack by surprise. He felt that a dawn strike would demoralize the unsuspecting enemy and result in a great victory. He knew, too, that Gall was out there. But Custer balked at crossing the river, which threw his favorite scout into one of his black moods. Bloody Knife told his fellow scouts that he had shown Long Hair a method of crossing the stream, but Custer did not deign to answer him. Instead, he ordered the command into camp.

The situation did not change on the morning of the 10th. Custer again did not see fit to take his chief scout's advice. It was a disgusted Bloody Knife who watched the troops' blundering attempts to cross on a raft. At sundown, an unwary party of Sioux rode to the river to water their horses, discovered the soldiers and wheeled away and out of range before a shot could be fired at them. At this turn of events Bloody Knife, angered beyond his limit, shouted at Custer that the whites harbored "little bird hearts," that they were afraid to fight the Sioux.139

A rude awakening befell the troops in the morning, when the concealed Sioux opened up on their camp with rifle fire from the opposite bank. A squad of sharpshooters was dispatched to keep them down while the troopers prepared to fight. Five or six hundred of the attackers crossed the river below the cavalry position and came upon the defenders in a magnificent charge. They were held off long enough for Custer to organize a counter charge to the music of the regimental band playing "Garry Owen." The force and spirit of the charge drove the surprised Sioux from the field. They were pursued for eight miles before the buglers blew the Recall. The returning troopers picked up such discarded articles as coffee, sugar, bacon, new type cartridges and a couple of Winchester rifles. Stanley was sure the depredators had obtained the booty at " ... that center of iniquity in Indian affairs, Fort Peck."

Custer figured that he had faced almost a thousand Indi-

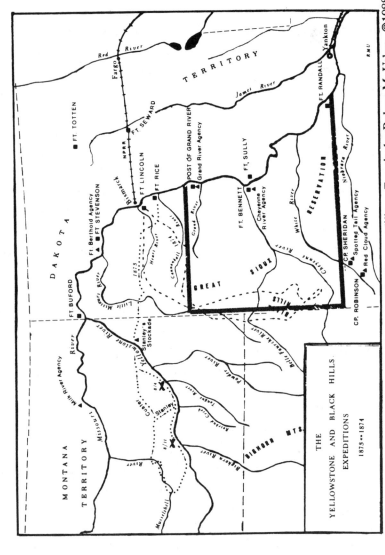

The Yellowstone and Black Hills Expeditions of 1873-74

From *Cavalier in Buckskin: George Armstrong Custer and the Western Military Frontier* by Robert M. Utley. ©1988 by the University of Oklahoma Press.

Bloody Knife: Custer's Favorite Scout

ans, inflicting on them losses in the two fights of 40 dead. Stanley officially reported four soldiers killed and four wounded in both engagements.

From that day on, the column was continually under observation by the Indians. The only other surprise came when many of the men were swimming one afternoon across the river from Pompey's Pillar, when a party of Sioux opened fire from around the great rock. Nobody was hit, but there was a churning of water and a scampering of naked white bodies flashing to the shelter of the bank.

The survey completed, Stanley sent Custer with six companies, the survey party and the scouts directly across country from the Musselshell River. Meanwhile, Stanley took the wagon train and the remainder of his command back along the Yellowstone, where they were sure to find forage. On September 6, 1873, Custer had the good fortune to shoot a fine, 800-pound bull elk on the Yellowstone under the guidance of Bloody Knife.

Libbie Custer told of another occasion where her husband and Bloody Knife had worked together to bring down a wildlife speciman. The head of the animal, she said, was one of many such trophies which adorned the walls of their home at Fort Lincoln:

> The head of a beautiful blacktailed deer was another souvenir of a hunt the General made with Bloody Knife, the favorite Indian Scout. When they sighted the deer, they agreed to fire together, the Indian selecting the head, the General taking the heart. They fired simultaneously, and the deer fell, the bullets entering heart and head.[140]

With the passing of the weeks they spent together during the expedition, a close camaraderie developed between Bloody

Knife and Custer, each probably recognizing in the other some of his own qualities. Both were bold men, courageous and resourceful. They saw the toughness in each other and the spirit of the vagabond, the latent urge to throw off all restraint and let a willful mind take its own course. Each accepted and respected the other for exactly what he was, as if to say, "Look, old fellow, I'm not fooling you and you're not fooling me. I know you for what you are. Let's get along." And they did.

****

When Bloody Knife returned to Fort Buford, it was with laurels which paid off in cash. General Stanley's high regard for his work prompted that officer to forward a laudatory letter to the commanding officer at the fort:

> I have directed the return to your post of the Indian scouts Bloody Knife and Fire Cloud. I take pleasure in commending the good conduct of these Indians. Bloody Knife has been particularly useful. Fire Cloud has been sick most of the march and has not rendered much service. Bloody Knife has been very highly spoken of in General Custer's dispatches for bravery in two Indian fights on the Yellowstone. Through the courtesy of the N.P.R.R. Co. I have secured for Bloody Knife sixty dollars, and for Fire Cloud forty dollars extra compensation for the time of their service on the expedition.[141]

Nor was that the only communication concerning the corporal that September. Lieutenant Richard T. Jacob, scout detachment commander, informed Indian Agent John Tappan at Fort Berthold of Bloody Knife's entirely natural request: "I have the honor to state that Bloody Knife request that you inform his wife that he has concluded to re-enlist at this Post, and that you will greatly oblige both him and myself by forwarding her to this Post by first opportunity."

Army red tape and paperwork were responsible for some light bookkeeping by the adjutant, Lieutenant Hiram H. Ketchum, on September 10 at Camp Thorne, which was serving as temporary headquarters of the Yellowstone Expedition in Montana Territory. Before him was the "Descriptive List and Account of Pay and Clothing" of each of the two scouts, Bloody Knife and Fire Cloud. The lists had been mailed to the Yellowstone Expedition and were now being brought up to date with campaign nearing its end.

In the case of Bloody Knife, Ketchum noted that he had furnished his own horse and equipment, that he was a scout by occupation, and the only charge against his account was for tobacco in August in the amount of 51 cents.

Fire Cloud's list described him as born in Montana Territory, age 23½, with brown eyes, black hair, a copper complexion, and a height of five feet, six inches. His occupation was listed as Warrior. An entry by Jacob indicated the scout was carrying a "B.L.B. Rifle Cal 50. and one hundred rounds of ammunition cal 50," belonging to the U.S. Army. Ketchum inserted charges for tobacco in the amount of $1.02.

Fire Cloud also was the target of an Army officer concerned with accountability for government property. A letter of the same date to the Yellowstone Expedition explained the officer's predicament:

> ... I have been informed that scout Fire Cloud, Detachment of Indian Scouts, belonging to this

Post, had exchanged his horse, as said horse does not belong to him. I respectfully request that when he returns to this Post, that you will see that he brings the horse in question with him.[142]

The letter was unsigned, but it either came from Lieutenant Jacob or the "mule chief," as the Indians called the Quartermaster.

➤ *Chapter 16* ◄

Activities at Fort Buford

While Bloody Knife and his sidekick were adventuring with the Yellowstone Expedition, the scouts left behind at Fort Buford were kept so busy that in July, Lieutenant Jacob was communicating with Assiniboins in an effort to augment his scout force. There was much work to be done. Mail must be carried to the expedition; deserters were being chased; a squad of scouts was assigned to Captain William Ludlow for his survey of the military reservation; 12 others escorted the Paymaster to the camp of the Northern Boundary Survey Commission; and there was always the lonely, dangerous guard duty atop the hills and bluffs surrounding the fort.

Twice in July, scouts were cited for leaving their picket posts. However, in most cases, Jacob got them off with plausible excuses. What he said to them privately remains a secret.

****

Over the years at lonesome, isolated Fort Buford, the enlisted men and some officers had become accustomed to satisfying their sexual urges with those laundresses who indulged in the world's oldest profession as a supplement to their incomes. The activity occurred in certain tipis in transitory Indian camps, or at the permanent Hidatsa village nearby. The scouts, however, would have nothing to do with the traffic in flesh and complained to Lieutenant Jacob, who in turn complained to Colonel Hazen on August 7, 1873:

> I have the honor to inform you that the scouts complain that some of the enlisted men of this command are in the habit of getting drunk, and visiting the scouts camp and abusing the women pertaining to said scouts. I therefore respectfully request that the necessary orders be issued to prevent this recurring.[143]

Hazen's endorsement was immediate:

> Existing orders already command men of this garrison to keep away from the scouts camp.

He followed it with another order:

> The Colonel cmdg. directs that three patrols daily be sent to the scout camp to arrest any unauthorized parties who may be found there. Scouts will report direct to the Officer of the Day, any man who disturbs them.

The scout roster divided into four squads present for duty on November 27, 1873 lists Bloody Knife as a lance corporal in charge of a squad of six men, two of whom were whites, Thomas Emmons and George Mulligan. If the white men considered it demeaning to serve under an Indian noncommissioned officer, there are no reports of it in the correspondence. In fact, some white men were anxious to serve in the Indian Scouts. It was not clear, either, how Emmons and Mulligan communicated with their immediate superior.[144]

Early in December, or what the Sioux call the Moon When Horns Break Off and the Arikara say is the Rattlesnake Moon, Bloody Knife was detailed up the Yellowstone to identify a store of supplies abandoned the previous summer by the steamboat, *Josephine*, at a period of low water. He found, as duly reported by the scrupulous Hazen, public property estimated to be in the value of $2000. Hazen decided it could be recovered in the spring.

General Stanley's suspicions about what he called that "center of iniquity in Indian affairs," Fort Peck, were confirmed in late December. George Mulligan and Crows Breast, the head chief of the Hidatsas, testified before a court of inquiry at Fort Buford, in the County of Buffalo in Dakota Territory, that they had witnessed the free trading of ammunition at the fur post. Crows Breast's deposition stated:

> I ... saw the traders giving ammunition to the hostile Indians and others. I saw it with my own eyes. I don't think it is right. Some of the same tribe have since taken six horses from us. The Interpreter for the Indian Agent at Fort Peck told us to trade for all the ammunition we could, to cache it if necessary, so that if we were stopped from trading it we would have plenty.[145]

Mulligan swore that the traders were " ... trading with Assiniboines, Yanktonnais and Unkpapa Sioux .. they had permission to trade ammunition from the Indian Agent Dr. Aldrich. They trade nothing else but powder, ball and caps, no fixed ammunition."

It was a fine point, to be sure. Army personnel defined fixed ammunition as the relatively new, self-contained metal cartridges. Loose ammunition was defined as the powder, ball, patches and paper used in percussion arms.[146] In his summation for the end of the year, Post Surgeon J.V.D. Middleton placed credit where it was due. In doing so, he probably unintentionally pleased Hazen with one statistic: "There have been no successful desertions during the year," he wrote, "although many have attempted it. The post is so isolated, deserters are easily overtaken by the scouts and mounted detachment."

****

Justice within the scout detachment apparently was as equalizing as it was in any other walk of life. On the twelfth day of January, or what the Arikara call the time of the Ground Cracked Moon and the Sioux the Moon When Things Are Awful, the Officer of the Day faithfully reported an incident to the Post Adjutant:

> Yesterday on inspecting the Scouts' quarters, I found Lance Corp'l Bloody Knife Det. Indian Scouts, under the influence of intoxicating liquor. He states that said liquor (whiskey) was obtained from one 'Mrs. Cooper,' an Indian woman half breed, living in the rear of Mr. Sparkes' Boarding House. I would respectfully request that some action be taken in this case; if the Scouts can obtain liquor it will be liable to lead to trouble between themselves and others.[147]

The word *Cancelled* was marked heavily through the report. Four days later Lieutenant Jacob became fed up with the insubordination of one of his noncommissioned officers:

> I ... request that Lance Sergeant R. Duran, Detachment of Scouts, may be reduced to the ranks for continual neglect of duty and disobedience of orders. I have on various occasions directed him to always see that Scouts in the Guard House had their meals taken to them, and he in Emmon's case has again failed to obey.[148]

This one was returned *Disapproved* from Post Headquarters. It would appear the scouts could do no wrong with friends in high places.

Private George Mulligan was bucking for rank. A typical order to the leader of a mail party was delivered to him on February 24, 1874:

> You will proceed to Fort Stevenson, D.T. with seven scouts in charge of mail and four pack horses. You will with two pack horses and three scouts return to this post at once with such mail matter as may be given you at Stevenson, leaving Lance Corp'l Spotted Eagle and three scouts with two animals at said post until such time as the Commanding Officer at Fort Stevenson may direct them to return. You will have rations and forage to include March 1, 1874. You will establish the camping places as follows: 1st night, half way between this Post and Grinnell's Wood Yard, 2nd night at Grinnell's Wood Yard, 3rd night, half way between Grinnell's and Berthold, 4th night at Berthold, 5th day at Stevenson, making same camps on return trip, and directing Corp'l Spotted Eagle to do the same.[149]

It was a typical Army detailed directive, leaving nothing to the judgment of a subordinate. Lieutenant Jacob signed it.

A tragic development in March created a flurry of activity for Jacob, who reported the incident to Colonel Hazen:

> It was reported to Lt. Crowell and myself that a squaw has hung herself on account of her destitute condition. We therefore questioned Lambert, the Post Interpreter, and Lance Sergt. Duran, Det. Ind. Scouts, both stating that a squaw has hung herself because she had nothing to eat, and that there was quite a number of old Indians around the Post that had no way of obtaining a living. Some of them get a little to eat by cutting wood for Laundresses and Companies. I therefore directed them to investigate and report to me the exact number of persons in that condition and I will report as soon as their report is received.[150]

Jacob recommended a course of action to Hazen that he hoped would prevent such a tragedy from repeating itself at Fort Buford:

> I would also state that the Scouts divide their Rations with said Indians, generally eating them all, except the Bread, the first day, and half starving the remainder of the ten days. I would therefore respectfully make the following recommendation: that rations for the Scouts be only drawn for a period of five days (instead of ten as at present), and then that the Scouts be allowed in the Post Commissary a credit of ten dollars per month, on orders signed by myself, I being responsible that the money is collected and paid to the ACS on pay-day. At present the Scouts obtain checks on the Post Trader and of course get only about one third of the amount they would obtain from the Commissary for the same money.[151]

Hazen lost no time in endorsing Jacob's proposal. He also directed that the destitute Indians be issued two rations of meat and bread every third day. To order them away from the Fort would be to sentence them to death from starvation, or to make of them simple prey for the ever-watchful Sioux.

At about the same time Jacob was warned to " ... limit the quantity of ammunition furnished the Scouts for hunting purposes, and see that they do not dispose of it improperly." It had come to the attention of the officers that the scouts, knowing their issued ammunition would be replaced, were in the habit of clandestinely trading it for liquor and food, then claiming it had been used in hunting. The scouts were also given to indiscriminate shooting when they were in the field.

Chapter 17

The Black Hills
Expedition of 1874

As of April 2, 1874, Fort Buford saw Bloody Knife no more. Lieutenant Jacob's brief petition of that date to his superior requested that Scout George Mulligan be appointed lance corporal because of Bloody Knife's discharge.[152]

Bloody Knife knew where he was going. *Siinani* Custer would take the trail again in the summer and *nee si RA pat* wanted to be with him. It is almost certain that he stopped at his home at Fort Berthold on his way to Fort Lincoln. He found life there much the same as ever, with his people still living in fear of Sioux raids. By May 30, he was standing in Lieutenant George D. Wallace's office at Fort Lincoln, re-enlisting for another six months.

A measure of his fame had preceded him. In an article printed in the *Bismarck Tribune* of April 29, extolling the virtues of the Arikara scouts in general, Bloody Knife was singled out for special mention. The editor wrote, "Bloody Knife, who was of such great value to Gen. Custer last summer on the expedition, is expected in a day or two to enlist."[153]

The day after re-enlistment, he went to work. Word came from Standing Rock that a Sioux war party was heading north. Custer burst out of Fort Lincoln with 500 men and 50 scouts. Three days of searching the prairie produced nothing. The Sioux had slipped by them and the Berthold Indians paid for it.

On June 13, a small band of the war party began sniping at the Arikara village. Warriors from the Three Tribes routed their Sioux tormentors and pursued them to a ridge about seven miles in the direction of Knife River. There they were suddenly confronted by 700 well armed and well mounted Sioux. Although surprised and outnumbered by four to one, the Berthold fighters battled so fiercely they were able to repulse the enemy and save themselves. It was a matter of basic survival. Five Arikaras and a Mandan were killed, scalped and mutilated on the field. The Three Tribes counted coup on six dead Sioux.[154]

****

The young post of Fort Abraham Lincoln bustled with activity. Bismarck streets were thronged with troops, teamsters, scouts, citizens, Indians, and a handful of strangers identified as professional men and scientists. Excitement ran high at the prospect of penetrating the sacred and forbidden medicine country of the Indians, the Black Hills, called *Paha Sapa* by the Sioux and *Wakaeiit* by the Arikara.

The expedition was billed as a reconnaissance and exploring mission by the U.S. government, for the purpose of securing military information. It was an ineffective blind for the real objective. Gold was the word on every tongue. Was it present in the Hills, as decades of rumors claimed it to be? Determined to know, the federal government put together an army strong enough to defend itself in the event of a fight, staffing it with scientists instructed to report on the flora, fauna and geology. It was then salted with professional miners, whose discoveries would be studied with

Fort Abraham Lincoln, Dakota Territory

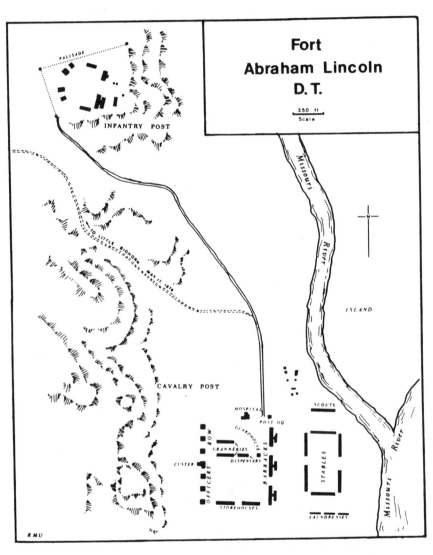

From *Cavalier in Buckskin: George Armstrong Custer and the Western Military Frontier* by Robert M. Utley. © 1988 by the University of Oklahoma Press.

the greatest interest.

In a letter written to his mother on June 14, Lieutenant Wallace told her, "The Infantry is taken along to guard the train and allow the Cavalry to cut loose and explore the country or chase Mr. Indians to their summer resorts."

Waiting for the expedition to start, Bloody Knife and the Rees explored the town of Bismarck. On one occasion on the street, one of two white men near them recognized their speech and introduced himself and his companion. He proved to be Luther North, an officer of the Pawnee Scouts. His companion was George Bird Grinnell, the naturalist, to whom North was acting as assistant.[155] It was the first of several visits they were to enjoy during the campaign. North wrote years later that they " ... became pretty good friends."

The scout detachment, commanded by Lieutenant Wallace, consisted of 22 Arikaras and 38 Santee Sioux from Nebraska. On the eve of the beginning of the expedition, the Santees had not arrived — in fact, they had not even left their agency. A telegraphic order was sent off and the missing contingent got to the post by train just in time. At one of the early campsites, a startled Army heard the Santees singing Sunday school songs.[156] There seems to be no record of whether the Rees and Santees practiced social intercourse.

It was a strong column that filed out of Fort Lincoln on July 2, 1874, with Lieutenant Colonel George Armstrong Custer in command. Ten of the twelve companies of the 7th Cavalry rode behind him. The other two, under Major Marcus Reno, were spending their second season as escort to the Northern Boundary Survey Commission. Two companies of infantry, one each from the 17th and 20th regiments, slogged along in the dust of the 110 wagons and the beef herd. There were also three Gatling guns, a Rodman cannon, and the ever-present 7th Cavalry band. Captain William Ludlow, Chief Engineer for the Department of Dakota, supervised the survey crew. Besides Grinnell and North, scientists along were Professor N.H. Winchell, geologist, and his assistant, Professor A.B. Donaldson. Doctor J.W. Williams, the Chief Medical Officer, was also a botanist. William H. Illingworth accompanied as photographer. There were two practical miners, H.N. Ross and W.T. McKay. Appointed as acting aide was Colonel Fred Grant, son of the President of the United States. Louis Agard was an interpreter. He shared guide duties with Charley Reynolds, a 32-year-old doctor's son from Illinois. All told, some 1200 men were on the march.[157]

West-southwestward the great dust cloud, kicked up by the thousands of hooves and feet, rolled over the semi-arid prairie, past the Heart and Cannonball rivers, and on to the Cave Hills. There the expedition stopped to explore the cavern from which the nearby hills took their name.

Shortly afterward, a small body of about 20 Indians was observed on the column's flank. Another party was seen the next day, and soon smoke signals were rising in the clear air. The scouts were sure the fleeing Indians were relaying information of the troops to a larger body and told the officers all the signs they saw portended war. More Indians were seen the next day, but no attack materialized.

Camp was pitched on July 14 in a beautiful little valley providing plenty of wood and water, to which Custer gave the name "Prospect Valley." Here the expedition laid over for a day of rest, repair and letter writing. Long Hair prepared dispatches and a private letter to his wife. At his order, Bloody Knife detailed two of his scouts to carry the mail back to Fort Lincoln, the bearers to leave camp after darkness fell. In his letter to his wife, Libbie, Custer mentioned that "Bloody Knife is doing splendidly." Since

Arikara village, 1832, drawn at the scene by renowned American artist George Catlin. The Pennsylvania native sketched this scene while aboard the *Yellow Stone,* the first steamboat to reach Fort Union at the confluence of the Missouri and Yellowstone rivers. Until 1832, all transportation to and from the confluence was by keelboat, canoe, dog sled or horseback. *(State Historical Society of North Dakota)*

Fort Clark, by Swiss artist Karl Bodmer. Located eight miles from present-day Stanton, North Dakota, Fort Clark was built in 1830-31 by the American Fur Company to serve a Mandan Indian earth lodge village built nearby in 1822. The Mandans abandoned the site in 1837 following a smallpox epidemic. It was occupied by the Arikaras from 1838-60, who abandoned the fort to join the Mandans and Hidatsas at Like-A-Fishhook Village. Fort Clark burned to the ground in 1861. *(State Historical Society of North Dakota)*

On-A-Slant Mandan Village, Fort Lincoln, circa 1940. The Mandans occupied earth lodges such as these from 1650 to 1750. Their Arikara and Hidatsa contemporaries lived in similar dwellings. *(State Historical Society of North Dakota)*

The ReaL Site of FishHook ViLLage, 1834–1886.
Drawn by Martin BearsArm.

Like-A-Fishhook Village, from a 1912 drawing by Martin Bears Arm. Note the pairing of many of the cabins with earth lodges, suggesting the cabins were used as winter dwellings. The numbers under each dwelling refer to the identification of the occupants. The founding date in the title is erroneous; it was a decade later. *(State Historical Society of North Dakota)*

Fort Berthold, Dakota Territory, circa 1869. The post was purchased by the American Fur Company in 1862. In 1868, it became the agency headquarters for the Arikara, Mandan and Hidatsa Indians, remaining so until 1874. Located on a bend below the mouth of the Little Missouri in present-day west central North Dakota, the site is now covered by the waters of the Garrison Reservoir. Photo by Stanley J. Morrow. *(State Historical Society of North Dakota)*

Arikara Village at Fort Berthold, Dakota Territory, circa 1869. Photo by Stanley J. Morrow. *(State Historical Society of North Dakota)*

Plains Indians of the 1800s

The photographs on these two pages were found stored in one of Lt. Colonel George Custer's footlockers located at the Custer family farmhouse near Monroe, Michigan.

Crow-Flies-High, an Hidatsa chief who, with other Hidatsas unhappy with reservation life, left Like-A-Fishhook Village and lived near Fort Buford, from about 1870 until 1884. That year, forced to move by the Army, they relocated down the Missouri and founded Crow-Flies-High Village near the mouth of the Little Knife River. A high-rising butte near New Town, North Dakota is named in his honor. *(Chester E. Nelson, Jr., Photo Collection)*

Two Crow, a warrior of the Blackfeet tribe. *(Chester E. Nelson, Jr., Photo Collection)*

Believed to be Charging Hawk, an Osage scout who served with Custer at the Battle of the Washita in November 1868. *(Chester E. Nelson, Jr., Photo Collection)*

Previously unpublished photograph of Black Buffalo, an Arikara scout. *(Chester E. Nelson, Jr., Photo Collection)*

Previously unpublished, believed to be a Mandan chief, name unknown. *(Chester E. Nelson, Jr., Photo Collection)*

Previously unpublished, believed to be a scout. *(Chester E. Nelson, Jr., Photo Collection)*

Bloody Knife posing during the 1873 Yellowstone Expedition. From all accounts, Bloody Knife did an outstanding job as chief scout and guide for General David S. Stanley during the summer survey that demonstrated the federal government's intent to establish the Northern Pacific Railroad through the Indian Country. Photo by William R. Pywell. *(National Archives)*

Bloody Knife, taken during the 1873 Yellowstone Expedition. Until 1981, due to an error in filing and identification, this photograph was believed to be that of an Coyotero Apache scout with the Wheeler Survey of the Southwest territories, conducted from 1871-74. Photo by William R. Pywell. *(National Archives)*

Bloody Knife on the 1873 Yellowstone Expedition. The Arikara and Lieutenant Colonel George Custer formed a close working relationship during this survey. The friendship lasted three years, until both men were killed at the Battle of the Little Bighorn the summer of the nation's Centennial observance. Photo by William R. Pywell. *(National Archives)*

ARMY OF THE UNITED STATES.

To all whom it may concern:

Know Ye, That *Sioux Stand (Ćat. hugh. nare)* a *Private* of ~~Captain~~ *1st Lieut John Enler d's* ~~Company~~ ~~of the~~ Detachment ~~Regiment~~ of *Indian Scouts* who, was enlisted, the *First* day of *October* one thousand, eight, hundred, and *Seventy three* to serve *Six Months* is hereby, discharged from the Army of the United States in consequence of *Expiration of term of Service* Said *Sioux Stand (Ćat. hugh. nare)* was born, in *Dakota* ~~in the State of~~ *Territory* is *30* years of age *5* feet *4* inches high *dark* complexion *black* eyes, *black* hair, and by occupation, when enlisted a *Scout* Given under my hand, at *Ft. Abm. Lincoln D.T.* this *First* day of *April* in the year of our Lord one thousand eight hundred and *Seventy four*

G A Custer
Lieut Col. 7th Cavalry Commanding Post
Bvt. Maj Gen. USA.

CHARACTER

Good
Jno. Carland
1st Lieut 6th Infantry
Comdg Detachment

A.G.O. No 98.

The discharge paper of Sioux Stand, an Arikara scout for the U.S. Army, dated April 1, 1874. The signature of the commanding officer is that of Lieutenant Colonel George A. Custer. *(Dorreen Yellow Bird Family Collection)*

Bloody Knife's exploits were copied by amateur scientist Philetus W. Norris about 1875 from the Arikara warrior's original war robe. The robe, made of several bison hides sewn together, depicted 24 different battle scenes. This war robe scene shows Bloody Knife urging on his horse with a whip, as he pursues a Crow warrior holding a shield. *(Smithsonian Institution, National Anthropological Archives)*

This scene from Bloody Knife's war robe depicts him scalping a man described as a U.S. Army cavalry officer, the only white man Bloody Knife claimed to have killed. The motive was to avenge the officer's alleged intimacy with Bloody Knife's wife, She Owl. *(Smithsonian Institution, National Anthropological Archives)*

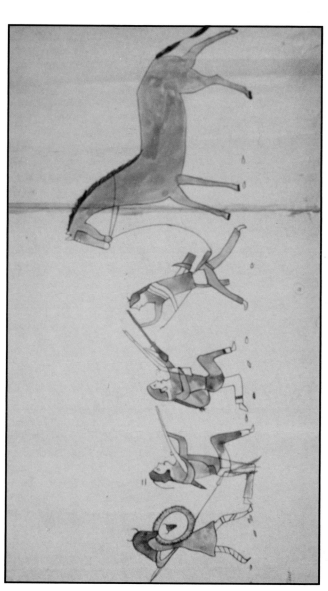

This war robe sketch shows Bloody Knife about to strike, but not kill, an enemy warrior, known as counting coup. A warrior allied with Bloody Knife, wearing the bison headdress, spears the other figure, who already has two coups counted against him, as indicated by the two marks above his head. The warrior with the bison headdress is probably a Mandan and member of that tribe's Bison Society. Judging from their hairstyles, the enemies are most likely Sioux. *(Smithsonian Institution, National Anthropological Archives)*

Little Sioux was 19 when he helped capture some Sioux ponies during the Reno fight at the Little Bighorn. A nephew of Bloody Knife, he is the great grandfather of Dorreen Yellow Bird, Arikara author of the Preface to this book. *(State Historical Society of North Dakota)*

Young Hawk, Soldier, Strikes Two and Sitting Bear (from left to right), all Arikaras. The first three served as scouts for Custer on the 1876 expedition and were with Major Marcus A. Reno during his desperate fight in the valley of the Little Bighorn. *(State Historical Society of North Dakota)*

Little Brave, an Arikara scout who was killed with Bloody Knife at the Battle of the Little Bighorn, June 25, 1876. He was 27. *(Little Bighorn Battlefield National Monument)*

Bobtailed Bull at Fort Berthold, October 1872. As a sergeant, he was second in command of the Indian scouts at Custer's Last Stand, after Lieutenant Charles A. Varnum. He was one of three Arikara scouts killed in the battle, along with Little Brave and Bloody Knife. He was 45. *(State Historical Society of North Dakota)*

Early 20th Century re-creation of an Indian sign left by the Sioux on their trail during the 1876 campaign. The skull of a buffalo bull is on one side of the pile of stones, and the skull of a buffalo cow is on the other side. A pole slants toward the skull of the buffalo cow to serve as a pointer. The Arikara interpreted this sign to mean that when the Sioux were confronted, they would stand and fight like a buffalo bull, while the soldiers would run from them like women. *(State Historical Society of North Dakota)*

Red Star, an Arikara scout who was 18 when he fought with Major Reno at the Little Bighorn Battle. Here he stands near the Little Bighorn River, at the crossing point of Reno's retreat to the bluffs, circa 1926. Known as Strikes-the-Bear at the time of the battle, he later changed his name to Red Star. *(State Historical Society of North Dakota)*

Gall, at Fort Yates, Dakota Territory, circa 1888. Gall's lifelong feud with Bloody Knife climaxed in the bloody showdown at the Little Bighorn on June 25, 1876. It was Gall's Hunkpapa Sioux camp that Reno encountered when he attempted to charge the southern end of the huge Indian village that Sunday. Fourteen years earlier, a war party led by Gall killed Bloody Knife's two brothers in the Badlands of what is now western North Dakota. Photo by George W. Scott. *(State Historical Society of North Dakota)*

Two poses of Sitting Bull. At left in 1883, at Fort Randall or Standing Rock, Dakota Territory, by Palmquist and Jurgens. *(State Historical Society of North Dakota)* At right in 1882, by Bailey, Dix and Mead. The legendary Hunkpapa Sioux medicine man adopted Gall as a younger brother after Gall lost his father at an early age. Some sources speculate that Bloody Knife and Sitting Bull were related. *(Chester E. Nelson, Jr., Photo Collection)*

These markers are located at the Indian Scouts' cemetery near White Shield, North Dakota. These scouts are not actually buried here. Bobtailed Bull and Little Brave may be buried in the mass grave near Last Stand Hill at the Little Bighorn Battlefield. Several stories exist as to what happened to Bloody Knife's body after the Custer Battle. One has it buried in the mass grave near Last Stand Hill; another claims it was decapitated by the victorious Sioux; another says it was left where it fell and never buried. *(Photos by Andrea Winkjer Collin)*

Indian Scout cemetery near White Shield, North Dakota, on the Fort Berthold Reservation. The cemetery is maintained by the Old Scouts Society, a group organized in the early 1930s by relatives of the Volunteer Scouts in the U.S. Army. *(Photo by Richard E. Collin)*

Frederick F. Gerard, a French trader who came to Fort Clark in 1849 and spent more than 40 years on the Upper Missouri. Serving as an interpreter and guide during the 1876 expedition that culminated in the Custer Disaster, Gerard wrote his three daughters from the mouth of the Bighorn River in early July 1876: "If I ever return to (Fort) Lincoln, I shall never go out again with an expedition." Photo by Orlando S. Goff. *(State Historical Society of North Dakota)*

Fort Rice, Dakota Territory, circa 1869. Established in 1864 by Brigadier General Alfred Sully during his expedition that year against the Sioux, the post was named for Brigadier General James Clay Rice, killed during the Civil War in the Battle of Laurel Hill in Virginia in May 1864. It served as a satellite post to Fort Abraham Lincoln after the latter's construction in 1873. Some of its troops accompanied units from Fort Lincoln on the expedition that resulted in the Little Bighorn Battle. Fort Rice was abandoned in 1878. Photo by Stanley J. Morrow. *(State Historical Society of North Dakota)*

Fort Stevenson, Dakota Territory. Pencil sketch by Philippe Regis de Trobriand, May 1868. It was on May 1, 1868 that Bloody Knife was sworn in for the first of his 11 hitches as an enlisted scout in the U.S. Army. Fort Stevenson, near present-day Garrison, North Dakota, was established on June 14, 1867. It helped protect navigation along the Missouri and aided in controlling the Sioux. It was abandoned on July 22, 1883. *(State Historical Society of North Dakota)*

Fort Stevenson, no date. Located some 12 miles below Fort Berthold, the site is now covered by the waters of the Garrison Reservoir. It was named after Brigadier General Thomas G. Stevenson, killed in the Civil War Battle of Spotsylvania in Virginia on May 10, 1864. After abandonment by the Army, it was used as an Indian school until 1894. *(State Historical Society of North Dakota)*

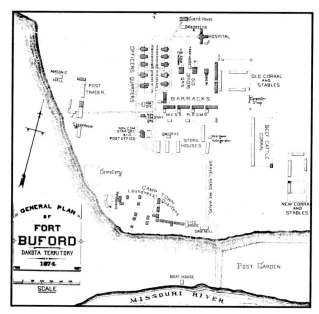

The interior of Fort Buford in 1874, the last year of Bloody Knife's service at the post. It was named for Major General John Buford, the Gettysburg veteran who died in December 1863. Fort Buford was where Sitting Bull and his followers laid down their arms on July 19, 1881, marking the final collapse of the coalition which had destroyed Custer and much of his 7th Cavalry five years earlier on the banks of the Little Bighorn. *(State Historical Society of North Dakota)*

Fort Buford, located near present-day Williston, North Dakota, circa 1869. Nine of Bloody Knife's 11 hitches as an enlisted scout in the U.S. Army were served here, from 1869-74. Fort Buford was established on June 15, 1866 just below the confluence of the Yellowstone and Missouri rivers, about two miles from Fort Union fur trading post. Located in the heart of buffalo country, Fort Buford was a scourge of the Sioux. The post was abandoned on October 1, 1895, and its troops transferred to Fort Assiniboine, Montana. *(State Historical Society of North Dakota)*

Rare photograph of First Lieutenant Charles A. Varnum, circa 1889. Varnum served with Custer on the Yellowstone and Black Hills Expeditions of 1873-74, as well as the disastrous campaign of 1876. At the time of the Custer Battle, Varnum was a 27-year-old second lieutenant in charge of the Indian scouts attached to the 7th Cavalry. Varnum, who fought with Reno, was the last surviving officer present at the Little Bighorn. He died on February 26, 1936, at 86. *(Chester E. Nelson, Jr., Photo Collection)*

Lieutenant Charles A. Varnum, West Point, 1872. *(Little Bighorn Battlefield National Monument)*

Billy Jackson, a quarter-blood Blackfoot who enlisted as an Indian scout after turning 18 in December 1874. He served for several years after the Bighorn-Yellowstone Expedition of 1876. He and Frederick Gerard were among those who became separated from Reno's command during the Battle of the Little Bighorn, hiding until the night of June 26, 1876, when they rejoined the troops on Reno Hill. *(Historical Collections/ University Archives, University of Colorado at Boulder Libraries)*

Previously unpublished photograph of Charles L. Gurley, the 6th Infantry second lieutenant who, on the morning of July 6, 1876, informed Libbie Custer and the other Army widows at Fort Lincoln of their husbands' deaths at the Battle of the Little Bighorn. Gurley was promoted to first lieutenant on July 19, 1881, coincidentally the same day Sitting Bull surrendered at Fort Buford. He resigned from the Army on December 31, 1882. *(Chester E. Nelson, Jr., Photo Collection)*

Mott Hooton was a first lieutenant of the 22nd Infantry at Fort Buford when he swore in Bloody Knife for the Arikara scout's second enlistment in the Army on May 21, 1869. Hooton served with distinction during a 39-year military career that spanned the first days of the Civil War to the aftermath of the Spanish-American War. Cited for "gallant service in action" at the Battle of Spring Creek in Montana Territory in October 1876, he retired in April 1902 as a brigadier general. *(Paul L. Hedren Photo Collection)*

Charley Reynolds, called "Lucky Man" by the Arikara for his hunting prowess, and "Lonesome" by the whites for his loner ways, served as a scout with Custer on his expeditions of the 1870s. It was Reynolds who brought word of Custer's discovery of gold in the Black Hills in 1874 to the American public, via dispatches filed with reporters at Fort Laramie. Reynolds perished two years later at the Little Bighorn, as part of Reno's command. *(Little Bighorn Battlefield National Monument)*

Fort Abraham Lincoln, Dakota Territory, circa 1876. Located three miles south of Bismarck, the post was established on June 14, 1872 and originally named Fort McKeen, for Colonel Henry McKeen, killed during the Civil War at the Battle of Cold Harbor, Virginia in June 1864. On November 19, 1872, it was renamed Fort Lincoln, in honor of the assassinated President. In 1873, it became a nine-company cavalry and infantry post, 655 soldiers total, with the infantry stationed near the mouth of the nearby Heart River. The fort was abandoned on July 22, 1891. *(State Historical Society of North Dakota)*

Fort Abraham Lincoln, Dakota Territory, 1876. Fort Lincoln served as Custer's final base of operations, beginning in 1873. The flamboyant "Boy General" of the Civil War departed here on May 17, 1876, for a rendezvous with destiny at the Little Bighorn. Photo by David F. Barry. *(Chester E. Nelson, Jr., Photo Collection)*

Rare photograph of Brevet Major General George A. Custer, January 2, 1865, by Alexander Gardner. Custer's actual rank at this time was captain; however, brevet ranks were distributed liberally during the Civil War to recognize wartime service. Custer received his major general brevet from Secretary of War Edwin M. Stanton for actions against the Confederates in the Shenandoah Valley in October 1864. In July 1866, Custer was promoted to the actual rank of lieutenant colonel, where he remained until his death a decade later. *(Chester E. Nelson, Jr., Photo Collection)*

Lieutenant Colonel Custer in January 1872. Images such as this of the dashing cavalryman in buckskins are one of the reasons why Custer maintains such a vivid hold on the public's imagination to this day. *(Chester E. Nelson, Jr., Photo Collection)*

Bloody Knife with Custer during the Yellowstone Expedition of 1873. Custer is seated in the chair; kneeling to his left and pointing to the map is Bloody Knife. Goose, another Arikara scout who was slightly injured at the Battle of the Little Bighorn, stands in the doorway. The other two scouts remain unidentified. The scouts are holding the latest model Army Colt .45 revolver, issued that year. *(Little Bighorn Battlefield National Monument)*

Bloody Knife is to Custer's right as the men pose with a grizzly bear brought down by the rifle fire of Bloody Knife, Custer and William Ludlow, standing at Custer's left. Standing behind Custer is his orderly, Private Noonan. Photo taken by William H. Illingworth on August 7, 1874, during the Black Hills Expedition. *(Little Bighorn Battlefield National Monument)*

A slightly different pose by the triumphant grizzly bear party. In this one, William Ludlow is seated. *(Little Bighorn Battlefield National Monument)*

Custer and a prize elk he killed on the Yellowstone Expedition, September 6, 1873. Custer mounted the kill, dubbed by some expeditioners as "The King of the Forest," and took it back to Fort Lincoln. Photo by William R. Pywell. *(Little Bighorn Battlefield National Monument)*

During the 1874 Black Hills Expedition, Custer's officer and scientific corps gathered for this portrait on August 13. Bloody Knife stands in the tent's doorway, while Custer reclines in front of the tent. Seated behind Custer's head is Major George "Sandy" Forsyth, 9th Cavalry, the commander during the Beecher's Island Fight in 1868 in Colorado Territory. In front of Bloody Knife, seated, is Major Joseph G. Tilford, 7th Cavalry. On the far left are William Ludlow, the expedition's chief engineer, and Captains George Yates and Tom Custer, two of Lt. Colonel Custer's company commanders who fell with him at the Little Bighorn. Captain Frederick Benteen is third from the right. Photo by William H. Illingworth. *(Little Bighorn Battlefield National Monument)*

On the steps of Custer's first home at Fort Lincoln in November 1873. From left, top row, are: Miss Agnes Bates, a friend of Libbie Custer's visiting from Monroe, Michigan; Lt. James Calhoun, who perished with his company and Custer at the Little Bighorn; Calhoun's wife, Margaret, the sister of Custer. Center row: Libbie Custer; her husband, Lt. Col. George A. Custer; Frederic Calhoun, then a civilian employee who survived his older brother, James, by 28 years (in front of Custer); and Capt. William Thompson, a former Iowa congressman who fought with Custer at the Battle of the Washita. Photo by Orlando S. Goff. *(Little Bighorn Battlefield National Monument)*

Group on the Custer home porch, July 1875. Left to right, front row: Lt. Tom Custer, Emma Wadsworth, Lt. Col. George Custer. Middle row: W.C. Curtis, Lt. R.E. Thompson, 6th Infantry. Back row: Herbert Smith, Libbie Custer, Margaret Custer Calhoun, Lt. James Calhoun. This was the second home of the Custers at Fort Lincoln. The first burned in February 1874 because of a defective chimney. This second home, which is the one that stands reconstructed today on its original site, was built in the spring of 1874. *(Little Bighorn Battlefield National Monument)*

Bloody Knife stands on the porch, wrapped in a blanket, at Custer's quarters at Fort Lincoln, July 1875. Left to right, front row: Lt. Tom Custer, Nellie Wadsworth, Lt. R.E. Thompson, 6th Infantry (facing left), Capt. Myles Keogh, Emma Wadsworth, Capt. Stephen Baker, 6th Infantry. Middle row: Mrs. Algernon E. Smith, Leonard Swett, a civilian friend of the Custers, Mrs. Myles Moylan (behind Emma Wadsworth), Boston Custer, the youngest of the four Custer brothers, Emily Watson, a Custer family friend, Lt. Col. Custer. Back row: Bloody Knife, Libbie Custer, Margaret Custer Calhoun (seated), Lt. Algernon E. Smith, and Lt. James Calhoun. Photo by Orlando S. Goff. (*Little Bighorn Battlefield National Monument*)

Rare photograph of the Wadsworth sisters, Nellie (left) and Emma (right), in 1875. Here they play to the camera of Fort Lincoln post photographer Orlando S. Goff, wearing the uniforms of their boyfriends, Lieutenants Tom Custer and William W. Cooke. Emma is wearing Tom's two Congressional Medals of Honor won in the last days of the Civil War. The Wadsworths were friends of the Custers from the east who stayed with them at Fort Lincoln from April through September 1875. *(Chester E. Nelson, Jr., Photo Collection)*

Libbie Custer with Nina Tilford, the daughter of Major Joseph G. Tilford, 7th Cavalry, at Fort Lincoln, circa 1875. Major Tilford, whose relations with Libbie's husband were cool, was stationed at nearby Fort Rice during the Fort Lincoln Custer era. *(Chester E. Nelson, Jr., Photo Collection).*

George A. Custer, circa March 1876, by Jose M. Mora, New York City. Custer was 36 years old and about to enter the final spring of his life. It was a season that would embroil him in a Congressional hearing investigating corruption charges against Secretary of War William W. Belknap. Note the rose in Custer's lapel. *(Chester E. Nelson, Jr., Photo Collection)*

Lieutenant Colonel Custer, circa March 1876, by Jose M. Mora, New York City. He was in the midst of preparations to lead the Bighorn-Yellowstone Expedition against the Sioux. In early May, he was removed as expedition commander and banned from even accompanying its troops into the field by an irate President Grant, livid at Custer for citing heresay evidence that implicated Grant's brother, Orvil, in the Belknap Scandal. Following a barrage of editorial criticism, the President relented enough to allow Custer to lead his 7th Cavalry on the campaign. (*State Historical Society of North Dakota*)

Lieutenant Colonel Custer in his study at Fort Lincoln, November 1873. Note the photograph of him, taken in May 1865, directly above his head. Photo by Orlando S. Goff. (*Little Bighorn Battlefield National Monument*)

George Armstrong Custer, June 1874, by photographer Huntington of Taylor's Gallery in St. Paul, Minnesota. *(Little Bighorn Battlefield National Monument)*

George A. Custer, May 8, 1875, by Edward M. Estabrooke, New York City. *(Little Bighorn Battlefield National Monument).*

Previously unpublished photograph of Lieutenant Colonel Custer at Fort Lincoln in 1875. Left to right: Frederic Calhoun, then a second lieutenant in the 14th Infantry; Nellie Wadsworth, Custer, and Emma Wadsworth. *(Chester E. Nelson, Jr., Photo Collection)*

there was no question about the scout's ability or efficiency, the reference must have been in regard to his behavior. In other words, *nee si RA pat* had not yet found an opportunity to get drunk.

More strong Sioux signs were uncovered in Castle Valley on July 26, turning Bloody Knife the scout into Bloody Knife the manhunter. With 20 Rees, the head scout quietly approached a camp of five lodges, where he placed his men in ambush and sent word back to Custer. Long Hair thundered up, a company behind him, and surrounded the camp with the hope of taking it peacefully in order to council with the Indians. Twenty-seven frightened Sioux found themselves virtual prisoners, even though interpreter Agard relayed Custer's assurance that they had nothing to fear. As an inducement to parley, Custer offered presents of flour, sugar, coffee and bacon. He told the Indians he wanted them to camp with the Army and furnish the whites with information about the country. This was agreed upon, but the captives continued to look askance at the smoldering Rees. The captives proved to be a band of Oglalas under their chief, One Stab.

Custer returned to the column, and later in the afternoon, the chief and three of his men showed up to collect their rations. As soon as it was done, two of them slipped away. One Stab and his remaining companion also tried to escape, but the chief was prevented from getting away by the scouts. The other Oglala fled in a fusillade of bullets and, although wounded, made it to freedom. The furious Rees boiled down the valley to the Sioux camp, only to find it deserted, its former occupants safely out of sight.[158]

Custer kept One Stab with him for several days, then released him unharmed, to the absolute disgust of the Rees. Professor A.B. Donaldson noted Bloody Knife's reaction: "Bloody Knife slunk to the rear of the marching column and scarce spoke a word all day, except to say that he felt ashamed and disappointed." It is easy to imagine that the remark lost a good deal of meaning in interpretation.

Ironically, it was One Stab who gave Custer the news that the Hunkpapas had been depredating on the Yellowstone, harassing the Yellowstone Wagon Road and Prospecting Expedition. The 150 citizens, with 22 wagons, had left Bozeman the previous February and by April 3 were on the Rosebud River, some 20 miles south of the Elk River. There they ran into trouble and Gall was a part of it. In four strong attacks in successive weeks, the Sioux, with an estimated strength of at least 600 fighting men, pestered the citizens and pressed their strikes so vigorously that the train was forced to turn about and return to Bozeman after losing one man killed and two wounded. One Stab said he had heard the raiders lost 10 warriors.

Somewhere on the trip — the exact date is not available — Long Hair bared his teeth to friends who did not expect it of him. Charley Reynolds and Bloody Knife, scouting the trail ahead, had directed the wagons over a high cut bank lined with a grove of trees. Some of the wagons got stuck, requiring a delay while they were muscled free. Custer galloped up in a rage and asked whose fault it was. Reynolds said it was Bloody Knife's, whereupon Custer tore his pistol from its holster and fired at both of them. Young Hawk, who told the story, said the two scouts were only saved by throwing themselves behind trees. When Custer calmed down long enough to holster the weapon, Bloody Knife went up to him where he sat on his horse and said ominously, "It is not a good thing you have done to me. If I had been possessed of madness too you would not see another day." Custer replied, "My brother, it was a madness of the moment that made me do this, but it is gone now. Let us shake hands and be friends again." Bloody Knife consented and it was as though the incident had never happened. [159]

In some respects, the story does not ring quite true. Although an incident of this sort probably happened, it was hardly in character for Charley Reynolds, as independent a man as Bloody Knife, to turn informer. And Bloody Knife, who could be overawed by no one, accepted a lame apology. His regard for his leader must indeed have been strong.

For Custer, however, the irrationality and irresponsibility of the act was in keeping with the character of the officer whose troops had mutinied in the Civil War; who in Louisiana led an enlisted man to believe he was about to be shot, until the moment the poor devil faced the firing squad; who shot deserters in Kansas; who himself committed the offense of absence without leave; and who was accused by his own officers of deserting a fellow officer at the Battle of the Washita in what is now Oklahoma in November 1868.

Lyrically descriptive phrases flowed from Custer's pen, however, when he wrote his reports and his letters to his wife, Libbie — whom he affectionately called " My Durl" and "My Darling Sunbeam"— back at Fort Lincoln. He ascended into raptures over the flowers, the water, the trees and scenery.

Despite the beauty, in some places travel was difficult. W.R. Wood, a surveyor, afterward wrote his observations:

> ... we had loads of trouble ... Sometimes we didn't make more than four or five miles a day. We had to stop and pick a way for the wagons to get through. I have seen them go all night long once or twice — there was no let-up with Custer. He went ahead and picked out a camping place and said, "I guess they can come this far." Then they fed the horses and went right on.

Wood was one of many witnesses to the conduct of Colonel Fred Grant, the President's son. "Grant ... was drunk nearly all the time," wrote Wood.[160]

On August 3, Custer decided to sent out the important reports to Fort Laramie. Charley Reynolds, true to his nickname of Lonesome, undertook the job alone. He had a tough trip, which included a water scrape and near discovery by Sioux warriors. But he made it, and by the grace of his own indomitable will and the railroad, he traveled back to Fort Lincoln long before the column arrived there.

From Bear Butte, Custer ordered six scouts to carry the mail ahead to Lincoln. Three of the party were Rees, the others were Santee Sioux. Strikes Two, a Ree assigned to lead one of the horses loaded with mailbags, later said at the moment of departure, Long Hair gave him a flask of whiskey.[161] Strikes Two did not say what was done with the liquor. He did state that the mailmen set off at sunset, rode all night, rested briefly, and continued on the trail all the next day. Why would Custer, a teetotaler himself and frequent caustic critic of those who drank, provide the guardians of the precious mailbags with a source of potential trouble? If true, it was an enigma.

The return trip began on August 6, 1874. The next day Custer killed a grizzly bear. The trophy may not have been downed in the manner in which he took credit for the kill. It was a one man job, he claimed. In the photograph taken with the carcass of the defurred monster, Custer included the members of the party with him at the time — his orderly, Private Noonan, Captain William Ludlow, and Bloody Knife. Fifty years passed by the time Luther North, the officer with the Pawnee Scouts, was shown the photo. He said that all of Custer's party were shooting at the animal and that it was hit by several bullets. "I believe the General claimed the honor," North recollected, "and as he was an expert with a rifle, (I) am inclined to think that he did." [162]

Even though the command traversed a different route on the way home, they were still reminded they were being watched. On August 16, a band of Indians was sighted and identified as Cheyennes. Bloody Knife talked with them and was told that Sitting Bull was gathering a hostile force near Prospect Valley with the intention of mounting an attack on the Army. Again the Rees prepared for war, but no Sioux appeared. They did cause quite a bit of trouble by firing the grass for several days march in advance of the troops. To escape the burned-over area, Custer sought the valley of the Little Missouri. From there, they made good progress homeward, reaching Fort Lincoln at 4:30 p.m. on August 30 with almost a thousand miles of traveling logged. The surveyors had covered approximately 1200 miles.

Only then did the men relax from the tensions created before their departure eight weeks earlier by the rumors that Sitting Bull was gathering an army of warriors about 70 miles to the south to contest the entrance of the expedition to the Black Hills.

High words of praise for the Arikaras came from Professor Donaldson:

> As scouts, they are invaluable. They have scoured the whole country over in advance of our marching column. If any hostile Sioux had been anywhere in front of us or on our flanks, these ubiquitous and cunning scouts would certainly have found them out. Where they scour the country, no ambush could be successfully laid. The Santees are more civilized, but not more useful. [163]

****

The Black Hills Expedition of 1874

Listening to her husband's comments about the expedition and its personalities inspired Libbie Custer to add to Bloody Knife's preserved laurels. She wrote, "Gen. Custer valued Bloody Knife, his favorite Indian scout, for his splendid service during the Black Hills Expedition of 1874. He had proved himself an invaluable and faithful scout."[164]

Long Hair himself remembered his indebtedness to Bloody Knife for a job well done. While he was in Chicago that autumn, he took the time and trouble to buy a gift for his number one scout. In addition, he put money where his mouth was. In a letter dated September 22, 1874 to Department Headquarters in St. Paul, Custer led off with the information that he had paid an extra $150 in special recognition to Charley Reynolds for the important and dangerous service he had rendered. The second paragraph referred to Bloody Knife:

> In the same order, an additional compensation was directed to be given to Blood Knife, the chief Indian scout, who accompanied the expedition. No one who accompanied but can certify to the invaluable assistance rendered by Bloody Knife as guide. He was unceasing in his daily efforts to find good and practicable routes for the command. Not only that, he frequently encountered unusual dangers, and being required to furnish his own horse, his extraordinary labors in looking for practicable routes far in advance of the expedition rendered his horse worthless, and for these combined reasons, the extra compensation was ordered to be given to him. I would add in this connection that at the termination of the Yellowstone Expedition of 1873, Gen. Stanley, for precisely similar services, although less deserving in each case, ordered these same two men, Reynolds and Bloody Knife, to be paid extra

compensation, and both received their pay soon after the order was issued.[165]

****

The far reaching consequences of the expedition's discoveries, through waves of national publicity, were immediately apparent in the clamor of white Americans to gain possession of the Black Hills. There was indeed gold at the "grass roots." Another consequence was that Custer's personal reputation, always at a high level, now attained new heights in the eyes of many. In the Sioux camps, however, his stock sank to an all-time low. The trail he blazed to the Black Hills and back became known to the unhappy Sioux as "The Thieves' Road." Among their people the name Long Hair was replaced with the unflattering epithet, Chief Of The Thieves.

It was toward the end of the year, on November 30, 1874, that Bloody Knife was discharged at Fort Lincoln. The official discharge document noted that he was possessed of an "excellent and reliable character." This marked the end of Bloody Knife's final enlistment as an Indian Scout. Custer would hire him as a civilian scout and guide for the fatal campaign against the Sioux 18 months later.[166]

➤ *Chapter 18* ◄

1875

Everyone knew by now that inexorable pressure was building toward an important confrontation between the soldiers and the warriors. The past four years of railroad survey and mining discovery expeditions significantly increased the tension between the two cultures. The astute Indian leaders knew that the last chance had arrived to stop the white man. An incident at the Standing Rock Agency involving the Hunkpapa warrior, Rain-in-the-Face, was a factor contributing to the unrest on that reservation.

As early as February 1874 at Standing Rock, agency interpreter John Brughiere had heard the young war chief brag of his coups in the killings of Honzinger and Baliran, when the two men wandered from the column during the Yellowstone Expedition of 1873. General Stanley at Fort Sully bided his time until December, when Rain-in-the-Face boldly appeared again at the agency. His presence there was reported by Charley Reynolds. The word went out to arrest him and immediately Custer dispatched his brother, Captain Tom Custer, and Captain George W. Yates and two companies of the 7th Cavalry from Fort Lincoln to arrest the one the whites viewed as a murderer. They picked him up on December 14, but not without a struggle, and Rain-in-the-Face was taken to the guardhouse at Fort Lincoln.

On April 18, 1875, he escaped, some said crying vengeance

on Tom Custer for that officer's mistreatment of him as a prisoner.[167] Regardless, the myth began there of the revenge of Rain-in-the-Face at the Little Bighorn, where he was said to have cut the heart from the body of Captain Custer and eaten it. The arrest and other incidents at the agency stirred up the Indians considerably, and a severe shortage of rations before winter ended made them deeply disillusioned and dissatisfied.

****

Bloody Knife was at loose ends in 1875, with no expeditions to guide. It is quite possible that he was hired in some capacity at Fort Lincoln, since it was evident that he spent much time with Custer. Apparently he was away for a part of the winter, spying on the Sioux bands, for in the waning of the Snow Moons, he reported to the Army that there were no Sioux warriors on the Little Missouri.

Efforts by Agent Sperry at Fort Berthold and Agent Burke at Standing Rock to organize a peace council between the Three Tribes and the Sioux came to fruition in May 1875 when the adversaries agreed to meet. The Berthold Indians had made the journey to Fort Lincoln in the dead of the preceding winter for the same purpose, only to give up and go home after waiting for a Sioux delegation which failed to appear. Now, however, both sides solemnly swore to bury the hatchet. There was a flood of oratory, singing and feasting by the 400 Sioux and 300 members of the Three Tribes. The ancient enemies touched the pen to a treaty of peace which lasted as long as it took either party to clear the fort gates.[168] It is notable that not one of the names of the Hunkpapas appears on the treaty.

The *Bismarck Tribune* of June 2, 1875 informed its readers

that following the treaty signing, the Berthold delegation visited the town.[169] Among those in the delegation was Bloody Knife, who drank himself into intoxication. The next morning, when he began to board the boat back to the fort, he was peremptorily ordered off. A fight with the boat crew resulted, in the course of which Bloody Knife retreated to the bluff and fired into the vessel. His shots were answered by a sergeant of the crew. The scout then took shelter in a coulee and sniped away at the boat from his new position. The *Tribune* ended its story by stating that " ... no one was injured." But certainly Bloody Knife's pride had been.

Much later that same day, Joseph Henry Taylor, at his home to the north, watched Bloody Knife and a small band of Rees dash up to the entrance to his stockade, ponies lathered from hard traveling. " ... my heart is strong," proclaimed the hung over and possibly still drunk Bloody Knife. "I have fought a steamboat this day." Taylor made a sarcastic remark impossible for the scout to miss. "Don't talk back," Bloody Knife commanded. "My heart is very bad." As he spoke, he cocked his rifle but was instantly disarmed and calmed by his companions. A somewhat chastened Taylor then was told the story of the boat which had refused them passage.[170]

Gall straddled both sides of the fence that year, enrolling with some of his followers at Standing Rock for rations, according to some sources.[171] A good deal of the time he was on the war path in and about the Black Hills, raiding freighters and stagecoaches.

Charley "Lucky Man" Reynolds, hearing the name given him by the Rees in recognition of his hunting prowess, spent the summer and early fall in the Montana Territory with Captain William Ludlow, exploring Yellowstone Park and the Judith Basin. Upon his return, Custer put him to work keeping an eye on the movements of the Three Tribes, instructing him to watch particularly the coming and going of Sioux spies and emissaries from the camps to the west and southwest.[172] The Sioux were still trying to effect a confederation of all warriors against all whites. At the same time, they continued to attack and kill Arikaras whenever they found the chance. Also that summer, a delegation of six leading Arikara and Mandans journeyed to Washington, D.C., where they conferred with the Commissioner of Indian Affairs. That official promised them an all-out war against Sitting Bull, and he agreed to furnish them with provisions with which to feed their starving people. The Commissioner at that time asked for and received permission to recruit scouts for the coming campaign against the Sioux.[173]

It was a quiet summer, nearly idyllic at Fort Lincoln, where Libbie Custer described her husband's preoccupation with his favorite scout:

> Bloody Knife was naturally mournful; his face still looked sad when he put on the presents given him. He was a perfect child about gifts, and the General studied to bring him something from the East that no other Indian had. He had proved himself such an invaluable scout to the General that they often had long interviews. Seated on the grass, the dogs lying about them, they talked over portions of the country that the General had never seen, the scout drawing excellent maps in the sand with a pointed stick. He was sometimes petulant, often moody, and it required the utmost patience on my husband's part to submit to his humors; but his fidelity and cleverness made it worthwhile to yield to his tempers.[174]

It would seem that even Joseph Henry Taylor found it impossible not to like and admire Bloody Knife. "Bloody Knife was no chief," Taylor wrote, "neither did he have the gift of command.

He was an excellent guide, a brave warrior and a true blue scout. No officer of the Army with whom he served ever charged him with disloyalty, whatever the provocation, nor in shirking any duty, however hazardous."[175]

In another statement, Taylor said that he had never met the scout's superior as a linguist in Arikara and Sioux, and that " ... in the sign language he was simply perfect ... Whatever his faults, (he) was no liar and if he talked at all, would talk straight."[176]

Proof of Taylor's opinions came late that autumn, when the great elk hunting partnership between the two ended before it really began because of a failing of the scout's. On a visit to the Arikara quarter at Fort Berthold, Taylor was approached by Bloody Knife with news of a herd of 40 elk just a few days travel away. The scout proposed that they hunt the animals on a partnership basis. Taylor was interested. The third night on the trail to the herd, the pair arrived at an abandoned shack for shelter, only to find it already occupied by two white hunters. The two parties pitched camp together in a friendly fashion. The two strange hunters then made the mistake of producing a keg marked "Port Wine," which they explained they had found on a frozen sand bar far out in the bed of the Missouri. They had been afraid to sample it for fear it might be poisoned. Linguist though he was, Bloody Knife was deficient in English, and the only intelligence he could make of the situation was that a keg of liquor was on hand and that it was full. Without understanding his role as guinea pig, he volunteered to start the keg around. When a suitable time had elapsed and he showed no ill effects, it might be presumed that *nee si RA pat* was joined in his solitary drinking by the rest of the hut's inhabitants. Taylor did not say.

But the next morning, when the white hunter was ready to stalk the waiting elk, Bloody Knife was not. Taylor said the warrior looked at the two owners of the keg as though to read their faces, switched his wistful glance to the container under their bunk, and " ...with an emphatic gesture, spoke out loudly: 'Right here I stay!'"[177] The elk hunt dissolved on the spot.

****

On December 6, 1875, the words responsible for ending Indian independence forever fell on a waiting West, when the Commissioner of Indian Affairs issued instructions to the Indian Agents to send word to the non-reservation tribes and bands of his ultimatum:

> ... that unless they shall remove within the bounds of their reservation (and remain there) before the 31st of January next, they shall be deemed hostile and treated accordingly by the military force.[178]

Thus was the stage set for the pageant of death on the Little Bighorn.

Chapter 19

The Bighorn-Yellowstone Expedition of 1876

Gall, by that fateful summer of 1876, had risen high in the estimation of his people. His following numbered in excess of 60 lodges, qualifying him for status as tribal chief. For years, he had proved himself a successful and much admired war chief. His physical appearance was exceptional. Libbie Custer wrote that he was " ... the finest specimen of the physical Indian ..." she had ever seen. Joseph Henry Taylor described him as " ... near six feet tall, a frame of bone, with the full breast of a gladiator and bearing of one born to command." Before him was the trail leading toward what the Sioux called the Greasy Grass, known to white men as the Little Bighorn.

On the opposite side, aiding and abetting the racial enemy, was Gall's old personal foe, Bloody Knife. In late winter, he made the journey from Berthold to Fort Lincoln. There he was informed on March 13, 1876 that he was hired, not as an Army enlisted scout, but as a citizen scout, by the Army Quartermaster Department. This entitled him to $50 a month, significantly more than the $13 monthly salary he had drawn as an enlisted scout. It also provided him with a government horse and accouterments. Custer's well known nepotism was closely matched by his loyalty to old comrades. Bloody Knife had good reason to feel a deep sense of satisfaction with what he had accomplished.[179]

****

After February 10, when it became obvious that the off-reservation Indians were not coming into the agencies, the Army was given the word to proceed with preparations for the campaign. Orders were shotgunned from St. Paul throughout the length and breadth of the Department of Dakota.

One of those orders found its way to Fort Totten, sending Totten's Contract Surgeon, James M. DeWolf, to Fort Lincoln for duty with the expedition. From Fort Lincoln he wrote his wife on April 19 that "Bloody Knife has come down to follow us out and pick up stragglers." Obviously, DeWolf was not familiar with the role of the scouts on campaign. As his medical case load, DeWolf was assigned by General Terry the 7th Cavalry and the Indian scouts. His initial opinion of the latter group was evident in his diary entry for May 9, when he had some of them in for a medical examination: "I have examined 22 Indians Scouts today (.)* Not a very nice job."[180]

It was the early part of May when General Alfred H. Terry arrived to command the expedition, accompanied by a defiant and angry Custer. Long Hair was now relegated to the leadership of only the 7th Cavalry as a result of his troubles with President Grant over the Belknap Scandal. Custer had testified in April before a Congressional committee investigating charges that Secretary of War William K. Belknap had sold post traderships. In his testimony, Custer repeated unsubstantiated rumors that the President's brother, Orvil, was among those involved in the Belknap corruption ring. This and other testimony by Custer enraged Grant, who sought vengeance against his former Civil War cavalry officer. The President had Custer removed from command of the Bighorn-Yellowstone Expedition, and at first refused to even let him accompany the 7th Cavalry into the field. Grant recanted only after a plea from General Terry, who acted on behalf of a despondent Custer.

In the meantime, the Arikara scouts were recruited, outfitted and organized into a cohesive body. Their noncommissioned officers were Bobtailed Bull and Soldier, and their commissioned officer Lieutenant Charles A. Varnum, whom they chose to call Peaked Face.

Not long after his return, Custer met with the scouts, recognized those he knew from previous campaigns, and complimented them all for volunteering to serve. He then presented Bloody Knife with a personal gift, a black handkerchief speckled with blue stars, and a medal which he said had been given to him in Washington for his brother.

Custer told the scouts he had been informed that this was to be his last Indian campaign. Accordingly, he felt that just one victory over even five tents of Sioux would make him the Great Father, the President of the United States. When that happened, he would take Bloody Knife with him to Washington, and his fast friend would become a chief of his people.[181]

At a later date, Lieutenant Varnum called a meeting with the scouts. With Gerard interpreting and Bloody Knife beside him, Varnum explained to the scouts the rules of discipline under which they were to operate.

The scout who did not get up when called, Varnum told them, would go without breakfast; the scout who did not help the cook by getting water and wood would go without meals; the scout who got drunk would be deprived of his horse and would have to travel on foot.[182] The 45 scouts were to fan out to the front and sides of the moving column to watch for presence of an enemy and guard against a surprise attack; they were to guard the outskirts of campsites at night and perform courier service and mail-carrying chores. Varnum closed by saying that he would always be camping with them.[183]

As fighters, most of the Arikaras had experience fending off the Sioux raids on their village and in war parties. The greater number of them were veterans of one or more hitches in the scouts in earlier seasons and on Custer's previous campaigns. Only seven of them were new recruits.[184]

The day before the expedition pulled out, Bloody Knife held a meeting of his own and relayed to the scouts the wishes of Long Hair. Custer, said Bloody Knife, wanted a big parade when the soldiers rode out from the fort on the morrow to lift up the hearts of Long Hair's woman and the other women of the place who were low in spirit. He wished the scouts to lead the parade. Bloody Knife also entrusted them with his own opinion that there was going to be a big fight and maybe many of them and many soldiers would be killed. With that, he let them go.

****

To the chanting of the Rees scouts' war songs and the stirring music of the 7th Cavalry band, the long column wound away from Fort Lincoln on Wednesday, May 17, 1876. As Custer had promised, the scouts were in the lead, with Peaked Face to the fore. Gerard had told the men they should sing to show the white women they were as brave and confident as the bluecoats. Behind the scout detachment rode the entire 7th Cavalry, all 12 companies proud in its strength. Plodding after came a platoon of three

The Great Sioux War of 1876-77

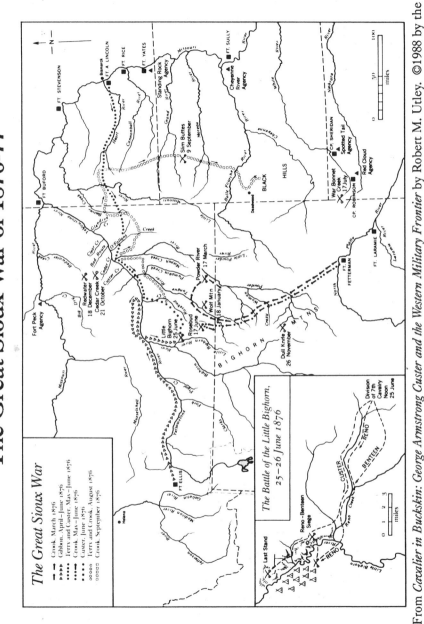

The Great Sioux War

▲—▲	Crook, March 1876
▲ ▲ ▲	Gibbon, April–June 1876
▷ ▷ ▷	Terry and Custer, May–June 1876
‼‼‼	Custer, May–June 1876
⬡⬡⬡	Custer, June 1876
●●●	Terry and Crook, August 1876
□□□	Crook, September 1876

The Battle of the Little Bighorn, 25–26 June 1876

From *Cavalier in Buckskin: George Armstrong Custer and the Western Military Frontier* by Robert M. Utley. ©1988 by the

Bloody Knife: Custer's Favorite Scout

Gatling guns, two companies of the 17th Infantry, and one of the 6th Infantry. A train of 150 wagons rumbled and squeaked, with the bawling beef herd in the rear. Twelve hundred men were on their way into deepest Indian country, while two other armies converged with them from the west and south. Possibly they would meet. Left behind, assisting in holding the forts, were 21 Arikara scouts at Fort Lincoln, 12 more at Fort Stevenson, and six at Fort Buford.

Far and wide, ahead and to the flanks ranged the highly mobile scouting force, performing their duties so efficiently and so well that constant remarks passed among the officers and men that the Rees were nearly irreplaceable. Being traders through heritage, they took advantage of their freedom to hunt on the job and sold the meat to the troops at the evening bivouacs. The hind quarters of a deer brought $2; front quarters, back or saddle, $1. Antelope, too, were plentiful. A band of scouts brought in seven of the swift creatures on May 21, and on the following day Bloody Knife and Charley Reynolds led another group into camp packing 14 antelope.

Surgeon DeWolf admitted to his wife and to his diary that he was satisfied with the work of the same scouts he had shrunk from examining. He wrote home on May 19: " ... we cannot be surprised very easily. The Indian Scouts are all camped tonight outside us." DeWolf's letter of May 29: "Scouts working ten miles out."[185]

Riding with Custer's Arikara scouts were five Sioux, including one poor soul named Broken Penis.[186] These scouts were all apparently Hunkpapas, married to Arikara women. Given the deep hostility between the two tribes, this may seem surprising. However, the Sioux and Arikara had a long history of occasional truces for purposes of trade. Like the marriage between Bloody Knife's

Arikara mother and Sioux father, these unions also most likely occurred during periods of peace.[187]

When camp was settled at Young Man's Butte on the night of May 23, Custer strode to the Ree camp to eat and visit with the detachment. Young Hawk was his favorite cook. Watching the conference from a distance, Mark Kellogg, the correspondent who filed dispatches primarily for the *Bismarck Tribune,* remarked in his diary that evening that "Gen. C— visits Scouts(.)* Much at home amongst them."[188] In truth, he was. The Arikara scout Red Star was reported to have said at one time that Custer had the heart of an Indian.

Partially in sign language, in which he was reasonably proficient, supported by Gerard's interpreting, Custer told the scouts that he wanted to fight the Sioux and Cheyennes and beat them. According to Red Star, Custer dreamed aloud before them:

> When we return, I will go back to Washington and on my trip to Washington, I shall take my brother here, Bloody Knife, with me. I shall remain at Washington and be the Great Father. But my brother, Bloody Knife, will return, and when he arrives home, he shall have a fine house built for him, and those of you present will be the ones appointed to look after the work that will be placed in charge of Bloody Knife. You will have positions under him to help in what he is to do and you can, when you wish to speak with me or send me word, gather at Bloody Knife's house and decide what the message will be. Then he will send it to me. He will be given the whole tribe of the Arikaras to be the head of. I will have papers made out for each of you here, then you will have plenty to eat for all time to come, and you and your children.[189]

It was typical of Custer to impose his will on others, and it must have been heady stuff for Bloody Knife to absorb. But what must the Rees have thought? In their village, Bloody Knife was no chief, nor had he performed any special services or acts for his people which would qualify him for such a position. Why should he be singled out for such an honor? Stolidly, they listened on.

Long Hair had prefaced his remarks about being the Great Father with the fact that he was displeased because the Hidatsas and Mandans were not represented in the detachment. He now came back to the subject and ordered the Rees to shoot and kill any Hidatsa they saw, but to divide their ammunition and rations with Mandans when they met people of that nation![190]

If the Ree scouts thought this final portion of Custer's talk was irrational and irresponsible, it does not appear they committed those thoughts to record.

****

For several days, an order had been in effect that no shooting would be allowed for fear of alerting enemy scouts. The rule was inadvertently broken one day by Billy Jackson when he shot at a snake in the river. In traditional Army style, young Jackson was punished by being sentenced to stand on one foot on an upended keg.

On May 30, Custer, at the head of four companies and a complement of scouts, swept a portion of the Little Missouri for warriors but found nothing. Deprecatingly, he wrote Libbie that night that "Bloody Knife looks on in wonder at me because I never get tired and says that no other man could ride all night and never sleep."[191]

On June 9, Terry met with Colonel John Gibbon, commander of the Montana Column, on the steamer *Far West,* on the Yellowstone, at which time a plan of campaign was devised. The first step was taken the next day when Major Marcus Reno, the one the Rees called Man With the Dark Face, was ordered to take six companies on a reconnaissance of the valleys of the Powder and Tongue rivers. With him went Mitch Bouyer, a mixed blood scout on loan from Gibbon, who was completely familiar with the country to be searched. Also along were three of the Arikaras.[192] On the 11th, the remainder of the Dakota Column marched to the Yellowstone where, after several days of jockeying for position, both Terry's and Gibbon's commands were united.

Here the Rees met Gibbon's complement of Crow scouts, whose fate was to be so closely interwoven with their own within a few days. The Crows seemed unimpressed. In the opinion of one of them, White Man Runs Him, the Arikaras appeared to be small men compared to other Plains tribes. He thought them dirty and careless in their personal habits. Unknowingly, his thinking was echoed by Peter Thompson, a 7th Cavalry private, who noted in his memoirs that " ... a dirtier set of rascals would be difficult to find."[193]

Reno advanced up the Powder River to the Tongue. He then violated orders by crossing over to the Rosebud, where he came upon a deserted Sioux camp. The size of it surprised and shocked the Rees. One of them, Forked Horn, warned the major, "If the Dakotas (Sioux) see us, the sun will not move very far before we are all killed." [194]

Camp Twenty was set up at the mouth of the Powder on June 11, where a trader was doing a land office business selling liquor to soldiers. Gerard at first sternly cautioned the scouts there would be no drinking. He later relented when Custer modified the order and permitted the scouts one drink only.

Camp broke at seven o'clock on the morning of the 15th for the march to Tongue River. As the Rees were preparing to move out, Custer and Bloody Knife rode up. "The General says we are all marching," said Bloody Knife. "There are numerous enemies in the country. If we attack their camp and are beaten, we must retreat in small groups. You scouts must not run away nor go back to your homes." Some confusion exists as to whether the order was Bloody Knife's idea or if it was issued by Custer through his chief scout.

The Man With the Dark Face completed his reconnaissance at the mouth of the Rosebud on June 19 and the next day was joined by Custer and Terry. Reno was not popular with the Arikaras and became less so at Camp Twenty, where an inspection of horses took place. The major decided that High Bear's mount was too badly galled to let the scout go on with his detachment. In the polite Indian manner of total disagreement, High Bear replied, "You see the sun there? If you say it does not move, I will not dispute you." The irony was lost on Reno. He turned to Gerard and said, "Tell him any man who is not a fool would agree with me, and that he will show himself a soldier by agreeing with me without question."

High Bear, like Bloody Knife unawed by Army shoulder straps, snapped back, "If only one of us is to go on, we will decide by a fight which one is to go. The man killed in the fight will not go." Infuriated, Reno then threatened to shoot High Bear. The scout drew his knife and started for the officer. Nearby, Bloody Knife had been watching the escalation of the argument. Now, he sprang between the wild-eyed contestants and shouted, "Long Hair is my brother and I forbid this fight!" To Reno he said more quietly, "I wish for my sake you would let him go."[195] Slowly, both men backed off and High Bear was allowed to go on.

Two of Reno's scouts reported on June 19 that they had come upon a large warrior trail leading west from the Rosebud to the Little Bighorn River. The news led to a council of the officers of the combined Dakota and Montana columns on the 21st. Terry's plan entailed a division of forces in order to effect a pincers movement in the vicinity of the Bighorn River, where it was believed the Sioux and Cheyennes were concentrated. It was arranged that Gibbon's troops would move southward up the Bighorn Valley. Custer's regiment was to search up the Rosebud. The hope was that somewhere between the two columns, the Sioux and Cheyennes would be trapped. From the evidence the scouts had seen, they were certain they were faced with at least 5000 warriors and they were concerned. The officers refused to believe them, contending there could not be more than 1000 or 1500 Indian fighting men in the country.

For his foray, Custer acquired on loan from Gibbon six of the latter's Crow scouts and Mitch Bouyer, whom the Rees called Man With the Calfskin Vest. The thorough familiarity of Gibbon's scouts with the country to be covered made them the logical choices for the job.

Custer, with his brother Tom, visited the scout camp that day to deliver dispatches. He ordered six of the Arikaras to be detailed to carry the mail to the Powder River base camp. Before he left, he talked briefly with the scouts through Gerard.

That evening, Mark Kellogg filed what turned out to be his last article with C.A. Lounsberry, the owner of the *Bismarck Tribune*. The 43-year-old journalist, who would fall with Custer less than four days later, reported that:

> We leave the Rosebud to-morrow, and by the time this reaches you, we will have met and fought the red devils, with what results remains to be seen. I

go with Custer and will be at (sic) the death.[196]

****

Eerie noises wafted through the morning air of June 22, 1876 from the direction of the Ree camp. Gerard had suggested they sing their death songs, knowing the peace of mind it brought them. So the scouts saddled and mounted and rode around, uttering their wailing sounds.

High noon came and with it, the departure of the 7th Cavalry. They paraded out of the camp before the approving eyes of General Terry and Colonel Gibbon. All 12 companies were on the march, their 29 Arikara and six Crow scouts moving ahead and to the sides, with Lucky Man Reynolds, Bloody Knife, Mitch Bouyer and Custer leading.

The "Royal Family," as the troops and the anti-Custer faction in the regiment called the Custer clique, filed by in their assigned positions in greater force than usual — Lieutenant Colonel Custer; younger brothers Tom and Boston Custer; brother-in-law Lieutenant James Calhoun; nephew Autie Reed; and bosom friend Captain Myles Moylan. The clan was gathered for the great victory they anticipated, which would be a windfall for all of them when it elevated their famous relative and friend to the White House. What heights could they not attain with the man's known penchants for loyalty and nepotism! The seventh member, Libbie Custer, or the "Queen of Sheba," as the troops called her, awaited developments at Fort Lincoln. The three Custer brothers, Autie Reed and James Calhoun would all be killed in battle 76 hours later.

Bloody Knife wore a white man's shirt and trousers, his hair hanging loose rather than braided, held from flying in the wind by a strip of flannel around his head, with three feathers affixed to the back.

From noon until four o'clock, the regiment pounded its way up the valley of the Rosebud, raising a dense cloud of choking dust. Water was the first consideration when they halted to camp.

Fred Gerard had been held at the Yellowstone to oversee the sending of dispatches with some Sioux scouts. Delayed two hours before the job was done, he then hastened to overtake Custer. He found the command 12 miles above the mouth of the Rosebud. As he made his way into camp, Custer's orderly saw him and told him Custer wished to see him. With Custer was Bloody Knife, considerably under the influence of trader's whiskey. The problem may have been that sign language communication between the two had broken down. As soon as he recognized the interpreter, Bloody Knife proclaimed loftily, "Tell General Custer that I don't believe he is out hunting for Indians; more likely on a pleasure trip! If he should find them, he would not dare to attack them!" A permissive Custer replied, " ... tell him that I am on an independent command and shall fight the Indians wherever I find them."[197] The chief scout seemed pacified and went off somewhere. He did not return to the scout camp. His absence was remarked on by the rest of them and they suspected he was drunk.

Later that evening, Lieutenant Edward S. Godfrey, making the rounds of his company site, came up to the scout campfire. Mitch Bouyer was there with Bloody Knife and Half Yellow Face, the leader of the Crow scouts, all having a talk. Bouyer asked Godfrey if he had ever fought the Sioux. Godfrey replied that he had. Bouyer then asked him how many of the Indians he expected to find. Godfrey repeated the officers' belief that they would find 1000 to 1500 Sioux. "Well, do you think we can whip that many?" persisted Bouyer. Godfrey guessed that they could. Bouyer's final remark was emphatic: "Well, I can tell you we are going to have a damned big fight!"[198]

Strangely, Godfrey made no reference to a drunken Bloody Knife.

Dull-eyed and haggard, the scout appeared at breakfast the next morning leading his horse. Whether his disciplinary infraction could not be proved, or whether the fact he was Custer's favorite kept him from being punished as Varnum had warned, no one seemed to know. Not for Bloody Knife the sentence of walking for a day, or standing until exhausted on an upended keg on one foot. It does seem a remarkable act of forbearance on Custer's part, especially in view of the adverse effect it must have had on the other scouts.

A couple of hours after breaking camp June 23, the regiment came upon the large lodgepole trail which Reno had been shown, and later in the day passed four big Indian campsites.

Among the stragglers that day was Dr. George E. Lord, the Fort Buford Post Surgeon who had been assigned for the campaign to the 7th Cavalry. The doctor was suffering agonies from cramps, which in his medical dictionary was defined as dysentery, but was more familiarly known by the descriptive frontier term "Dakota quickstep." He was in distinguished company. Back on the Yellowstone, Colonel Gibbon was sick with the same complaint. They and the others had consumed too much alkali-impregnated water.

****

More Sioux campsites were sighted when the march resumed on the morning of the 24th. At one especially large location there were unmistakable signs of a sun dance circle. The Rees interpreted from the evidence found there and elsewhere on the route that the Sioux knew the bluecoats were coming and were confident they could beat them. Another large trail was discovered toward the end of the afternoon. All of the scouts were now openly worried and uneasy about the size of the unseen camp. The Crows too became sullen. Charley Reynolds and Mitch Bouyer were solemn.

About four o'clock in the afternoon, Custer called a halt. With his guidon orderly following at a respectful distance, he went to the Ree campfire, where he sat with the smoking scouts. He informed them that the Crows brought word of a large Sioux camp. What did they think of the news? Stabbed leaped from his place at the fire and danced as though dodging bullets, advising Long Hair that white soldiers should fight like Indians. It was foolish to stand erect as the easiest of targets. Custer then flattered the Indians' fighting qualities and said he hoped his brothers would take many horses away from the Sioux. Then he warmed to his subject:

> And on this expedition, if we are victorious when we return home, Bloody Knife, Bobtailed Bull, Soldier, Strikes Two and Stabbed will be proud to have following behind them on parade marches those who have shown themselves to be brave young men. When your chief, Son of the Star, sees you on this parade, I am sure he will be proud to see his boys ... if we are successful, when we return, my brother Bloody Knife and I will represent you at Washington and perhaps we will take you in person to Washington.[199]

Perhaps Custer failed to notice that his words had not heartened the Rees at all.

Bivouac was made that evening about eight o'clock. In the

scout quarter the always taciturn Lucky Man Reynolds was now morose. A painful inflammation on his hand was giving him much trouble. Because of a premonition that he would be killed, he had not wanted to leave the Yellowstone. Twice he had asked Terry to be relieved of the duty. But the General had talked him into going on. Now he sensed that Custer was getting into a situation that was too big for the 7th Cavalry to handle alone. Quietly, he opened his war bag and gave away all his possessions. The gesture embarrassed the Rees, to whom most of the articles were given, but they accepted them to ease Reynolds' feelings.

An hour later, Custer ordered Varnum to take Bouyer and Reynolds with four of the Crows and a half dozen Rees and scout ahead through the night in an effort to locate the Sioux camp.

Sometime after midnight, the regiment was roused to take up the trail again, halting shortly after two o'clock in the morning with the first streaks of dawn. Bloody Knife rode with Custer, Gerard and Half Yellow Face. Custer voiced a fear that some of the Sioux would escape, to which his chief Ree scout replied flatly that he would find all the Indians he wanted in the huge Sioux camp ahead.

It was Sunday, June 25, 1876.

Chapter 20

The Battle
of the Little Bighorn

In the early morning, the Arikara scout Red Star rode into the bivouac area with a message from Varnum that the Sioux camp was in sight. Excitement reigned as the Rees again sang their death songs. Stabbed, 45, complimented the youthful, 18-year-old Red Star, building up his confidence by praising his lonely and dangerous but important ride with the message through a country infested with the enemy. The group around Custer included Bloody Knife, Red Star, Gerard and Tom Custer. After the message had been read, Custer, nodding toward his brother Tom, said to Bloody Knife, "Your brother there is frightened. His heart flutters with fear, his eyes are rolling from fright at this news of the Sioux. When we have beaten the Sioux, he will then be a man."[200]

Red Star was tying up his horse's tail for war. Bloody Knife told Custer defiantly that he " ... would find enough Sioux to keep us fighting for two or three days!" Custer answered that he thought they could get through them in one day.

By nine o'clock, the command moved out. Custer, Bloody Knife, Tom Custer and Gerard rode ahead with three of the Rees to the vantage point called the Crow's Nest. Custer climbed to the top but could see nothing with either the naked eye or field glasses. He was assured by Reynolds, Bouyer and the scouts that the village was there and that it was a big one. Reynolds told him that the largest gathering of Indians he had ever seen was in the camp. Stabbed, a sort of elder councillor, rode among the Ree scouts, making medicine as he exhorted them to be brave and to behave well. Dismounting, he brought out some clay, which he mixed with spit in his hands and rubbed on the bodies of each of the Arikaras while he prayed.

Custer had decided earlier to wait until dawn of June 26 for the attack. Part of his strategy was to surround the camp in the darkness as he had done at the Washita eight years earlier. The Crows, however, were sure the troops had been detected. They urged Custer to change his mind and attack at once. Half Yellow Face was particularly insistent. Finally, Custer gave in.

Assembling the scouts, he gave them their instructions. "Make up your minds to go straight to their camp and capture their horses. Boys, you are going to have a hard day. You must keep up your courage; you will get experience today."[201] Custer believed that if the enemy warriors could be put afoot, they would be forced to stand and fight.

Under a punishing sun, in an almost windless atmosphere, the regiment at noon started over the divide, down into the fateful valley of the Little Bighorn.

About a mile passed beneath the weary hooves of the horses and ponies. Near the headwaters of Reno Creek, Custer called a halt. He conferred with Lieutenant William W. Cooke, the adjutant, then gathered the officers and divided the column into four sections. Reno was assigned the leadership of a battalion consisting of companies A, G and M, totaling about 140 soldiers. He was also accompanied by Bloody Knife, Charley Reynolds and 26 other scouts. Captain Frederick Benteen assumed command of Companies D, K and H, some 115 strong. Custer gathered about 215 soldiers in five companies — C, E, F, I and L — under his direct control. Also with him were his 18-year-old nephew, Autie Reed, Assistant Surgeon George E. Lord, Mitch Bouyer, four Crow scouts, and newspaper correspondent Mark Kellogg, who was primarily representing the weekly *Bismarck Tribune*.[202] Company B, commanded by Captain Thomas McDougall, guarded the pack train and brought up the rear. The pack train unit, including Company B, numbered about 130 men.[203] They had been assigned from each of the 7th Cavalry's 12 troops to handle the heavily ladened column, which included mules carrying some 24,000 rounds of ammunition.

Mitch Bouyer approached Custer and said there were more enemy Indians ahead of them than he had ever seen in his more than 30 years on the Upper Missouri. He felt strongly that if Long Hair attacked the village, none of the troops would come out alive. Stirred to anger, Custer shot back that if Bouyer was afraid, he did not have to come along. Bouyer, angered in turn, replied, "I can go anywhere you can!" That would indeed be the case, as Bouyer followed Custer into his last battle and to their deaths.

Bloody Knife fastened his gaze on his most powerful god, the sun, and said prophetically, "I shall not see you go down behind the mountains tonight."[204]

A little later he said musingly, "I am going home today, not the way we came, but in spirit, home to my people."

Private Peter Thompson, in recalling the officers' conference, remembered that Fred Gerard "... so far forgot himself as to go and sit down near the place where the consulting officers were gathered. General Custer looked at him and said, 'Go where you belong and stay there.' "[205] Gerard's mournful, bloodhound features registered surprise and embarrassment. He got up and moved away.

Not long after the noon hour, the battalions separated. Benteen's section moved out a quarter of an hour before the balance of the regiment. Custer set a fast pace when his five companies and Reno's command pushed forward. It was sometime after two o'clock when they came to a lone tipi, where they found the scouts who were supposed to be an hour ahead of the column. The scouts had stopped at the tipi, slit it open and found inside the dead body of a Sioux warrior. They all rode around the lodge, singing and striking it with their quirts. One of them entered and drank the soup and ate some of the meat left to nourish the departed on his journey to the Land of Shadows. There Gerard, slightly in the lead, observed a body of Indians moving downstream. He called out to Custer, "There go your Indians running like devils!"

Long Hair was angry with the scouts for stopping without permission and now he ordered them to pursue the Indians Gerard had sighted. They refused. Furiously, he roared at them, "I told you to dash on and stop for nothing! You have disobeyed me! Move to one side and let the soldiers pass you in the charge! If any man of you is not brave, I will take away his weapons and make a woman of him!" One of the Rees cried in answer, "Tell him if he does the same to all of his white soldiers who are not so brave as we are, it will take him a very long time indeed!" A shout of laughter from the other scouts greeted this sally, but they indicated they were now ready to fight.[206]

Young Hawk, expecting to be killed and scalped, carefully arranged his hair.

Either Bloody Knife or Bouyer again approached Custer and warned him there were more Sioux ahead than there were bullets in the belts of his soldiers. But Custer, now thoroughly aroused, could not be convinced that it would be a disasterous mistake to move ahead.

It was at this halt, Gerard said afterward, that Custer ordered Reno to take his battalion and try to bring the Indians to battle. "I will support you," he promised. Then, probably remembering the instructions he had issued to the scouts about running off the Sioux pony herd that was in the bottoms, he added, "Take the scouts with you."[207]

It was 3:15 p.m.

****

To the creak of leather and the jangle of metal they were off, Custer with his five companies following Reno's battalion for about two miles, then branching to the right and down the Little Bighorn. Another couple of miles at a fast trot and Reno reached the river, delaying for 10 or 15 minutes while the horses were watered. A number of the 28 scouts now with Reno had fallen behind because their overworked mounts could not keep up with the fast traveling troops.[208]

Excited Rees called to Gerard that Indians were coming at them from the direction of the village, which was then about two or three miles away. The interpreter, thinking Long Hair should be informed of the strength of the opposition, turned back to find him. Within minutes, he met Lieutenant Cooke, who told him that he would so inform Custer. Reno used some time to re-form his men once they had forded the stream. Twelve of the scouts had not crossed, but instead had turned to the right to go after a Sioux horse herd. Of the 16 then with Reno, six of them also turned right to run off another pony herd.[209]

The order to advance was given and the bluecoats rode

The Battle of the Little Bighorn, June 25, 1876

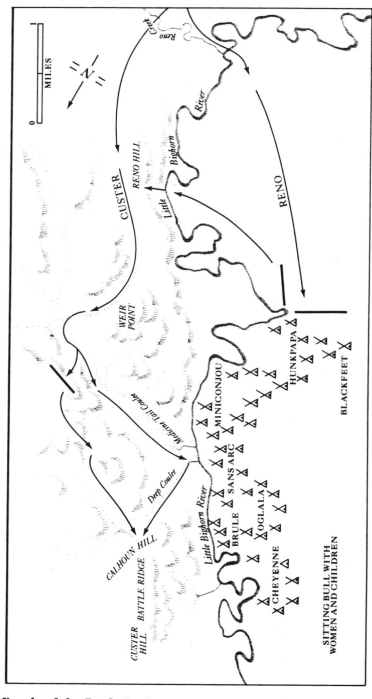

From *The Lance and the Shield: The Life and Times of Sitting Bull* by Robert M. Utley. Map by Jeffrey L. Ward. Reprinted by permission of Henry Holt and Co., Inc.

MILES

N

RENO HILL

CUSTER

Reno Creek

Little Bighorn River

RENO

WEIR POINT

Medicine Tail Coulee

Deep Coulee

CALHOUN HILL

BATTLE RIDGE

CUSTER HILL

Little Bighorn River

HUNKPAPA

BLACKFEET

MINICONJOU

SANS ARC

BRULE

OGLALA

CHEYENNE

SITTING BULL WITH WOMEN AND CHILDREN

The Battle of the Little Bighorn

down the valley still at a quick trot, with troops A and M thrown into a line and G riding in reserve. Reno signaled the gait to be increased to a headlong charge, the 10 remaining scouts under Varnum fanning out ahead and to the extreme left, aiming for the main pony herd. On the dry earth, the charging battalion of 130 soldiers and scouts raised a throbbing thunder of sound and a tremendous cloud of dust. A second dust cloud rose over the Indian village where the warriors, little boys and women were bringing in the war horses.

Reno had no idea he was striking the Hunkpapa end of the camp. He could not have picked a worse spot. Around Sioux lodge fires, the Hunkpapas were renowned as the End of the Circle Band. Theirs was the place of highest honor and most danger when the nation traveled, that of rear guard. They were the toughest and most recalcitrant of all the Sioux. And now their war chiefs, Gall, Black Moon and Crow King, were gathering the fighting men to wipe out the Chargers, the Pony Soldiers.

As the thundering blue line came within carbine range of the village after a mile or more of hard riding, Reno for the first time realized the immensity of the camp. Anticipating that he would be overwhelmed if he advanced any further, he halted the command and dismounted the men to fight on foot. Hundreds of warriors were flitting to their front and to their left. The 90 men left on the firing line after the horseholders had taken the mounts to the comparative shelter of a small stand of timber directed their fire at the confused melee in the Indian camp. Dust and campfire smoke was so thick it was difficult to select targets. But the big, heavy 405-grain bullets shattered lodge poles into splinters, ripped holes in the skin coverings, sent trade kettles clanging over the packed dirt floors, and knocked over a number of the dwellings, setting them on fire. They tore their way indiscriminately into yielding, copper-colored bodies, and in one unhappy lodge, smashed into lifelessness two women and three children of war chief Gall.

Even with the poor visibility, Reno was becoming increasingly aware of the awesome power before him.

Off to the left, the small squad of scouts who had gone after ponies had brought in some of the captured animals. Bloody Knife had secured three horses from near the point of the Hunkpapa camp, which he drove in among the scouts. Evidently, his intention was to go back for more. Three of the Rees were in contact with him. Red Bear, unable to see his chief scout because of the dust, heard him call out, "Someone take these horses back to the hill. One of them is for me."[210] Young Hawk and Little Sioux, neither of whom seemed aware in the excitement of the fight that he was given the responsibility for the captured horses, related similar stories.

Little Sioux paid no attention to the ponies, possibly because at the same moment he saw that Bobtailed Bull, his sergeant scout, the last man at the extreme left of the line, was being cut off from the rest of them by a band of Cheyenne horsemen. While making a desperate effort to make it to the safety of the timber, Bobtailed Bull's horse was shot out from under him. The Arikara scout was chased across a wet slough and into some underbrush, where he died before a hail of Cheyenne bullets.[211]

Young Hawk said that Bloody Knife came directly toward him, apparently after he had rid himself of the horses, and said, "What Custer has ordered about the Sioux horses is being done. The horses are being taken away."[212] Young Hawk recalled that Bloody Knife was wearing his medicine, the black handkerchief with the blue stars given to him by Custer, as well as a bear's claw with a clam shell fastened to it. According to Young Hawk, Bloody Knife did not return for more ponies, but instead took up a post in the fighting line near Little Sioux.

The position of the scouts on Reno's left flank was a bad one, exposed as they were to the Sioux and Cheyennes oncoming now from both the left and the front, intent on retrieving their horses and overwhelming the handful of soldiers.

The first phase of the raids on the Sioux herds had taken place before the troops dismounted. After fighting on foot for some time, it became obvious that no more horses could be captured, since the enemy was approaching close and had already rolled up the left flank held loosely by the scouts. The surviving Rees came in to join the troops. With his left gone and Indians infiltrating his right and rear, Reno ordered a retreat to a stand of timber on the riverbank. The fast firing soldiers had already dug into the last reserves of ammunition on their persons. There was more in the saddlebags. Only 15 or 20 minutes had elapsed since the battle began, yet already greasy white clouds exuding the rotten egg stench of black powder smoke hung low over the field, mingling with the smoke and dust. Arrows feathered the ground in the area vacated by the retreating troops.

The timber proved to be a reasonably good defensive position, but it was more frightening than being in the open. Arrows whispered, sighed and rattled their paths through the brush and trees, some stopping with thumps in limbs and trunks. A steady fall of leaves, twigs and small branches rained down, sliced off by the passage of the heavy bullets, some thumping into tree trunks and branches, leaving a trail which could almost be seen. The sustained, full-throated, swelling roar of thousands of voices, pierced with the shrill war cries of blood-sensing warriors, the screams of women and children, the fearful shrieks of wounded and dying horses and men, interspersed with the deep boom of the heavy rifles and carbines smothered the valley, depressing all thought.

Men cowered in the thickets.

By now, the warriors had almost completely surrounded the command. Large parties of them, many of them fresh from the victory over General Crook at the Battle of the Rosebud a week earlier, dashed mounted in to attack. Others worked their way through the brush on foot. They were as disorganized as the troops but infinitely more numerous. An officer tried to get Billy Jackson to take a message to Custer. Jackson balked, telling the officer that no man would be able to get through.[213]

Infiltration increased and firing grew heavier. Reno, thinking he was still in a bad place, selected a spot on the top of the bluffs on the opposite side of the stream to set up a stronger defensive line. In the fury of battle, he had lost his hat and tied a white handkerchief around his head. He called out an order to leave the timber, telling the company commanders to concentrate their men and horses in a small, 10-acre clearing, mount the men and prepare to charge away from the village through the ring of warriors surrounding them. Not all the officers and men heard the order. Consequently, while those who did hear it gathered and mounted, the defensive line diminished considerably, allowing the attackers to move up in strength.

The Arikara scout, Little Brave, already poorly mounted and bleeding heavily from a wound in his arm, was overtaken and killed near Reno's crossing on the east bank of the river.[214]

Charley Reynolds, left behind in the timber, was killed as he attempted to ride to the safety of the bluffs. He apparently had his horse shot from under him. After the battle, Reynolds' body was found near the animal, with several empty cartridge shells nearby, indicating he had put up a desperate last stand.[215]

Bloody Knife, accustomed to being at Custer's side in a fight, was sitting on his horse about 10 feet to the right and just slightly in front of Major Reno. At that moment, a large party of Sioux burst through the timber to within 30 feet of the assembled troops and fired a ragged volley point blank at them. A trooper screamed and fell from his horse. One or more bullets caught Bloody Knife in the head, one of them squarely between the eyes.[216] Reaction caused him to throw an arm up as his head jerked backward. He toppled from his horse, slid to the ground and was still. Warm blood and brains spattered on Reno's face and body. On the ground, Bloody Knife did not hear the shaken, unnerved Reno order the troopers to charge for the bluffs.

It was 3:55 p.m.

Epilogue

Dust and white powder smoke were barely settling and clearing in the river bottoms when the Indian women went to work on the dead and wounded bluecoats. When they found Arikaras, they were singularly vicious.

The *Bismarck Tribune* noted this tribal hostility in an extra published the morning of July 6, 1876: "Bloody Knife surrendered his spirit to the one who gave it, fighting the natural and hereditory (sic) foes of his tribe, as well as the foes of the whites."[217]

What was the aftermath for Bloody Knife? Several versions exist. One of them concerns two young Hunkpapa sisters who went out to the battlefield in search of trophies. They found the scout's body and recognizing it as that of an enemy, cut off the head and carried it back to the Sioux camp, swinging it between them by the hair. Their mother, when she saw it, gasped in horror and begged them to take it away. She recognized it as the head of her brother, Bloody Knife. The girls were displaying the head of their uncle! Knowing of the bad blood between Gall and the Ree scout, the mother was convinced that Gall had killed him.

A minor refinement on the same story had the young women placing the head on a pole and transporting it around the camp in triumph.

Joseph Henry Taylor wrote that Gall, because of the tragic loss of so many members of his family, was in mourning, taking no part in the scalp dance. "Chief Gall, stoic that he was, had remained impassive to the scenes about him after the day's work of blood was over, and he might have continued so throughout the night had not the severed head of Bloody Knife been brought before him. A broad smile crossed his face as he spoke out joyously, 'Now that my vilest enemy is dead, I can join you in the dance.' "[218]

Young Hawk told that on the night of June 27, he and Forked Horn went to the deserted Sioux camp for meat they knew had been abandoned by the Sioux. There they met a white man of Gibbon's command who showed them a scalp he had found in the camp, and he asked if it were a Sioux scalp. From the lightly graying hair and other recognizable features, the two Arikaras identified it as that of Bloody Knife. They asked the man to throw it away, since it was the scalp of a Ree. The man demurred, saying that if it was Bloody Knife's scalp, he wanted to keep it for his father who had known the chief scout in earlier years at a military post at the mouth of the Yellowstone. The man gave them each a pony from a small herd of Sioux horses he had captured.

The next day, while the Rees assisted in the location and burial of the dead, Young Hawk, accompanied by some of the other Rees, was shown a scout's body in the bushes. They could not tell who it was because the face and head " ... were all pounded to pieces," but they thought it was the body of Bloody Knife.

Another report originating among the whites stated that Terry's troops found the head of Bloody Knife in the abandoned village.

Yet another version came from one of the troopers in Reno's command, Private Theodore W. Goldin of Company G. Goldin wrote a friend in Minnesota in early 1934 that he had been in the party that identified the body of Bloody Knife the morning of June 27, 1876:

> ... It was not far from where he fell or was last seen alive. He was scalped and there were a number of arrows in his body ... He was not decapitated. (Charley) Reynolds was scalped but not mutilated, as he lay some distance from any of the others, partly hidden by a clump of brush.[219]

Goldin was one of 24 troopers awarded the Congressional Medal of Honor, the highest military award for bravery in battle. He was among a group of volunteers who left the relative safety of Reno Hill and, while under heavy sniper fire from the Indians, retrieved water from the Little Bighorn for the wounded.

Many years afterward, when Dr. Henry R. Porter, Contract Surgeon and the only surviving doctor of the Custer command, was in private practice in Bismarck, the son of his partner noticed a small bottle on the physician's desk one day. Floating in colorless liquid were " ... dark brown twisted threads." The youth asked Dr. Porter what the substance was. "Those, Willie," the doctor replied, "are the brains of Bloody Knife!"

Round-eyed with wonder, the boy listened while Porter related his story of being on the scene of the "wounding" of the Ree scout, an injury which disabled him. According to Porter, the doctor charged bravely back alone into the mass of warriors to try to save his Ree friend. The ranks of the warriors were so thick they could not shoot or strike him without hitting their own men. "Porter sprang from his horse and lifted the wounded scout in his arms. As he tried to remount, a second bullet hit Bloody Knife in the head, blowing his brains into the pocket of Porter's blouse."[220] And he had saved the grisly strands!

Countless myths have arisen out of the Little Bighorn fight and this could easily be one of them. There is no other ready answer.

And, finally, Billy Jackson told a biographer long afterward that he and Fred Gerard assisted in the burials of "Charlie Reynolds, Bloody Knife and others of Reno's troops" at the battle site. Jackson did not mention mutilation.[221]

She Owl

At the moment Bloody Knife was shot, the United States Army Quartermaster Department owed him exactly $91.66 in pay for services rendered as a citizen scout. On April 4, 1879, an Arikara woman, She Owl, appeared before Indian Agent Thomas P. Ellis at Fort Berthold and after being sworn to the truth, stated in a deposition that she had never received the pay due her husband at the time of his death. She Owl further stated that she had been married to Bloody Knife for 10 years, that her eldest child was about nine years old, and that she was " ... the sole and only legal representative of said Bloody Knife." Indestructible old Pierre Garreau was the interpreter. She Owl got the money due her, but not until 1881, five years after her husband fell at the Little Bighorn.[222]

Gall

Gall had about four and a half years of freedom left to enjoy after the triumph over Custer and Bloody Knife. Using the fiery language of the day, John Finerty of the *Chicago Times* described *Pizi* in that period as, "A ruthless vagabond who looked like a horse-stealing gypsy and was, by repute, a double-dealing, skulking rascal."

In 1877, Gall fled into Canada with Sitting Bull. Surprised by troops while trading at Poplar River, Montana Territory, in January 1881, he was captured after a short skirmish, held as prisoner for several months at Fort Buford, then sent to the Standing Rock Reservation. With Major Edward S. Godfrey, Gall attended the 10th Anniversary Reunion of the Little Bighorn fight at the battlefield on June 25, 1886, where he described the action and said that killing the soldiers was like "chasing buffalo." In 1889, he became a judge of the Indian Court at Standing Rock. Gall died at Oak Creek, South Dakota, on December 5, 1894. He was believed to be about 54 years old.

Frederick F. Gerard

When Reno and his troops fled so precipitately from the timber in the river bottom, Gerard, Lieutenant Charles C. DeRudio, Billy Jackson and Sergeant Thomas O'Neill, none of whom had heard the order to get out, were left behind in the flight. After hiding out and narrowly averting discovery by the prowling Indians several times, they made their way to Reno's perimeter on the bluff the night of the 26th.

Later, while the battlefield was being studied by the officers, a report circulated that it was thought Sitting Bull's body had been found. Having seen the chief on one occasion, Gerard was called upon to assist in the identification. His opinion, after examining the copper-skinned corpse, was that it was not that of Sitting Bull, since one of the Sioux leader's legs was supposed to be shorter than the other. Actually, Sitting Bull limped from an old war wound in his left foot. As it turned out, Gerard was right, but not because his diagnosis was correct.

On May 1, 1876, sixteen days before the expedition started, Gerard wrote his three daughters from Fort Abraham Lincoln that he had taken a life insurance policy in the amount of $1500, with the girls as share and share alike beneficiaries. He also let them know of the two lots he had bought in Bismarck in their names, shrewdly placing the property in trust for his own use until his death. In this letter, and in another written earlier, he told the girls that he would accompany the expedition against the Sioux.

His first letter to them after the battle was written from the mouth of the Bighorn River, dated July 6, 1876. A single sentence from that letter is worth preserving: "If I ever return to Lincoln, I shall never go out again with an expedition."[223]

Gerard served as post interpreter at Fort Lincoln until 1882. The next year, he opened a store in Mandan, Bismarck's sister city across the wide Missouri. He sold the store in 1890 when he entered the employ of Pillsbury Mills in Minneapolis as an advertising agent. Gerard died on January 13, 1913, at the age of 84.

Billy Jackson

Billy Jackson's wish to become an Indian scout came true at Fort Lincoln on December 10, 1874, just after he had turned 18 years of age. From that date he served continuously until several

Bloody Knife: Custer's Favorite Scout

years later following the expedition of 1876. Like Gerard, he became separated from the Reno command in the valley during the fight. Teaming up with Gerard, DeRudio and O'Neill, he successfully hid out until the night of the 26th, when the foursome joined the forces on Reno Hill.

His brother, Robert Jackson, had not been on the campaign, but he joined Billy on the Yellowstone some weeks afterward when the scouts were distributed among the other commands The two continued to perform scouting duties in Montana Territory posts for several years.

When his Army service was over, Billy, a one-quarter Blackfeet, returned to the Blackfeet Reservation in Montana Territory, where he went into the horse and cattle ranching business. There he became known to his fellow tribesmen as *Siksikakoan*, or Blackfeet Man. In his waning years, he became well acquainted with author James Willard Schultz, who wrote his biography. Billy died on the reservation in the winter of 1899 at the age of 43.[224]

Sitting Bull

Tatanka Iyotanka, or Sitting Bull, a name of honor around the Sioux council fires, spent the months following the great Indian victories at the Rosebud and the Little Bighorn traversing central and eastern Montana Territory with the ambitious Colonel Nelson A. Miles snapping at his heels.

In 1877, he crossed into Canada, the Grandmother's Land of Queen Victoria, where for the moment he was safe. As the years passed, increased pressures from Washington, where they wanted him, and from Ottawa, where they did not want him, caused him to reassess his position. Reluctantly, and firmly believing that he would be killed like Crazy Horse, he decided to surrender in order to save his people from starvation.

On July 19, 1881, 187 of the faithful of his once-proud, free Sioux filed behind him into Fort Buford to give themselves up.[225] Conflicting and ironic thoughts must have passed through his mind as he saw everywhere around him the scenes of former triumphs — the many countings of coups in the killing of the white soldiers and citizens; the driving off of the white man's whoa-haws; the burning of his haystacks; the destruction of his woodpiles.

The next morning, with his 11-year-old son Crowfoot in attendance, he met the Post Commander, Major David H. Brotherton of the 7th Infantry, an old adversary, in the major's office.[226] Through his son, he surrendered his rifle, refusing to submit to the humiliation himself.

Two years as a virtual prisoner at Fort Randall followed, then comparative independence at Standing Rock. In 1885, he appeared for a season with Buffalo Bill's Wild West Show. When the Ghost Dance Movement erupted among the heartsick Sioux in 1889-90, he became a devotee. He was killed by Indian Police when they attempted to arrest him at his home on Grand River, South Dakota, on December 15, 1890. He was 56 years old.

The next day, the Army general who led the Bighorn-Yellowstone 1876 campaign against Sitting Bull's confederacy died of heart failure in New Haven, Connecticut. Alfred H. Terry was 64 years old.[227]

The Ree Scouts

Several of the Ree scouts made the retreat with Reno to the top of the bluff. Others joined them there later. Bloody Knife, Bobtailed Bull and Little Brave had been killed.[228] Another, the

21-year-old Goose, had been severely wounded by a direct hit in the hand during the rout in the valley. A Crow scout, White Swan, had also been badly wounded in the leg and hand while fighting with Reno in the valley.[229]

Most of the Rees left behind in the early stages of the fight, and a number of those on the bluffs, concluded that their best course of action would be to return to their base camp. With Gerard missing, nobody could understand them and they did not know what to do. They arrived there in separate groups on June 28.

The Ree scouts have been much and mistakenly maligned for "fleeing," even though they do not deserve such a blot on their history. They were not hired to fight. Their duties were to trail the enemy and find him, stampede and make off with hostile pony herds, and possibly take part in skirmishing. They were also to protect the command from surprise on the march, and when encamped, aid in locating the trail and choosing good campsites. That they performed their jobs efficiently and thoroughly is obvious since there were no complaints, other than from those who did not understand their plight.[230]

They were wise enough to understand that an awful mistake was being made, although their repeated warnings fell on deaf ears. To their everlasting credit, they charged and fought for Custer, despite their grave concerns about the odds against them. They made a valiant effort to capture the Sioux pony herd. An indication of their value was demonstrated when many of them were transferred to service under other field commanders during the time the badly demoralized 7th Cavalry was being reorganized in the field.

They served through many of the campaigns and scraps until after the Battle of Muddy Creek in Montana Territory on May 7, 1877. It was at Muddy Creek that Colonel Nelson A. Miles captured 51 lodges of Minniconjou Sioux under Lame Deer. The Lame Deer Fight, together with the surrender of Crazy Horse and 899 of his followers the day before at Camp Robinson, Nebraska, and other mass surrenders the same spring at all the Sioux agencies, marked the virtual end of the Great Sioux War of 1876-77.[231]

From their first enlistments in 1868 through the next two decades, the U.S. Army benefited from the services of scouts from the Three Tribes, with the Arikaras providing a majority of the scouts. One Indian served for 10 years. Another enlisted for a total of 18 hitches between 1871 and 1880. Since enlistment periods were for six months, or at the discretion of higher officers, a long period of service or succession of enlistments were not always in consecutive order.

From reports available today, it is probable that not a single one of the Arikara scouts who rode with Custer was ever able to draw even a token pension from the federal government.

In 1890, according to the federal government, the population of the Three Tribes on the Fort Berthold Reservation was 1388. The federal census of 1990 registered a population of 2999.

Lieutenant Charles A. Varnum

As Custer's Chief of Scouts, Lieutenant Varnum commanded some 40 Indian Arikara, Crow and Sioux scouts during the Little Bighorn campaign. Upon his return to Fort Lincoln in September 1876, he assumed command of Company C, formerly Captain Tom Custer's troop.

In 1880, he was re-assigned to H Company, which he commanded off and off for the next decade. Varnum received a promotion to captain in 1890, following the retirement of Thomas McDougall, who had commanded the pack train at the Little Bighorn battle. Varnum was present at the Battle of Wounded Knee in December 1890, when the Ghost Dance phenomenon exploded in a blaze of rifle and cannon fire near the Pine Ridge Agency in South Dakota. The carnage left more than 200 Sioux dead and wounded. Seventh Cavalry casualties came to 25 dead and 39 wounded.[232]

The next day, Varnum was part of the 7th Cavalry that fought Sioux warriors from a nearby camp at White Clay Creek. He ignored an order to abandon his position, instead leading a charge that recaptured higher ground and allowed other units to withdraw from the field without further loss. Seven years later, Varnum received the Congressional Medal of Honor for his actions at the Battle of White Clay Creek.

Varnum spent three years as a professor of military science at the University of Wyoming, leaving in 1898 to rejoin his B Troop as they left for Cuba during the Spanish-American War. Health problems forced him to leave six months later for detached service in Denver, where, in 1901, he was promoted to major. On October 31, 1907, Varnum was retired from the Regular Army for disability. However, he remained on the active duty roster. In 1918, he was promoted to colonel and helped with the World War I mobilization efforts at Fort Mason in San Francisco. It was there he retired from active duty in April 1919, after 47 years of Army service.

Varnum holds the distinction of being the last surviving officer who fought with the 7th Cavalry at the Little Bighorn. He died on February 26, 1936, at the age of 86, in San Francisco.[233]

The last surviving enlisted man present at the battle was Charles A. Windolph, a private who served in Captain Frederick Benteen's H Company. Windolph received the Congressional

Medal of Honor for exposing himself to Indian fire while fellow soldiers retrieved water for the wounded from the Little Bighorn River. The German immigrant died at Lead, South Dakota, on March 11, 1950, at the age of 98. He is buried in the Black Hills National Cemetery at Sturgis, South Dakota.[234]

The last 7th Cavalry survivor of the Yellowstone-Bighorn Expedition of 1876 was Jacob Horner of Bismarck, North Dakota. A private in Company K, he was stationed at the confluence of the Yellowstone and Powder rivers as a guard at the regiment's supply camp, more than 200 miles distant, at the time of the battle. Horner's four-year hitch in the Army ended with an honorable discharge at Fort Totten, near present day Devils Lake, North Dakota, on April 7, 1881. He lived the next 70 years in Bismarck, where he worked as a butcher and served six years as a city alderman.[235] Horner died on September 21, 1951, fifteen days shy of his 97th birthday.[236]

There were serveral Indian participants who survived Horner and Windolph. The last two died in 1955. One was Sitting Bull's deaf-mute son, John, who died that May. The last surviving warrior was Dewey Beard, sometimes called Iron Hail, who died in November.[237] A Minniconjou Sioux, he was 14 years old at the Little Bighorn; he lost most of his family at the Battle of Wounded Knee in 1890. The last Indian witness to the battle is believed to have been a Cheyenne named Charles Sitting Man, who watched the Custer Fight as a child and lived until 1962.[238]

Elizabeth B. Custer

Elizabeth Custer, better known as "Libbie," survived her husband by almost 57 years, long enough to witness the dawn of the New Deal and the Presidency of Franklin D. Roosevelt.

The Battle of the Little Bighorn dealt her a tremendous personal loss, claiming not only her 36-year-old husband, but two of his brothers, his brother-in-law and his nephew as well. That summer, legislation was introduced in Congress to provide a monthly widow's pension of $50 for Libbie, as well as a second fund to provide $80 a month to Custer's parents, Emanuel, 70, and Maria, 69, in Monroe, Michigan. Both bills failed.[239]

Libbie, who was married to Custer for 12 years, spent much of her long widowhood writing, lecturing and traveling to promote her husband's life, especially his Army career while on the frontier. She wrote a trilogy of books based on those frontier experiences, all of them bestsellers, between 1885 and 1890: *Boots and Saddles, Following the Guidon* and *Tenting On the Plains.*

In 1910, President William Howard Taft attended ceremonies with Libbie to unveil a 34-foot high bronze statue honoring her husband in her hometown of Monroe, Michigan.

Libbie died on April 4, 1933, in New York City, four days short of her 91st birthday. Two days after her death, she was buried at West Point beside her beloved "boy," as she often addressed him in correspondence.

Major Marcus A. Reno

Reno never really recovered from the debacle on the Little Bighorn, becoming a scapegoat for those who believed he failed Custer as the second-in-command in two fundamental ways — for ordering a retreat after charging toward the southern end of the Indian village, thus freeing hundreds of warriors to meet Custer's attack at the opposite end of the huge encampment, and for not attempting to locate and aid Custer after the retreat to the bluffs.

After assuming command at Fort Abercrombie, near present-day Wahpeton, North Dakota, Reno received the first of two court martials in 1877. The charges included taking "improper and insulting liberties" with a fellow officer's wife, which included attempting "to draw her person close up to his own (and) placing his arm around her waist ..." The military board recommended he be dismissed from the service. However, President Rutherford B. Hayes commuted the sentence to two years' suspension without pay.[240]

Two years later, in an effort to clear his name from the charges leveled at him as a result of the Little Bighorn, Reno requested that a U.S. Army Court of Inquiry be convened to investigate the events surrounding the battle. After four weeks of testimony from many of the surviving officers, enlisted men and civilians, the Court ruled there was nothing in Reno's conduct which required censure. The ruling was upheld by President Hayes on March 5, 1879.

Reno testified at the Court hearing in Chicago about the sudden death of Bloody Knife. Eyewitnesses at the battle claimed that when Reno's face was splashed with the brains and blood of the Arikara scout, he panicked and immediately started on his horse for the bluffs across the river. Reno attempted to counter that charge:

> I saw Bloody Knife shot, and also a man of M Company to whom the attention of the Doctor was at once directed. Bloody Knife was within a few feet of me; I was trying to get from him by signs where the Indians were going. I did not immediately leave the glade and the timber and go on a gallop to the river. I had given orders for the formation and I went through the timber and up on the plain to satisfy myself about the Indians there. Capt. Moylan was at my side. Before Bloody Knife was killed, the

formation was being made to leave the timber.[241]

Reno received his second court martial that same year, again on charges of "conduct unbecoming an officer and gentlemen." This conduct included peeping through a parlor window at the daughter of a colonel while she was visiting with her parents and hitting a lieutenant with a billiard cue. This time, President Hayes refused to reverse the recommendation of the court, which was to dismiss Reno from the Army. After 23 years of service, Reno was dishonorably discharged in 1880.[242] On March 30, 1889, Reno died in Washington, D.C., following an operation for mouth cancer. He was 54 years old.

In 1967, the Army Board for Correction of Military Records heard an appeal from Reno's great-grandnephew to overturn the dishonorable discharge. The board did so, terming his dismissal "unjust" and ordering that his records be changed to show an honorable discharge. It was no small victory, for it allowed the long-maligned major to be buried with full military honors at the then-Custer Battlefield National Cemetery.[243]

Reno's second-in-command while on the bluffs overlooking the Little Bighorn in 1876, Frederick Benteen, was also the target of a court martial years after the battle. In 1887, he was convicted of sustained drunkenness and "unsoldierlike conduct" while serving as the commander of Fort Du Chesne in Utah Territory. The charges against him included cursing the fort's civilian employees while drunk and urinating near a group of women.[244] A year later, Benteen received a disability discharge and retired to Atlanta, Georgia, where he died on June 22, 1898. He was 63.

The Leighton and Jordan Yellowstone Store Ledger

A number of revealing entries are to be found in the pages of the charge account book kept at the trader's store situated during the latter phase of the campaign at the mouth of the Tongue River on the Yellowstone, the later site of Fort Keogh. Goods for the lucrative business, organized by a group of Bismarck men, were supplied by Leighton and Jordan. Both men were Fort Buford traders who sent along Robert C. Matthews to represent them.

Listings of the items sold in the personal accounts show a wide variety of food articles available which can only be considered exotic in that part of Indian country in that day and age. It was unusual to find such fare as lemons, pickles, eggs, tinned salmon and oysters up for sale on campaign. The answer was found in the easy accessibility to the troops by steamboat. With the paddle wheelers shuttling back and forth to Fort Buford every few days, it was a relatively simple matter to keep the traders supplied with everything they needed.

Very few enlisted men are entered on the rolls. But Private Peter Thompson undoubtedly reflected the opinions of all frontier military men at the Heart River camp on the expedition's first day out, when the men were paid. "But oh!," he wrote. "We here again met the blood sucking sutler with his vile whiskey, rotten tobacco and high priced notions. It was plain to be seen that he would reap a rich profit on this expedition."

Liquor was consumed in astonishing quantities. It seemed to be the fashion to buy it by the gallon at $6, although it was certainly not cheaper in what today would be trumpeted as the "large economy size." After the long, dry spells in the field, soldiers were possessed of deep thirsts, and an inclination for them to relieve their tensions is no surprise.

It may not come as a surprise either that of the 14 surviving officers of the 7th Cavalry carried in the Leighton and Jordan charge accounts, none could compete with Major Marcus Reno in the consumption of whiskey. In a 22-day period beginning August 1, 1876, the man who was the target of a whispering campaign as the scapegoat of the Little Bighorn debacle purchased a total of seven gallons and two large bottles of whiskey. The expenditure came to $45.75, with the large bottles priced at $1.25. His account records three gallons bought on August 1; two more on the 18th, plus the two large bottles; a gallon again on August 21; and another on the 22nd. There are few listings other than whiskey entered in Reno's account.

His nearest competitor was Lieutenant Edwin P. Eckerson, with three gallons entered as purchased on August 1, August 19, and August 23. Eckerson then needed a Seidlitz Powder on September 3, which cost him 75 cents.

Next in volume came Captain Myles Moylan and Lieutenant George D. Wallace with two gallons each. Moylan's stock was laid in at dates spaced well apart, while Wallace's were both registered on the same day. Wallace bought fish lines and hooks at 50 and 25 cents respectively, at five each. Presumably, his fishing excursion was a damp and happy one.

A touch of refinement is indicated in the taste of Captain Thomas H. French. He invested in a gallon of the cheap stuff, but added two quarts of brandy, at $3 a bottle. Lemons, at $1.25, number not specified, were included on French's shopping list.

Lieutenants Charles A. Varnum and Edward G. Mathey each got a gallon of whiskey on separate dates. No whiskey is recorded as having been purchased by the following: Captains Benteen and McDougall, Lieutenants Edward S. Godfrey, Winfield S. Edgerley, Luther R. Hare, Henry T. Nowlan and Charles C. DeRudio. The latter, however, was a roll-your-own smoker — he bought cigarette papers and tobacco.

The total amount of whiskey bought by 7th Cavalry officers in August 1876, exclusive of Reno's purchases, amounted to 10 of the big jugs, a gallonage nearly equalled by Reno alone.

Fred Gerard opened his account on July 2. Most of his drinking was done at the crude bar, judging from the number of charges against his name in the single drink category. The two exceptions came on August 23, when he bought a quart for $1.50, and on the 24th, when he had his canteen filled at $2.50. There is a possibility that at some time he loaned Billy Jackson $9, since the latter apparently paid that amount against Gerard's bill on August 3.

It must be remembered that the preceding listings are from credit accounts only, and not from cash sales.[245]

Appearances can be deceiving, but it would seem that not all of the 7th Cavalry officers were drowning their sorrows over the late, great fight at the Little Bighorn. On the other hand, those who did were doing a good job of it.

****

Appendix

The following are summaries of the battles, fights and skirmishes mentioned in this book. Much of the information is taken from Ben Innis' unpublished The Great Buffalo Country Dictionary, Calendar and Atlas of Historical Events from 1670-1971.

1854

The Grattan Massacre — The killing of a stray emigrant cow was the cause of this fight. In an attempt to collect compensation for the animal and to take action against the responsible Indian, Second Lieutenant John L. Grattan led 30 men from the 6th Infantry, along with two howitzers, into the Brule Sioux village of Conquering Bear near Fort Laramie on August 19, 1854. After training his howitzers on the Sioux tipis, Grattan parleyed with Conquering Bear, in an effort to have him hand over the warrior responsible for butchering the stray cow.

After 45 minutes of fruitless discussion, Grattan lost patience and ordered his men to open fire. The howitzers were set too high and the charges harmlessly damaged the tops of the tipis. Outraged, the Sioux attacked Grattan and his 30 men, killing all of them.[1] Conquering Bear was killed, along with a number of other Indians. Spotted Tail and Red Cloud also took part in the fighting. The incident is thought to have precipitated the start of the intermittent western Indian Wars which continued over the next four decades.

1855

The Battle of Blue Water — In the aftermath of the Grattan Massacre, Secretary of War Jefferson Davis ordered Colonel William S. Harney into the field to help bring peace to the troubled Nebraska Territory. With a command of about 600 men from the 2nd Dragoons, the 4th Artillery and the 6th and 10th Infantry, Harney came upon the Brules Sioux camp of Little Thunder, camped on Blue Water Creek near the North Platte River. Little Thunder was the successor to the fallen chief of the Grattan Disaster, Conquering Bear. The camp contained warriors responsible for the series of raids and killings against the whites on the Platte road during the winter of 1854-55. Following failed peace negotiations between Harney and Little Thunder, Harney ordered his men to attack the village the morning of September 3, 1855. When the fighting ceased, Brule casualties totaled 85 dead and five wounded, about one third of the entire camp's population. Harney reported losses of four killed and seven wounded.

While searching the destroyed lodges, soldiers discovered the scalps of two white women and the clothing of some of Grattan's troops.[2]

1859

The Battle of Rainy Buttes — This was a skirmish between the Hunkpapa Sioux and Crows in the spring of 1859 that included Sitting Bull. The Hunkpapas, camped along the upper Cannonball River in what is now southwestern North Dakota, were on the move north when a group of about 50 Crows charged them from a ridge. A young Sioux boy was killed, and the Hunkpapa warriors quickly counterattacked. Sitting Bull's father, Jumping Bull, was among those killed in the fighting. Sitting Bull rode to the scene of his father's death, saw what had happened, and pursued the responsible Crow until killing him.[3]

1862

The Minnesota Uprising — An Indian war precipitated by the failure of agents and traders serving the Santee Sioux in the Minnesota River Valley to furnish the Indians with their annuities in the summer of 1862. Agent Thomas Galbraith refused to distribute the goods until he had his customary kickback from the supplier in hand. There was not help from trader Andrew Myrick, either, when the Sioux turned to him. He told them to eat grass or their own carrion. By July, the Sioux were starving.

The explosion came on August 17, 1862, when four young warriors killed five white settlers. The next day, a large war party led by Little Crow attacked the Lower Agency, where they killed 20 whites and took a dozen women captive. Myrick was among the victims, his lifeless mouth stuffed with grass.

The uprising spread, laying waste to a 250-mile stretch of southern Minnesota. Indians ambushed a relief column from Fort Ridgely. A total of 24 soldiers fell, but assaults on the fort itself on

August 20 and 22 failed. Other battles were fought at New Ulm on August 19 and 23 and at Birch Coulee on September 2. Fort Abercrombie went under siege for almost two months. Estimates of Indian forces ranged from 1500 to 2000. In the final fight at Wood Lake, where 1600 whites congregated under General Henry H. Sibley, the Santees were decisively defeated. Many captives were recovered. The scrap caused the surrender of large numbers of Indians.

The battles at Birch Coulee and Wood Lake broke the power of Little Crow and drove thousands of Indians into Dakota Territory. On December 9, 1862, General John Pope, from Division Headquarters at Milwaukee, stated that all danger from the Indians had ceased.

White casualties in the Minnesota Uprising ranged upward from 644 citizens and 113 soldiers killed. Indian losses were not available. Some 30,000 white refugees sought protection from the uprising; 8000 settlers suffered property losses totaling more than $2 million.

A military court convened in Sibley, Minnesota, and sentenced 303 Indians to death. However, President Abraham Lincoln commuted the sentences of all but 38, who were hanged in Mankato, Minnesota on December 26, 1862.

The Minnesota Uprising resulted in U.S. Army campaigns against the Sioux in Dakota Territory, one under General Sibley in 1863, the other led by Sibley from the east and General Alfred Sully from the south in 1864. A minor foray by Sully followed in 1865.

1863

The Battle of Big Mound — Nature took a hand in this battle fought near present day Tappen, North Dakota, on July 24, 1863. The opposing forces were General Henry H. Sibley's more than 3000 volunteer Minnesota, Dakota Territory and Iowa troops of the Northwestern Indian Expedition of 1863 and an army of 1500 Sioux. A tremendous thunderstorm added to the din created by artillery and rifle fire. The Sioux were routed and pursued for 15 miles over the prairie. It was the first of three fights in a span of five days. The Battle of Dead Buffalo Lake followed two days later and the Battle of Stony Lake took place on July 28. Sibley at that point destroyed the Sioux camp. His casualties for the three battles listed at seven killed and three wounded, while he estimated Sioux losses at 150, including 80 in the Big Mound Fight.

The Battle of Dead Buffalo Lake — The second in a series of three large-scale Indian fights engaged in by General Henry H. Sibley's column of the Northwestern Indian Expedition of 1863, the others being at Big Mound and Stony Lake. An army of 800 Sioux was defeated by the more than 3000 volunteer troops from Minnesota, Iowa and Dakota Territory, near what is now Dawson, North Dakota on July 26. Sibley estimated the Sioux lost 100 warriors at Dead Buffalo Lake to his artillery and small arms fire. He claimed a total troop loss for all three fights at seven killed and three wounded.

The Battle of Stony Lake — The last big fight in a series of three fought by General Henry H. Sibley's Northwestern Indian Expedition column of 1863 against the Sioux, the others being at Big Mound and Dead Buffalo Lake. Some 2000 warriors arrayed themselves against the more than 3000 Minnesota, Iowa and Dakota Territory volunteers and their artillery and were soundly defeated near what is now Driscoll, North Dakota on July 28, 1863. Sibley claimed his total losses in the three successive engagements, all fought within five days, amounted to seven killed and three wounded. Some white sources reported Sioux losses of 100 or more in each fight, but Sibley said his men killed a total of 150 warriors in all three clashes.

The Battle of Whitestone Hill — It was the fourth major defeat for the Sioux in the summer of 1863, and the worst. General Alfred Sully, leading the southern column of the Northwestern Indian Expedition of 1863 in what is now southern North Dakota, caught the Indians at Whitestone Hill on September 3. His soldiers killed about 100 Indians, destroyed their 400-lodge village and sent the survivors retreating across the prairie. Sully's 3000 troops routed the 1500 Santees, Hunkpapas, Yanktonnais and Blackfoot Sioux under Yanktonnai chief Two Bears, and captured 156 of them. Army fatalities came to 22.

Sully's force consisted entirely of militia, mostly from Nebraska and Iowa, and one artillery battery.

1864

The Battle of Killdeer Mountain — On July 28, 1864, General Alfred Sully, commanding 2200 troops of the Northwestern Indian Expedition of 1864, attacked a camp of 1600 lodges of Hunkpapas and other Sioux in what is now west central North Dakota. Sully used his eight pieces of artillery to distinct advantage against the warriors, variously estimated at from 1500 to 5000 strong. In a six-hour fight, the troops drove the Indians for five miles, then completed the job by destroying their camp and burning everything in it. White sources reported soldier losses from two to five killed and 10 wounded. The Sioux later said they lost 31 warriors, against military claims of 100 to 150.

The battle was one of the largest fought between Indians and soldiers in the history of Plains Indian warfare.

The Battle of the Badlands — A vicious, three-day running fight through the Little Missouri River Badlands in present-day southern North Dakota between a Sioux force numbering in the thousands and the 2000 troops of General Alfred Sully's Northwestern Indian Expedition of 1864. From August 7-9, the Indians attacked from the butte tops, pouring down a deadly shower of bullets and arrows on the troops toiling along the bottoms with their clumsy wagon train. When the warriors realized the column could not be stopped, they broke off the fight. Artillery assumed a large role. Estimates of Indian dead range from 100 to 311, plus many wounded. No accurate report exists regarding soldier casualties, but some statements record only 12 wounded; another reported nine dead and 100 wounded.

Most of the troops involved were the same who had gone up against the Sioux at Killdeer Mountain two weeks earlier. Sully continued his expedition on to the Yellowstone River.

No admirer of the Badlands' isolated and twisted topography, Sully reputedly said the place reminded him of "Hell with the fires burned out."

1865

The Cole-Walker Battles — In the summer of 1865, an expedition under the command of General Patrick E. Connor moved through the Black Hills and Powder River country. It was near the Powder that the Sioux ran into two of Connor's three divisions, commanded by Colonel Nelson Cole and Lieutenant Colonel Samuel Walker. Their force of some 2000 men pushed painfully through the Indian country as their horses and mules gave out and food became a scarce commodity. On September 5, 1865, several hundred Hunkpapa, Blackfeet, Minniconjou and Sans Arc Sioux warriors attacked the soldiers from both sides of the Powder River. As the besieged Army columns moved up the Powder Valley, the attacking Sioux withdrew. However, further fighting lay ahead, as the Oglala and Cheyenne villages of Red Cloud and Little Wolf were alerted to the presence of the advancing army.

It was not until late September that Cole and Walker were able to re-unite their columns with Connor's, and by then the Powder River Expedition of 1865 had turned into failure. In their series of fights with the Sioux along the Powder River, Cole and Walker lost 13 men, with another five wounded. They also sustained a loss of nearly 1000 horses and mules, as well as huge quantities of equipment and supplies. Cole estimated that his bluecoats had killed or wounded as many as 500 Indians. However, Walker admitted that "I cannot say as we killed one."[4]

1866

The Fetterman Fight — At Fort Phil Kearny, Wyoming Territory, Captain William J. Fetterman boasted that he could ride through the whole Sioux nation with 80 men. Fetterman, a 30-year-old veteran of General William T. Sherman's march through Georgia in the Civil War, had arrived at the fort in early November.

His big chance came on December 21, 1866, when besieging Sioux, Cheyennes and Arapahoes attacked the fort's wood train some distance away. Fetterman was ordered out with a body of 81 men of the 18th Infantry and 2nd Cavalry to its relief. A 10-man decoy party led by Crazy Horse lured Fetterman's troops over a ridge and into Red Cloud's waiting ambush. The 1500 to 2000 warriors slaughtered Fetterman's command to the last man. A military source listed 60 Indians killed. Another report stated that the fight cost the Sioux 11 warriors, the Cheyennes two and the Arapahoes one. Newspaperman John Finerty was told much later by Indians that they had lost 180 men.

Several newspapers, in their accounts of the battle, spelled Fetterman's name incorrectly, a common affliction of frontier reporting. *The New York Times* referred to him as Feetman and Filterman; *The Daily Leavenworth Times* called him Feiterman; *The Montana Post* contributed Fetterneau; and *The Alta California* listed him as Tetterman.[5]

The destruction of Fetterman's entire command crackled through military and civilian channels with lightning impact. Before the Fetterman Disaster, the American public had been lulled by enterprising entrepreneurs and an overconfident federal government into believing that westward expansion was continuing with relative ease. The Fetterman Fight shattered that illusion.

President Andrew Johnson appointed a commission composed of military and civilian officials and headed by General John Sanborn to investigate the debacle. Commission members chose to focus more on the larger issue of federal Indian policy, rather than battlefield logistics. Congress responded to the Sanborn Commission's call for policy revisions by creating the Indian Peace Commission in 1867. Among its members were Generals Sanborn and William T. Sherman, then the nation's number two general after Ulysses S. Grant. By the time the commission first met in August 1867, the Indians completely dominated the Powder River country and so threatened the Bozeman Trail that a Wells Fargo representative predicted not even a pound of freight would pass through overland Montana Territory that year.[6]

After much negotiation, a treaty was signed at Fort Laramie in 1868 by the commission and the Sioux. It called for the abandonment of the Bozeman Trail and its three forts by the Army. Celebrating his victory, Red Cloud set the torch to Fort Phil Kearny when its gates closed for the last time on July 31, 1868.

1868

The Battle of Beecher's Island — A company of 50 picked white Plainsmen commanded by Major George A. (Sandy) Forsyth was attacked in camp by a mixed force of about 600 Cheyennes, Sioux and Arapahoes led by Roman Nose on September 17, 1868. The fight took place on a low island in the Arickaree Fork of the Republican River in northeastern Colorado Territory. After several unsuccessful charges, the Indians besieged the whites until the latter were relieved by cavalry on September 25. Six whites, including the command's surgeon, were killed. Forsyth and 16 others were wounded. Forsyth reported Indian losses at 32 killed and 100 wounded. Other reports stated that 100 Indians were killed. Indian sources say no more than six of their own were killed.[7] The Cheyenne chief Roman Nose was killed.

The battle was named for Lieutenant Frederick H. Beecher, second in command, who was killed. He was a nephew of the popular Protestant preacher and reformer, Henry Ward Beecher.

The Battle of the Washita — Not the first nor the last of the narrow escapes from disaster which charmed Custer's military career until the disaster on the Little Bighorn. With the 7th Cavalry band blaring "Garry Owen" into the frozen air on November 27, 1868, eleven troops of the regiment charged Black Kettle's Cheyenne village of about 50 lodges on the Washita River of Indian Territory, in what is now western Oklahoma. Custer claimed in his report that 103 warriors were killed. The camp was destroyed and 900 ponies were shot. Black Kettle was among the dead. Of the 800 soldiers under Custer, 27 were killed, including Major Joel Elliott and a detachment of 18 men. Toward the end of the fight, it was discovered that the village was just one end of a 10-mile long series of camps containing an estimated 600 to 1000 lodges of other Cheyennes, Kiowas, Comanches, Apaches and Arapahoes. Toward nightfall, the troops extricated themselves from serious danger by means of a forced march from the field. Custer's regiment was a part of General Philip Sheridan's winter campaign of 1868. Indians called the attack "The Washita Massacre." The fight led to a rift in loyalties within the 7th Cavalry. Custer was charged by some with deserting Major Elliott and his small command in the face of the enemy.

The same tactics Custer used with such disastrous results at the Little Bighorn in 1876 he enjoyed with resounding success at the Washita. In both cases, he did not reconnoiter the Indian village before him to determine its size, which was irrelevant to him. He was supremely confident his 7th Cavalry could defeat any Indian force before it. He also divided his relatively small regiment into several columns to attack the encampment. The famed "Custer's Luck" harvested winning headlines with these bold tactics on the snow-packed prairies of the western Indian Territory in 1868; it brought catastrophic defeat on the sunbaked plains of southern Montana Territory eight years later.

1869

The Battle of Summit Springs — Northeastern Colorado Territory was the scene of the fight in which the Cheyennes lost their chief Tall Bull on July 11, 1869. Colonel Eugene A. Carr commanded the eight companies of the 5th Cavalry and 50 Pawnee scouts which inflicted a serious defeat on the Cheyennes and a few Sioux and Arapaho.[8] Carr reported 52 Indians were killed, with only one soldier wounded. Buffalo Bill Cody served as chief scout. The battle marked the end of the organized and effective resistance of the Dog Soldiers, the most elite and militant of the Cheyenne soldier societies.[9]

1872

The Pryor Creek Fight — Angry Sioux, Cheyennes and Arapahoes, attempting to put a stop to the plans of the Northern Pacific Railroad, raided the company's surveying party early on the morning of August 14, 1872. The outfit was escorted by components of the 2nd Cavalry and other units. At the time of the assault, they were opposite the mouth of Pryor Creek on the Yellowstone River. The fight continued until noon, involving such leaders as Sitting Bull, Crazy Horse and Black Moon, an Hunkpapa Sioux chief killed at the Little Bighorn. The Indian force totaled anywhere from 400 to 1000, depending on which witness told the story. The white force was about 400. Two whites were killed, including one civilian and one soldier. Five soldiers were wounded. Black Moon said later that 40 Indians were killed.

1876

The Battle of Powder River — Six companies of the 2nd and 3rd Cavalry under Colonel Joseph J. Reynolds, with Frank Grouard as guide, surprised what they thought was a Sioux village on the morning of March 17, 1876, near the Powder River in southeastern Montana Territory. It turned out to be a Cheyenne camp, but Reynolds captured and burned the village and also captured the Indian herd of 700 ponies. Counterattacking fiercely, the Cheyennes drove the troops from the field. Eventually, they recaptured their pony herd. Reynolds was forced to abandon his dead and some wounded. The detachment then found its way back to General George Crook's column. Four soldiers were killed and six wounded. Indian losses were reported to be anywhere from two to 23 killed and as many as 33 wounded.

Crook later preferred charges against Reynolds for his actions in the affair, claiming that it forced Crook's army to fall back to Fort Fetterman and end its expedition against the Indians. Reynolds was found guilty in a court martial that led to his retirement from the service.

The Battle of the Rosebud — General George Crook's battle report did not indicate that he lost the fight, but neither is there much evidence to show that he won. Charitably, it could be considered a draw. Thousands of Sioux and Cheyennes under Crazy Horse and Two Moons attacked Crook's army of 1300 soldiers, civilians and Indian scouts in a six-hour battle on June 17, 1876, on the Rosebud River in southeastern Montana Territory. The white forces, consisting of elements of the 2nd and 3rd Cavalry and the 4th and 9th Infantry, could not advance. However, they did manage a cautious retreat when the fighting ceased.

Newspaperman John Finerty with the *Chicago Times* wrote

that 5000 Indians opposed Crook. Later, Crazy Horse said he began the fight with 1500 fighting men and was reinforced to bring the number of 6500. Crook was able to use less than 1000 of his men for the actual fighting. He reported a loss of 10 soldiers killed, but the figures of 28 troopers, citizens and Indian scouts dead and 56 wounded arise from other sources. The Indians admitted 11 killed and five wounded. However, 13 Indian bodies were reported to have been found on the field, and the Army felt they had killed at least 18 warriors. A year later, Crazy Horse said he lost 36 men. Another source listed from 100 to 150 Indians killed.

Most of the warriors who faced Crook were fighting Custer eight days later at the Little Bighorn. Crook's force was the southern column of the three armies of the Bighorn-Yellowstone Expedition converging on Sioux and Cheyenne country in an attempt to encircle and decisively defeat the Indian nations.

The Battle of the Little Bighorn — Larger battles were fought on the Western Plains between Indians and the U.S. Army, but no other had a more shattering or continuing impact on the American public than Custer's Last Stand of 1876. Lieutenant Colonel George A. Custer was charisma personified to millions of Americans, and because there were no white witnesses to the complete annihilation of his portion of the command, the battle rages to this day on paper, with no end of supposition in sight.

The facts are this: Custer was killed; four members of his immediate family — two brothers, a brother-in-law and a nephew — died with him. A number of line officers also died, one of them Second Lieutenant James G. Sturgis, the son of the actual commander of the 7th Cavalry, Colonel Samuel D. Sturgis. Also killed were "Lonesome" Charley Reynolds, Mitch Bouyer and Bloody Knife, all valuable scouts. Two of the regiment's three surgeons were killed. All told, some 270 soldiers, scouts and Indian allies lost their lives in three days of fighting, from June 25-27, on the banks of the Little Bighorn River in south central Montana Territory. That includes the 47 men killed under the command of Major Marcus Reno and Captain Frederick Benteen. Indian fatalities have been estimated to range from 33 to 300. In all likelihood they were surprisingly light, probably not totaling more than 50 out of the 1500 to 3000 warriors engaged.

Leading the entire 7th Cavalry in search of what was thought to be an extremely large concentration of Sioux and Cheyennes, Custer divided his regiment into four sections for the attack when he discovered the camp. He sent Major Marcus A. Reno to charge the south end of the village, while he rode with his battalion to strike at a northern point. Other than a couple of fleeting glimpses of him, he was never seen alive again. Reno's attack was doomed from the beginning in the face of the overwhelming force of Indians which confronted him. His troops were routed and driven across the river to the blufftops, where they were besieged for two days. They gained reinforcements late in the first afternoon with the arrival of Captain Frederick Benteen's section, as well as the pack train under Captain Thomas McDougall.

The Sioux military genius, Crazy Horse, along with Gall, Crow King and medicine man Sitting Bull, exerted a constant, heavy pressure on the surviving soldiers, only packing up their village and departing with the approach of General Alfred Terry's column on June 27.

The Custer Disaster sparked a furious, all-out campaign to subdue the nomadic Plains tribes. Paradoxically, although the Little Bighorn was unquestionably a huge Indian victory, its main consequence was the breaking of Indian power and its dispersal to the reservation system. The 7th Cavalry wore the scars of the debacle until the tragedy of Wounded Knee in December 1890, where they were accused of indulging in an act of revenge.

The Skirmish at Warbonnet Creek — More of a skirmish than a battle. At Warbonnet Creek in northwestern Nebraska on July 17, 1876, Colonel Wesley Merritt and a portion of the 5th Cavalry intercepted and chased back to their reservations a large band of Sioux and Cheyenne warriors trying to join the tribes after the victories at the Battle of the Rosebud and the Battle of the Little Bighorn the month previous. At Warbonnet Creek, the Cheyenne war chief Yellow Hand, or Yellow Hair, was killed, claimed by Buffalo Bill as the scout's victim. Cody was said to have swung the scalp in the air and shouted, "First scalp for Custer!"

The Battle of Slim Buttes — Captain Anson Mills, scouting in advance of General George Crook's column, with elements of the 3rd Cavalry and the 9th and 14th Infantry, discovered the camp of Sioux chief American Horse in present day northwestern South Dakota and attacked the 37 lodges at dawn on September 9, 1876. The camp contained about 600 Sioux, mostly Oglalas. The Indians were driven out, the camp destroyed and 175 ponies captured.

Nearby, Crazy Horse's camp was informed of the fight and reinforcements were rushed to the Indians, but it was too late. By that time, the remainder of Crook's army had come up. American Horse, shot in the stomach, surrendered and was treated by Army surgeons before dying near midnight. It was estimated the fight cost the Indians five warriors. From one to three whites were said to be killed and 14 wounded. At the time, Crook was returning to home base after the Bighorn-Yellowstone Expedition of 1876.

Items discovered at the village included several pieces of

equipment belonging to the 7th Cavalry and troopers who had fallen at the Little Bighorn. Among them were the guidon flag of Company I, one of the troops wiped out with Custer;[10] a gauntlet marked with the name of Company I's commander, Captain Myles Keogh; three horses owned by the 7th Cavalry; several McClellan army saddles; an officer's shirt; and some letters written to and by soldiers of the 7th Cavalry.[11]

The Battle of Cedar Creek — Following the twin victories at the Rosebud and Little Bighorn, the large Sioux coalition forged by Sitting Bull and his followers was kept on the move by a U.S. Army eager for revenge. By early October 1876, a large force of Hunkpapas, Minniconjous and Sans Arcs crossed the Yellowstone River and tried to stop the 22nd Infantry's supply trains from moving between Glendive in Montana Territory and the Tongue River.

Colonel Nelson A. Miles marched down the Yellowstone with nearly 500 men of his 5th Infantry, looking for Sitting Bull. On October 20, he located the medicine man's camp near the head of Cedar Creek. That day and again on the next, the two leaders conducted fruitless negotiations. Sitting Bull demanded that all whites leave the Indian country, and Miles insisted that the Sioux retire to the reservations.[12]

Both sides broke off the talks, and Miles moved to the attack. As the Sioux camp began to move on, its warriors stayed behind to protect the withdrawal of their families. It was a quick, relatively bloodless clash. One warrior was killed, and two soldiers wounded. Miles pursued the camp, overtaking it on the Yellowstone. By this time, however, Sitting Bull had split away, taking 30 lodges and moving north toward the Missouri River.[13]

The Dull Knife Fight — At dawn on November 25, 1876,

Colonel Ranald S. Mackenzie, in command of six companies of the 4th Cavalry, two of the 5th Cavalry, two of the 3rd and one of the 2nd, and a detachment of Indian scouts, attacked Dull Knife's Cheyenne camp on Willow Creek at the edge of the Bighorn Mountains in central Wyoming Territory. The battle raged until the afternoon, as an estimated 500 warriors faced 700 soldiers. The Indians left the field toward the end of the day after losing 25 warriors, including three of Dull Knife's sons. Six soldiers were killed and 25 wounded. The Army also captured 500 ponies.

Among the findings among the 200 destroyed lodges was military equipment belonging to the 7th Cavalry, including a guidon made into a pillow case, testimony to the Cheyenne involvement at the Little Bighorn five months earlier.[14] The camp was destroyed and the Cheyennes were left destitute in sub-zero weather. The survivors made their painful way to the camp of Crazy Horse on the Upper Tongue River.

The Battle of Red Water — As Sitting Bull and his followers moved north toward the Missouri River in late October 1876, Colonel William B. Hazen and four companies of the 6th Infantry moved out of Fort Buford to intercept them. After hearing that the Sioux were camped near the Fort Peck Agency, in a destitute state, Hazen decided to leave one company at the agency and returned to Fort Buford. With winter coming on, he was certain Sitting Bull would soon have to give up.

Colonel Nelson A. Miles, however, continued the pursuit. Through November and into December, his 5th Infantry moved through the Missouri and Yellowstone country, searching for Sitting Bull and the other Sioux who refused to come into the reservations. One of Miles' officers, Lieutenant Frank Baldwin, found Sitting Bull's trail and clashed with his followers in early December. On December 18, 1876, Baldwin's battalion came upon Sitting Bull's camp of 122 lodges near the headwaters of Red Water Creek. There the Army struck, scattering the inhabitants and dealing a severe blow to Sitting Bull's supply storage for the winter.[15]

The following spring, Sitting Bull moved into Canada, by coincidence the same week that Crazy Horse surrendered at Fort Robinson in Nebraska. The medicine man who forged the coalition that crushed Custer would remain in Canada until surrendering at Fort Buford near present day Williston, North Dakota, on July 19, 1881.

1877

The Battle of Wolf Mountain — Following skirmishes on January 1, 3 and 7, 1877, the 500 troops of the 5th and 22nd Infantry, commanded by Colonel Nelson A. Miles, crossed swords with a strong warrior force of 600 Sioux and Cheyenne under Crazy Horse in southern Montana Territory on January 8. It was more like a long-range sniping duel than a pitched battle, with two pieces of artillery mounted in wagons contributing to what could be called a victory for the Army, since the Indians retreated. Three soldiers were killed and eight wounded. It was thought that about 15 Indians were killed, although they later stated they lost five warriors. The fighting ended about noon, five hours after it began, because of a heavy snowstorm.

The Lame Deer Fight — Also known as the Battle of Muddy Creek. On May 7, 1877, Colonel Nelson A. Miles attempted to parley with the Sioux chief Lame Deer at the latter's camp of 51 lodges in southeastern Montana Territory. Backing up Miles were four companies of the 2nd Cavalry, two of the 5th Infantry and four of the 22nd Infantry. In the midst of negotiations, a misunderstanding occurred and shooting started. When the white powder smoke cleared, four soldiers were dead and seven wounded. The Indians lost 17 warriors, their village was destroyed and 500 ponies were captured.

This battle, combined with Crazy Horse's surrender the day before at Camp Robinson, Nebraska and the mass surrenders at all the Sioux agencies, marked the virtual end of the Great Sioux War of 1876-77.[16]

The Battle of the Big Hole — A pitched battle fought deep in the mountains of extreme southwestern Montana Territory between the fleeing Nez Perces and units of the 7th Infantry and 2nd Cavalry aided by citizen volunteers, all under the command of Colonel John Gibbon. The troops charged the village, near the Big Hole River, at 4 a.m. on August 9, 1877. Even though surprised, the Indians recovered sufficiently to put the attackers on the defensive and capture a cannon. Although Nez Perce losses after two days of tough fighting came to 89 dead, compared to the 24 soldiers and six civilians killed and 35 soldiers and four civilians wounded, the conflict was considered an Indian victory.[17] The Nez Perces, later reporting they had suffered 69 fatalities, specified that only 32 were fighting men and the remainder women and children. The battle was the third of five major engagements in the Nez Perce campaign.

The Battle of Canyon Creek — The fourth in the bigger fights of the Nez Perce War. Colonel Samuel D. Sturgis and six companies of the 7th Cavalry, portions of three companies of the 1st Cavalry, and a small detachment of the 4th Artillery engaged the retreating Indians near Clark's Fork on the Yellowstone River in south central Montana Territory on September 13, 1877. Three soldiers were killed. The Army claimed it killed 21 Indians. The Nez Perces said they lost only one man.

The Battle of Bear Paw Mountain — A six-day fight and the fifth and final major battle of the classic Nez Perces flight of 1877. Chief Joseph had camped his people near present-day Havre, Montana, believing he was safely across the Canadian border. Colonel Nelson A. Miles, with a mixed force of 5th Infantry, 2nd and 7th Cavalry and some Cheyenne and Crow scouts, attacked the camp on September 30, 1877. He was repulsed. The battle settled into a state of siege. Twenty-four of the soldiers were killed and 42 wounded. Indian losses were put at 17 killed and 40 wounded. The dead included some of the war chiefs.

One of the Nez Perce chiefs, White Bird, and a sizeable group escaped to Canada. On October 5, Chief Joseph surrendered the remnants of his people to Miles and General Otis O. Howard. It was then that Joseph uttered his touching farewell to the escape effort: "From where the sun now stands, I will fight no more forever."

1890

The Battle of Wounded Knee — On the morning of December 29, 1890, a detachment of troops attempted to disarm the 400 people of chief Big Foot's Sioux band camped on Wounded Knee Creek in South Dakota. The Army hoped to bring the Indians into the Standing Rock Agency to be watched during the Ghost Dance troubles. The force was composed of eight companies of the 7th Cavalry, a company of Cheyenne scouts and a battery of Hotchkiss cannon, all under the command of Colonel James W.

Forsyth. Through a misunderstanding, a shot was fired that precipitated a wild fight which spread over the hills for miles as the troops pursued the retreating Sioux. Men, women and children were slain indiscriminately. When the carnage ceased, 25 soldiers lay dead and another 39 were wounded. More than 200 Sioux were killed.[18] Several days later, a burial party interred the bodies, including that of Big Foot, in a common grave.

Major General Nelson A. Miles, who was in command of Army field operations during the Ghost Dance unrest, was severely critical of Forsyth's handling of the incident. He relieved the colonel of his command and convened a Court of Inquiry. However, the Secretary of War cleared Forsyth and restored him to his command.

The Battle of White Clay Creek — Also known as the Battle of Drexel Mission. On the day after the showdown at Wounded Knee, Sioux warriors from a large encampment along White Clay Creek near the Pine Ridge Agency set fire to some sheds near the Drexel Mission church four miles north of the agency. Colonel James Forsyth's 7th Cavalry arrived at the scene, only to have its two squadrons separated and pinned down by Indian fire. To the rescue came the 9th Cavalry under the command of Major Guy V. Henry, who drove the Sioux from their positions and saved the day for Forsyth's beleaguered regiment. Seventh Cavalry casualties came to two killed and five wounded.[19]

White Clay Creek and Wounded Knee marked the last major confrontation between the U.S. Army and the Indians. In the period of heaviest conflict, from 1866-90, Army casualties numbered 69 officers killed, 68 wounded, and 879 enlisted men killed, 990 wounded, for a total of 948 soldiers killed and 1058 wounded. Indian casualties, pulled from military records and therefore questionable, total 4371 killed, 1279 wounded and 10,318 captured.[20]

There was one final minor battle in the Indian Wars a few years later in northern Minnesota. It occurred on October 5, 1898, when a federal marshal with about 100 soldiers of the 3rd U.S. Infantry attempted to arrest the Chippewa chief Bugonaygeshig at Sugar Point on the east shore of Leech Lake. The troops were called out to arrest Bugonaygeshig to testify in a Federal case against illegal whiskey sales to the Chippewas. The chief refused to go. He said that after testifying in a similar case in Duluth the year before, he had been released to walk home, a distance of more than 100 miles.[21]

Sources vary as to which side fired the first shot. The ensuing battle resulted in the death of the commanding officer, Major Melville C. Wilkinson, and six enlisted men. Another 10 soldiers and four civilians were wounded.[22] There were no confirmed Indian casualties. Many of Bugonaygeshig's 35-member band, known as Pillagers, were arrested, but the chief escaped.

In his message to the 1899 session of the Minnesota Legislature, Governor David M. Clough's observations about the Battle of Sugar Point could apply to any number of similar outbreaks during the Indian Wars:

> A series of acts and neglects most wrongful to the Indians of Minnesota, by a blunder more criminal in its results than the neglects and acts which preceded it, took a small party to Leech Lake in this state ... The climax to a long course of folly and wrong in dealing with the Pillagers precipitated bloodshed and led to the death of a number of brave and noble-hearted men. This in turn came very near causing an outbreak of all the Minnesota Chippewas.[23]

On January 3, 1899, President William McKinley issued full pardons for the members of Bugonaygeshig's band arrested as a result of the battle at Leech Lake.

Notes

1. Robert M. Utley, *Frontiersmen in Blue: The United States Army and the Indian, 1848-1865*, p. 114.
2. Robert M. Utley, *Frontiersmen in Blue: The United States Army and the Indian, 1848-1865*, pp. 116-117.
3. Robert M. Utley, *The Lance and the Shield: The Life and Times of Sitting Bull*, pp. 24-25.
4. Robert M. Utley, *Frontiersmen in Blue: The United States Army and the Indian, 1848-1865*, pp. 330-332.
5. Richard E. Collin, *The Fetterman Disaster*, p. 10.
6. James C. Olson, *Red Cloud and the Sioux Problem*, p. 60.
7. Robert M. Utley, *Frontier Regulars: The United States Army and the Indian, 1866-1891*, p. 148.
8. Ibid., pp. 156-157.
9. Ibid., pp. 126, n15.
10. Jerome A. Greene, *Slim Buttes: An Episode of the Great Sioux War*, p. 163, n13.
11. Ibid., pp. 72-73.
12. Robert M. Utley, *Frontier Regulars: The United States Army and the Indian, 1866-1891*, p. 273.
13. Robert M. Utley, *The Lance and the Shield: The Life and Times of Sitting Bull*, pp. 172-173.
14. Robert M. Utley, *Frontier Regulars: The United States Army and the Indian, 1866-1891*, p. 275.
15. Ibid., p. 274.
16. Paul L. Hedren, *The Great Sioux War, 1876-77*, p. 19.
17. Robert M. Utley, *Frontier Regulars: The United States Army and the Indian, 1866-1891*, p. 307.
18. Ibid., pp. 406-407.
19. Ibid., p. 408.
20. Ibid., p. 412, n19.
21. *The WPA Guide to Minnesota*, p. 461.
22. Roger Pinckney, "Old Bug's Necklace," *American History*, December 1994, p. 75.
23. William Watts Folwell, *A History of Minnesota*, Volume IV, p. 323.

Notes

The Heritage of Bloody Knife

1. George F. Will, "Magical and Sleight of Hand Performances by the Arikara," *North Dakota Historical Quarterly*, Vol. 3, No. 1, p. 50.
2. Dale L. Morgan, *Jedediah Smith*, p. 37.
3. Bernard DeVoto, *Course of Empire*, p. 37.
4. George E. Hyde, "The Mystery of the Arikaras," *North Dakota History*, Vol. 19, No. 1 (January 1952), p. 40
5. Adrian R. Dunn, "A History of Old Fort Berthold," *North Dakota History*, Vol. 30, No. 4 (October 1963), p.9. Hereinafter referred to as: Dunn, "Fort Berthold."
6. George E. Hyde, "The Mystery of the Arikaras," *North Dakota History*, Vol. 19, No. 1 (January 1952), p. 40.
7. Dale L. Morgan, Jedidiah Smith, p. 50.
8. George E. Hyde, "The Mystery of the Arikaras," *North Dakota History*, Vol. 18, No. 4 (October 1951), p. 374.
9. Bernard DeVoto, *The Journal of Lewis and Clark*, p. 48.
10. Ray H. Mattison, "Historic Oahe Sites," *South Dakota Historical Collections*, Vol. 27 (1954), p. 98.
11. Wayne Gard, *The Great Buffalo Hunt*, p. 46.
12. O.A. Stevens, "Bradbury and Nuttall, Pioneer Dakota Botanists," *North Dakota History*, Vol. 26, No. 4 (October 1959), p. 159.

The Arikara War of 1823

13. Alexis Praus, editor, *The Sioux, 1798-1922: A Dakota Winter Count*, p. 12.
14. Don Berry, *A Majority of Scoundrels*, p. 27.
15. Ibid., p. 42.

The Rees in Transition

16. Russell Reid and Clell G. Gannon, "Journal of the Atkinson-O'Fallon Expedition," *North Dakota History*, Vol. 4, No. 1 (October 1929), p. 31.
17. Annie Heloise Abel, *Chardon's Journal at Fort Clark*, p. xvii.
18. John Myers Myers, *Pirate, Pawnee and Mountain Man*, p. 224.
19. Ray H. Mattison, *Fort Union: Its Role in the Upper Missouri Fur Trade*, p. 14.

Smallpox Disaster

20. Bernard DeVoto, *Across the Wide Missouri*, p. 285.
21. Annie Heloise Abel, *Chardon's Journal at Fort Clark*, p. 138.
22. Bernard DeVoto, *Across the Wide Missouri*, p. 295.
23. Annie Heloise Abel, *Chardon's Journal at Fort Clark*, p. 24.

Bloody Knife and Gall: The Early Years

24. John S. Gray, "Bloody Knife, Ree Scout for Custer," *Chicago Westerners Brand Book*, Vol. XVII, No. 12 (1960-61), p. 89. Hereinafter referred to as: Gray, "Bloody Knife."
25. Dunn, "Fort Berthold," p. 26.
26. Ibid.
27. Will G. Robinson, "Digest of Indian Commissioner Reports," *South Dakota Historical Collections*, Vol. 26 (1952), p. 487.
28. Ibid., p. 491.
29. John Palliser, *The Solitary Hunter*, p. 206.
30. "Biographical Sketch of F.F. Gerard," *Collections of the North Dakota Historical Society*, Vol. 1 (1906), p. 344. Hereinafter referred to as: Sketch, "F.F. Gerard."
31. Thaddeus A. Culbertson, *Journal of an Expedition to the Manvaises Terres and the Upper Missouri in 1850*, p. 95.
32. Joseph Henry Taylor, *Frontier and Indian Life and Kaleidoscopic*

Lives, p. 291. Hereinafter referred to as: Taylor, *Frontier and Indian Life.*

Grounds For Revenge

33. Rudolph Friederich Kurz, *Journal of Rudolph Friederich Kurz,* p. 167.
34. John E. Sunder, *The Fur Trade on the Upper Missouri, 1840-1865,* p. 141.
35. Sketch, "F.F. Gerard," p. 344.
36. Gray, "Bloody Knife," p. 89.
37. Will G. Robinson, "Digest of Indian Commissioner Reports," South Dakota Historical Collections, Vol. 27 (1954), p. 212.
38. Ray H. Mattison, "The Letters of Henry A. Boller," *North Dakota History,* Vol. 33, No. 2 (April 1966), p. 203.
39. Ibid., p. 109.
40. Ben H. Innis, *Sagas of the Smoky Water,* p. 58.
41. Elmer Ellis, "The Journal of H.E. Maynadier," *North Dakota Historical Quarterly,* Vol. 1, No. 2 (January 1927), p. 50.
42. Taylor, *Frontier and Indian Life,* p. 291.

Skirmishes with the Sioux

43. Stanley Vestal, *Sitting Bull, Champion of the Sioux,* p. 44.
44. John E. Sunder, *The Fur Trade on the Upper Missouri,* 1840-1865, p. 225.
45. Helen McCann White, editor, *Ho! For the Gold Fields,* p. 49.
46. Ray H. Mattison, "Old Fort Stevenson," *North Dakota History,* Vol. 18, Nos. 2-3 (January-April 1951), p. 55. Hereinafter referred to as: Mattison, "Old Fort Stevenson."
47. Ralph M. Shane, "A Short History of the Fort Berthold Indian Reservation," *North Dakota History,* Vol. 26, No. 4 (October 1959), p. 196. Hereinafter referred to as: Shane, "History, Fort Berthold."
48. Mary Jane Schneider, *North Dakota's Indian Heritage,* p. 66.
49. Carolyn Gilman and Mary Jane Schneider, *The Way to Independence: Memories of a Hidatsa Indian Family, 1840-1920,* p. 314.
50. Taylor, *Frontier and Indian Life,* p. 291.
51. Dunn, "Fort Berthold," p. 51.

War Breaks Out

52. Shane, "History, Fort Berthold," p. 205.
53. Dunn, "Fort Berthold," p. 60.
54. Ben H. Innis, *Sagas of the Smoky Water,* p. 308.
55. Dunn, "Fort Berthold," p. 53.
56. Ibid., p. 54.
57. Robert Huhn Jones, *The Civil War in the Northwest,* p. 60.
58. Dunn, "Fort Berthold," p. 54.
59. Ibid., p. 52.
60. Will G. Robinson, "Digest of Indian Commissioner Reports," *South Dakota Historical Collections,* Vol. 27 (1954), p. 350.
61. Dunn, "Fort Berthold," p. 54.
62. Louis Pfaller, "The Killdeer Mountain and Badlands Battles," *North Dakota History,* Vol. 31, No. 1 (January 1964), p. 49.
63. "The Indian Operations," Report of Brigadier General Alfred Sully of October 7, 1864, *Army and Navy Journal,* November 19, 1864, p. 199.
64. "Northwest Indian Expedition," Report of Brigadier General Alfred Sully of August 29, 1864, *Army and Navy Journal,* November 5, 1864, p. 170.
65. Ethel A. Collins, "Pioneer Experiences of Horatio F. Larned," *North Dakota Historical Collections,* Vol. 7 (1925), p. 34.
66. Mattison, "Old Fort Stevenson," p. 56.
67. Ben H. Innis, *The Great Buffalo Country Dictionary, Calendar and Atlas of Historical Records and Events from 1670-1971,* p. 167. Hereinafter referred to as: Innis, *The Great Buffalo Country Dictionary.*

A Measure of Revenge

68. Gray, "Bloody Knife," p. 56.
69. Mattison, "Old Fort Stevenson," p. 56.
70. Taylor, *Frontier and Indian Life,* p. 292.
71. Dunn, "Fort Berthold," p. 56.
72. Mattison, "Old Fort Stevenson," p. 56.
73. John S. Gray, "Arikara Scouts with Custer," *North Dakota*

History, Vol. 35, No. 2 (April 1968), p. 444. Hereinafter
referred to as: Gray, "Arikara Scouts with Custer."
74. Fairfax Downey and J.N. Jacobsen, *The Red Bluecoats*, pp. 11-12.
75. Innis, *The Great Buffalo Country Dictionary*, p. 214.
76. Records of the U.S. General Accounting Office, *Register of Miscellaneous
   Claims*, Vol. 18, p. 414, RG 217, National Archives.

The Army Moves In
77. Mattison, "Old Fort Stevenson," p. 57.
78. *War Department Records of Fort Buford, Dakota Territory, Letters Sent*,
   National Archives. Hereinafter referred to as: *Buford, Letters Sent*.
79. Philippe Regis de Trobriand, *Military Life in Dakota: The Journal of
   Philippe Regis de Trobriand*, p. 123. Hereinafter referred to as: Kane,
   Military Life in Dakota.
80. Ray H. Mattison, editor, "An Army Wife on the Upper Missouri: The
   Diary of Sarah H. Canfield, 1866-1868," *North Dakota History*, Vol.
   20, No. 4 (October 1953), p. 207.
81. Taylor, *Frontier and Indian Life*, p. 289.

The Indian Scouts
82. O.G. Libby, *The Arikara Narrative*, p. 44. Hereinafter referred to as: Libby,
   Narrative.
83. *Register of Enlistments of Indian Scouts*, general M 233, National Archives.
   Hereinafter referred to as: *Register of Enlistments of Indian Scouts*.
84. Kane, *Military Life in Dakota*, p. 279.
85. Dunn, "Fort Berthold," p. 60.
86. M.M. Quaife, editor, *Yellowstone Kelly*, p. 25.
87. Lewis F. Crawford, *Rekindling Camp Fires*, p. 172.
88. *Register of Enlistment of Indian Scouts*.
89. M. M. Quaife, editor, *Yellowstone Kelly*, p. 45.

Scouting at Fort Buford
90. Robert M. Utley, *Frontier Regulars: The United States Army and the Indian,
   1866-1891*, p. 104.
91. *War Department Records of Fort Buford, Dakota Territory, Medical Records*,
   National Archives. Hereinafter referred to as: *Buford, Medical Records*.
92. Ibid.
93. *Buford, Letters Sent*, February 9, 1869.

94. Ibid., August 15, 1869.
95. Taylor, *Frontier and Indian Life*, p. 288.
96. *Buford, Letters Sent.*
97. *Buford, Medical Records.*
98. John M. Taylor, *Garfield of Ohio*, p. 219.
99. *Buford, Letters Sent.*
100. Dunn, "Fort Berthold," p. 63.
101. Buford, Medical Records.
102. *War Department Records of Fort Buford, Dakota Territory, Document File*, National Archives.
103. James Willard Schultz, *William Jackson, Indian Scout*, p. 75. Hereinafter referred to as: Schultz, *William Jackson.*
104. *Buford, Medical Records.*
105. Wesley R. Hurt and William E. Lass, *Frontier Photographer*, p. 21.
106. *Fort Berthold Indian Agency Records, War Department, January 27, 1871*, National Archives.
107. *War Department Records of Fort Buford, Dakota Territory, Cemetery Records*, National Archives.
108. Sketch, "F.F. Gerard," p. 347.
109. *Buford, Letters Sent.*
110. Ibid.
111. Biographical sketch of Dr. Benjamin F. Slaughter, *North Dakota Historical Quarterly*, Vol.1, No. 2 (January 1927), p. 39.
112. Jessamine Slaughter Burgum, *Zezula*, p. 51.
113. *Buford, Medical Records.*
114. *Buford, Letters Sent.*

Scouts and Traders
115. *Buford, Medical Records.*
116. *Buford, Letters Sent.*
117. *Buford, Medical Records.*
118. Will G. Robinson, "Digest of Indian Commissioner Reports," *South Dakota Historical Collections*, Vol. 28 (1956), p. 267.
119. *War Department Records of Fort Buford, Dakota Territory, Post Returns*, National Archives.
120. *Buford, Medical Records.*
121. Ben H. Innis, *Sagas of the Smoky Water*, p. 282.
122. Ibid., p. 283.

123. Ibid., p. 277.

White Men in Red Country
124. Jessamine Slaughter Burgum, *Zezula*, p. 62.
125. *Buford, Medical Records.*
126. *Buford, Letters Sent.*

The Yellowstone Expedition of 1873
127. Joseph Mills Hanson, *Conquest of the Missouri*, p. 159.
128. *Buford, Medical Records.*
129. Schultz, *William Jackson*, p. 99.
130. Ibid., p. 100.
131. Ibid., p. 101.
132. Jessamine Slaughter Burgum, *Zezula*, p. 55.
133. Ibid., p. 78.
134. Schultz, *William Jackson*, p. 101.
135. Charles Edmund DeLand, "Basil Clement (Claymore)," *South Dakota Historical Collections*, Vol. 10, No. 1, p. 360.
136. Jay Monaghan, *The Life of General George Armstrong Custer*, p. 343.
137. *Buford, Letters Sent.*
138. Elizabeth B. Custer, *Boots and Saddles*, 1885 edition, p. 282.
139. Gray, "Bloody Knife," p. 94.
140. Elizabeth B. Custer, *Boots and Saddles*, 1961 edition, p. 144.
141. *War Department Records of Fort Buford, Dakota Territory, Letters Indian Scouts*, National Archives. Hereinafter referred to as: *Buford, Letters Indian Scouts.*
142. *Buford, Letters Sent.*

Activities at Fort Buford
143. *Buford, Letters Indian Scouts.*
144. Ibid.
145. Ibid.
146. Innis, *The Great Buffalo Country Dictionary*, p. 252.
147. *Buford, Letters Indian Scouts.*
148. Ibid.
149. Ibid.
150. Ibid.
151. Ibid.

The Black Hills Expedition of 1874

152. Ibid.
153. Article, *Bismarck Tribune*, Dakota Territory, Wednesday, April 29, 1874, p. 19.
154. Taylor, *Frontier and Indian Life*, p. 121.
155. Donald F. Danker, editor, *Man of the Plains*, p. 184.
156. Gray, "Bloody Knife," p. 94.
157. George W. Kingsbury, "Custer's Black Hills Expedition," *History of Dakota Territory*, p. 884.
158. Ibid., p. 887.
159. Libby, *Narrative*, p. 194.
160. W.R. Wood, article on his experiences with the Black Hills Expedition of 1874, North Dakota Historical Society files, No. B 54.
161. Libby, *Narrative*, p. 170.
162. Donald F. Danker, editor, *Man of the Plains*, p. 192.
163. Gray, "Bloody Knife," p. 94.
164. Elizabeth B. Custer, *Boots and Saddles*, 1885 edition, p. 302.
165. War Department Records of Fort Lincoln, Dakota Territory, Letters Sent, National Archives.
166. Gray, "Arikara Scouts with Custer," p. 447.

1875

167. John S. Gray, "What Made Johnny Bruguiere Run?" *Montana Magazine*, Vol. 14, No. 2 (Spring 1964), p. 40.
168. Dunn, "Fort Berthold," p. 69.
169. Article, *Bismarck Tribune*, Dakota Territory, Wednesday, June 2, 1875, "Indians."
170. Taylor, *Frontier and Indian Life*, p. 289.
171. P.E. Byrne, *Soldiers of the Plains*, p. 31.
172. Taylor, *Frontier and Indian Life*, p. 109.
173. Libby, *Narrative*, p. 38.
174. Elizabeth B. Custer, *Boots and Saddles*, 1885 edition, p. 235.
175. Taylor, *Frontier and Indian Life*, p. 287.
176. Ibid., p. 290.
177. Ibid., pps. 290-296.
178. P. E. Byrne, *Soldiers on the Plains*, p. 25.

The Bighorn-Yellowstone Expedition of 1876

179. Gray, "Bloody Knife," p. 95.
180. James M. DeWolf, "The Diary and Letters of James M. DeWolf," *North Dakota History*, Vol. 25, Nos. 2-3 (January-April 1958), p. 37. Hereinafter referred to as: DeWolf, "The Diary and Letters of James M. DeWolf."
181. Libby, *Narrative*, p. 58.
182. Ibid., p. 197.
183. Schultz, *William Jackson*, p. 124.
184. Gray, "Arikara Scouts with Custer," p. 474.
185. DeWolf, "The Diary and Letters of Dr. James M. DeWolf," p. 43.
186. Thomas W. Dunlay, *Wolves for the Blue Soldiers*, p. 261.
187. Ibid., p. 140.
188. John C. Hixon, "Custer's Mysterious Mr. Kellogg," *North Dakota History*, Vol. 17, No. 3 (July 1950), p. 168.
189. Libby, *Narrative*, p. 62.
190. Libby, *Narrative*, p. 63.
191. Elizabeth B. Custer, *Boots and Saddles*, p. 306.
192. Edgar I. Stewart, *Custer's Luck*, p. 225.
193. Peter B. Thompson, article on his experiences with the Dakota Column as an enlisted man with the 7th Cavalry in 1876, North Dakota Historical Society files, No. B 34.
194. Libby, *Narrative*, p. 70.
195. Ibid., p. 73.
196. Oliver Knight, *Following the Indian Wars*, p. 206.
197. Frances Chamberlain Holley, *Once Their Home*, p. 262.
198. W.A. Graham, *The Custer Myth*, p. 135.
199. Libby, *Narrative*, p. 81-82.

The Battle of the Little Bighorn

200. Ibid., p. 90.
201. Ibid., p. 93.
202. Oliver Knight, *Following the Indian Wars*, p. 188.
203. John S. Gray, *Centennial Campaign*, p. 172.
204. Schultz, *William Jackson*, p. 134.
205. Peter B. Thompson, article on his experiences with the Dakota Column as an enlisted man with the 7th Cavalry in 1876, North

Dakota Historical Society files, No. B 34.

206. Libby, *Narrative*, p. 122.

207. Ibid., p. 172.

208. Gray, "Arikara Scouts with Custer," p. 470.

209. Ibid.

210. Libby, *Narrative*, p. 122.

211. Dale T. Schoenberger, "Custer's Scouts," *Montana Magazine*, Vol. 16, No. 2, (Spring 1966), p. 45. Hereinafter referred to as: Schoenberger, "Custer's Scouts."

212. Libby, *Narrative*, p. 96.

213. W.A. Graham, *The Custer Myth*, p. 293.

214. Schoenberger, "Custer's Scouts," p. 47.

215. Edgar I. Stewart, *Custer's Luck*, pp. 369-370.

216. Edgar I. Stewart, *Custer's Luck*, p. 363.

Epilogue

217. Article, *Bismarck Tribune*, Dakota Territory, Thursday, July 6, 1876, p. 1

218. Taylor, *Frontier and Indian Life*, p. 297.

219. John M. Carroll, *The Benteen-Goldin Letters on Custer and His Last Battle*, p. 47.

220. Article, *Bismarck Tribune*, North Dakota, Tuesday, August 15, 1939, Section 3, p. 4.

221. Schultz, *William Jackson*, p. 155.

222. *Records of the U.S. General Accountant's Office, Register of Miscellaneous Claims*, Vol. 18, p. 414, RG 217, National Archives.

223. Frederick F. Gerard, letters to daughters, March 8, 1876, May 1, 1876, and July 6, 1876, North Dakota Historical Society files, No. B 147.

224. Walter McClintock, *The Old North Trail*, p. 7.

225. Usher L. Burdick, *Tales From Buffalo Land*, p. 26.

226. John C. Ewers, *Indian Life On the Upper Missouri*, p. 176.

227. Rod Gragg, *The Old West Quiz & Fact Book*, p. 168.

228. Gray, "Arikara Scouts with Custer," pp. 476-477.

229. Schoenberger, "Custer's Scouts," p. 47.

230. Gray, "Arikara Scouts with Custer," p. 472.

231. Paul L. Hedren, *The Great Sioux War, 1876-77*, p. 19.

232. Robert M. Utley, *Frontier Regulars: The United States Army and the Indian, 1866-1891*, pp. 406-407.

233. John M. Carroll, *Custer's Chief of Scouts: The Reminiscences of Charles A. Varnum*, pp. 15-17.
234. Windolph, Charles A., *I Fought with Custer*, as told to Frazier and Robert Hunt, pp. xiii-xv.
235. Roy P. Johnson, "Jacob Horner of the 7th Cavalry," *North Dakota History*, Vol. 16, No. 2 (April 1949), pp. 76-77.
236. Lawrence A. Frost, *Custer Legends*, p. 214.
237. Evan S. Connell, *Son of the Morning Star: Custer and the Little Bighorn*, p. 350.
238. Rod Gragg, *The Old West Quiz & Fact Book*, p. 177.
239. Lawrence A. Frost, *General Custer's Libbie*, p. 228.
240. John Upton Terrell and Colonel George Walton, *Faint the Trumpet Sounds*, p. 221.
241. Ibid., pp. 263-264.
242. Ibid., p. 299.
243. Wayne Michael Sarf, *The Little Bighorn Campaign, March-September 1876*, p. 194.
244. Rod Gragg, *The Old West Quiz & Fact Book*, p. 175.
245. *Leighton and Jordan Post Trader's Ledger*, Yellowstone Store.

Notes

Bibliography

I. Articles

Bell, Gordon L., and Beth L. Bell, "General Custer in North Dakota," *North Dakota History*, Vol. 31, No. 2 (April 1964), pp. 101-113.

Brininstool, E.A., "Charley Reynolds: Hunter and Scout," *North Dakota Historical Quarterly*, Vol. 7, Nos. 2-3, pp. 72-81.

Collins, Ethel A., "Pioneer Experiences of Horatio F. Larned," *North Dakota Historical Society Collections*, Vol. 7 (1925).

Connolly, James B., "Father DeSmet in North Dakota," *North Dakota History*, Vol. 27, No. 1 (January 1960), pp. 5-24.

DeLand, Charles Edmund, "Basil Clement (Claymore)," *South Dakota Historical Collections*, Vol. 10, No. 1, pp. 245-389.

"Gall," *South Dakota Historical Collections*, Vol. 1, pp. 151-155.

Godfrey, Edward S., "Custer's Last Battle," *Contributions to the Montana Historical Society*, Vol. 9 (1923), pp. 141-212.

Gray, John S., "Arikara Scouts with Custer," *North Dakota History*, Vol. 35, No. 2 (April 1968), pp. 442-478.

_____, "Bloody Knife, Ree Scout for Custer," *Chicago Westerners Brand Book*, Vol. 17, No. 12 (1960-61), pp. 89-96.

_____, "Captain Clifford's Story of the Sioux War of 1876," *Chicago Westerners Brand Book*, Vol. 26, No. 11 (1969-70), pp. 81-88.

_____, "Last Rites for 'Lonesome' Charley Reynolds," *Montana Magazine*, Vol. 13, No. 3 (July 1963), pp. 40-51.

_____, "On the Trail of 'Lonesome' Charley Reynolds," *Chicago Westerners Brand Book*, Vol. 14, No. 8 (1957-58), pp. 57-64.

_____, "What Made Johnny Bruguiere Run?," *Montana Magazine*,

Vol. 14, No. 2 (April 1964), pp. 34-49.

"Indians of North Dakota," *North Dakota Historical Society Collections,* Vol. 1, (1906) pp. 433-475.

Lennan, I.P., "The Fisk Expedition of 1864," *North Dakota Historical Society Collections,* Vol. 2 (1908), pp. 431-439.

Mattison, Ray H., "Fort Rice: North Dakota's First Missouri River Military Road," *North Dakota History,* Vol. 20, No. 2 (April 1953), pp. 87-108.

_____, "Old Fort Stevenson," *North Dakota History,* Vol. 18, Nos. 2-3 (April-July 1951), pp. 53-91.

_____, "Report on Historic Sites in the Oahe Reservoir, Missouri River," *South Dakota Historical Collections,* Vol. 27 (1954), pp. 1-159.

Noyes, Lee, "Major Marcus A. Reno at the Little Bighorn," *North Dakota History,* Vol. 28, No. 1 (January 1961), pp. 5-11.

O'Harra, Cleophas C., "Custer's Black Hills Expedition of 1874," *South Dakota Historical Collections,* (1929), pp. 221-286.

Parker, Donald D., "Expeditions Up the Missouri," *South Dakota Historical Collections,* Vol. 33 (1966), pp. 458-487.

Pfaller, Rev. Louis, "The Peace Mission of 1863-1864," *North Dakota History,* Vol. 37, No. 4 (October 1970), pp. 293-313.

Pickney, Roger, "Old Bug's Necklace," *American History,* Vol. 29, No. 5 (December 1994) pp. 40-43, 75.

Robinson, Will G., "Digest of the Indian Commissioner Reports," *South Dakota Historical Collections,* Vol. 26 (1952), pp. 456-533.

_____, "Digest of the Indian Commissioner Reports," *South Dakota Historical Collections,* Vol. 27 (1954), pp. 160-515.

_____, "Digest of the Indian Commissioner Reports," *South Dakota Historical Collections,* Vol. 28 (1956), pp. 179-344.

_____, "Digest of the Indian Commissioner Reports," *South Dakota Historical Collections,* Vol. 29 (1958), pp. 307-500.

_____, "Digest of the Indian Commissioner Reports," *South Dakota Historical Collections,* Vol. 31 (1962), pp. 1-73.

Rogers, J. Daniel, "Bloody Knife's Last Stand," *Natural History,* June 1992, pp. 36-43.

Schoenberger, Dale T., "Custer's Scouts," *Montana Magazine,* Vol. 16, No. 2 (April 1966), pp. 40-49.

Stevens, A.O., "Audubon's Journey Up the Missouri River, 1843,"

North Dakota Historical Quarterly, Vol. 10, No. 2 (April 1943)
pp. 63-82.

_____, "Bradbury and Nuttall, Pioneer Dakota Botanists," *North Dakota History*, Vol. 26, No. 4 (October 1959), pp. 159-169.

Thompson, Peter B., article on his experiences with the Dakota Column as an enlisted man with the 7th Cavalry in 1876, North Dakota Historical Society files, No. B 34.

Truax, Allen L., "Manuel Lisa and His North Dakota Trading Post," *North Dakota Historical Quarterly*, Vol. 6, No. 4 (July 1932), pp. 292-301.

Will, George F., "Magical and Sleight of Hand Performances by the Arikara," *North Dakota Historical Quarterly*, Vol. 3, No. 1(October 1928), pp. 50-65.

Wood, W.R., article on his experiences with the Black Hills Expedition of 1874, North Dakota Historical Society files, No. B 54.

II. Books

Abel, Annie Heloise, editor, *Chardon's Journal at Fort Clark, 1834-1839*. Pierre, South Dakota: Department of History, State of South Dakota, 1932.

_____, editor, *Tabeau's Narrative of Loisel's Expedition to the Upper Missouri*. Norman, Oklahoma: University of Oklahoma Press, 1939.

Alter, J. Cecil, *Jim Bridger*. Norman, Oklahoma: University of Oklahoma Press, 1962.

Athearn, Robert G., *Forts of the Upper Missouri*. Englewood Cliffs, New Jersey: Prentice-Hall, Inc. 1967.

Audubon, John James, *Audubon and His Journals*, edited by Maria Audubon and Elliott Coues. NewYork: Charles Scribner's Sons, 1897.

Berry, Don, *A Majority of Scoundrels*. New York: Harper and Brothers, 1961.

Boller, Henry A., *Among the Indians: Eight Years in the Far West, 1858-1866*, edited by Milo Milton Quaife. Chicago: R.R. Donnelley and Sons Company, 1959.

Brady, Cyrus Townsend, *Indian Fights and Fighters*. Lincoln, Nebraska: University of Nebraska Press, 1971.

Brininstool, E. A., *A Trooper With Custer*. Columbus, Ohio: Volume 1, The Hunter-Trader-Trapper, 1926.

Brown, D. Alexander, *The Galvanized Yankees*. Urbana, Illinois: University of Illinois Press, 1963.

Brown, Mark H., *The Plainsmen of the Yellowstone*. Lincoln, Nebraska: University of Nebraska Press, 1961.

Burdick, Usher L., *Tales From Buffalo Land*. Baltimore: Wirth Brothers, 1940.

Burgum, Jessamine Slaughter, *Zezula*. Valley City, North Dakota: Gretchell and Nielsen, 1937.

Byrne, P.E., *Soldiers of the Plains*. New York: Minton, Balch and Company, 1926.

Camp, Walter, edited by Kenneth Hammer, *Custer in '76: Walter Camp's Notes on the Custer Fight*. Provo, Utah: Brigham Young University Press, 1981.

Carroll, John M., *The Benteen-Goldin Letters on Custer and His Last Battle*. Lincoln, Nebraska: University of Nebraska Press, 1974.

_____, *Custer's Chief of Scouts: The Reminiscences of Charles A. Varnum*. Lincoln, Nebraska: University of Nebraska Press, 1982.

Chittenden, Hiram Martin, *The American Fur Trade of the Far West*, Vol. 2. Lincoln, Nebraska: University of Nebraska Press, 1986.

Connell, Evan S., *Son of the Morning Star: Custer and the Little Bighorn*. San Francisco: North Point Press, 1984.

Crawford, Lewis F., *Rekindling Camp Fires*. Bismarck, North Dakota: Capital Book Co., 1926.

Culbertson, Thaddeus A., *Journal of an Expedition to the Mauvaises Terres and the Upper Missouri in 1850*. Edited by John Francis McDermott. Washington, D.C.: Smithsonian Institution, Bureau of American Ethnology. Bulletin 147, 1952.

Custer, Elizabeth B., *Boots and Saddles*. New York: Harper and Brothers, 1885.

_____, *Boots and Saddles*. Norman, Oklahoma: University of Oklahoma Press, 1961.

_____, *Following the Guidon*. Norman, Oklahoma: University of Oklahoma Press, 1966.

_____, *Tenting On the Plains*. New York: Harper and Brothers, 1915.

DeBarthe, Joe, *Life and Adventures of Frank Grouard*, edited by Edgar I. Stewart. Norman, Oklahoma: University of Oklahoma Press, 1958.

Denig, Edwin Thompson, *Five Indian Tribes of the Upper Missouri*, edited by John C. Ewers. Norman, Oklahoma: University of Oklahoma Press, 1961.

DeVoto, Bernard, *Across the Wide Missouri.* Boston: Houghton Mifflin Company, 1947.

_____, *The Course of Empire.* Boston: Houghton Mifflin Company, 1962.

_____, editor and interpreter, *The Journals of Lewis and Clark.* Boston: Houghton Mifflin Company, 1953.

Dick, Everett, *Tales of the Frontier.* Lincoln, Nebraska: University of Nebraska Press, 1963.

Downey, Fairfax, and Jacobsen, Jacques Noel, Jr., *The Red Bluecoats: The U.S. Army Indian Scouts.* The Old Army Press, Fort Collins, Colorado, 1973.

Dunlay, Thomas W., *Wolves for the Blue Soldiers.* Lincoln, Nebraska: University of Nebraska Press, 1982.

Ewers, John C., *Indian Life on the Upper Missouri.* Norman, Oklahoma: University of Oklahoma Press, 1968.

Ferris, Robert G., editor, *Founders and Frontiersmen.* Washington, D.C.: National Park Service, 1967.

Finerty, John F., *War-Path and Bivouac, or The Conquest of the Sioux.* Norman, Oklahoma: University of Oklahoma Press, 1961.

Folwell, William Watts, *A History of Minnesota, Volume IV.* St. Paul, Minnesota: Minnesota Historical Society, 1930.

Frazer, Robert W., *Forts of the West: Military Forts and Presidios and Posts Commonly Called Forts, West of the Mississippi River to 1898.* Norman, Oklahoma: University of Oklahoma Press, 1965.

Frost, Lawrence A., *The Custer Album: A Pictorial Biography of General George A. Custer.* Seattle, Washington: Superior Publishing Company, 1964.

_____, *General Custer's Libbie.* Seattle, Washington: Superior Publishing Company, 1976.

_____, *Custer Legends.* Bowling Green, Ohio: Bowling Green University Popular Press, 1981.

_____, *Custer's 7th Cavalry and the Campaign of 1873.* El Segundo, California: Upton & Sons, Publishers, 1986.

Gard, Wayne, *The Great Buffalo Hunt.* Lincoln, Nebraska: University of Nebraska Press, 1959.

Gilman, Carolyn, and Schneider, Mary Jane, *The Way to Independence:*

Memories of a Hidatsa Indian Family, 1840-1920. St. Paul, Minnesota: Minnesota Historical Society Press, 1987.

Gragg, Rod, *The Old West Quiz Book & Fact Book.* New York: Harper and Row Publishers, 1986.

Graham, Colonel W. A., *The Custer Myth.* New York: Bonanza Books, 1953.

_____, *The Story of the Little Big Horn.* New York: Bonanza Books, 1959.

Gray, John S., *Centennial Campaign: The Sioux War of 1876.* Norman, Oklahoma: University of Oklahoma Press, 1988.

_____, *Custer's Last Campaign: Mitch Boyer and the Little Bighorn Reconstructed.* Lincoln, Nebraska: University of Nebraska Press, 1991.

Greene, Jerome A., *Slim Buttes, 1876: An Episode of the Great Sioux War.* Norman, Oklahoma: University of Oklahoma Press, 1982.

_____, *Yellowstone Command: Colonel Nelson A. Miles and the Great Sioux War, 1876-1877.* Lincoln, Nebraska: University of Nebraska Press, 1991.

Grinnell, George Bird, *The Fighting Cheyennes.* Norman, Oklahoma: University of Oklahoma Press, 1963.

Hanson, Joseph Mills, *The Conquest of the Missouri.* New York: Murray Hills Books, Inc., 1946.

Hedren, Paul L., edited by, *The Great Sioux War, 1876-77: The Best from Montana The Magazine of Western History.* Helena, Montana: Montana Historical Society Press, 1991.

Heitman, Francis B., *Historical Register and Dictionary of the United States Army, From Its Organization September 29, 1789 to March 2, 1903.* Urbana, Illinois: University of Illinois Press, 1965.

Historical Section, Army War College, *Indian Battles and Skirmishes on the American Frontier, 1790-1898.* New York: Argonaut Press for University Microfilms, Ann Arbor, Michigan, 1966.

Hodge, Frederick Webb, *Handbook of American Indians North of Mexico.* New York: Rowman and Littlefield, 1971.

Holley, Frances Chamberlain, *Once Their Home.* Chicago: Donahoe and Henneberry, 1890.

Hoxie, Frederick E., edited by, *Indians in American History.* D'Arcy McNickle Center for the American Indian, the Newberry Library, Arlington Heights, Illinois: Harlan Davidson, Inc. 1988.

Hurt, Wesley R., and William E. Lass, *Frontier Photographer: Stanley*

J. Morrow's Dakota Years. Lincoln, Nebraska: University of Nebraska Press and University of South Dakota, 1956.

Hutton, Paul Andrew, edited by, *The Custer Reader*. Lincoln, Nebraska: University of Nebraska Press, 1992.

Hyde, George E., *Red Cloud's Folk: A History of the Oglala Sioux Indians*. Norman, Oklahoma: University of Oklahoma Press, 1937.

Innis, Ben H., *Sagas of the Smoky Water: True Stories Reflecting Historical Aspects of the Missouri-Yellowstone Confluence Region, 1805-1910*. Williston, North Dakota: Centennial Press, 1985.

Jones, Robert Huhn, *The Civil War in the Northwest*. Norman, Oklahoma: University of Oklahoma Press, 1960.

Kelly, Luther S., edited by M.M. Quaife, *Yellowstone Kelly: The Memoirs of Luther S. Kelly*. New Haven: Yale University Press, 1926.

Kimball, Maria Brace, *A Soldier-Doctor of Our Army*. Boston and New York: Houghton Mifflin Company, 1917.

Kingsbury, George W., edited by George Martin Smith, *History of Dakota Territory*. Chicago: S.J. Clarke Publishing Company, 1915.

Knight, Oliver, *Following the Indian Wars: The Story of the Newspaper Correspondents Among the Indian Campaigners*. Norman, Oklahoma: University of Oklahoma Press, 1960.

Koury, Captain Michael J., *Diaries of the Little Big Horn*. Bellevue, Nebraska: The Old Army Press, 1968.

Kurz, Rudolph Friederich, edited by J.N.B. Hewitt, *Journal of Rudolph Friederich Kurz*. Lincoln, Nebraska: University of Nebraska Press, 1970.

Leonard, Zenas, edited by John C. Ewers, *Adventures of Zenas Leonard, Fur Trader*. Norman, Oklahoma: University of Oklahoma Press, 1959.

Libby, O.G., editor, *The Arikara Narrative of the Campaign Against the Hostile Dakotas, June 1876*. North Dakota State Historical Society Collections, Vol. 6. Cedar Rapids, Iowa: The Torch Press, 1920.

Maximilian, Prince of Wied, edited by Reuben Gold Thwaites, *Travels In the Interior of North America, Early Western Travels*, Volume 22. New York: AMS Press, 1966.

_____, edited by Reuben Gold Thwaites, *Travels In the Interior of North America, Early Western Travels*, Volume 23. New York: AMS Press, 1966.

_____, edited by Reuben Gold Thwaites, *Travels In the Interior of North America, Early Western Travels*, Volume 24. New York: AMS Press, 1966.

McLintock, Walter, *The Old North Trail: Life, Legends and Religion of the Blackfeet Indians*. Lincoln, Nebraska: University of Nebraska Press, 1968.

Members of the Potomac Corral of the Westerners, *Great Western Indian Fights*. Lincoln, Nebraska: University of Nebraska Press, 1960.

Merington, Marguerite, edited by, *The Custer Story: The Life and Letters of General George A. Custer and His Wife Elizabeth*. Barnes and Noble Inc., published by arrangement with Devin-Adair Publishers, Inc., 1994.

Miller, David Humphreys, *Custer's Fall*. New York: Bantam Books, 1957.

Monaghan, Jay, *Custer: The Life of General George Armstrong Custer*. Lincoln, Nebraska: University of Nebraska Press, 1971.

Morgan, Dale L., *Jedediah Smith and the Opening of the West*. Lincoln, Nebraska: University of Nebraska Press, 1953.

Myers, John Myers, *Pirate, Pawnee and Mountain Man*. Boston: Little, Brown and Company, 1963.

McLaughlin, James, *My Friend, the Indian*. Boston and New York: Houghton Mifflin Company, 1926.

Nelson, Bruce, *Land of the Dacotahs*. Minneapolis: University of Minnesota Press, 1946.

North, Luther, edited by Donald F. Danker, *Man of the Plains*. Lincoln, Nebraska: University of Nebraska Press, 1961.

Oglesby, Richard Edward, *Manuel Lisa and the Opening of the Missouri Fur Trade*. Norman, Oklahoma: University of Oklahoma Press, 1963.

Olson, James C., *Red Cloud and the Sioux Problem*. Lincoln, Nebraska: University of Nebraska Press, 1965.

Palliser, John, *Solitary Rambles and Adventures of a Hunter in the Prairies*. London: George Routledge and Company, 1856.

Porter, Mae Reed, and Odessa Davenport, *Scotsman in Buckskin*. New York: Hastings House, 1963.

Rickey, Don, Jr., *Forty Miles a Day on Beans and Hay*. Norman, Oklahoma: University of Oklahoma Press, 1963.

Robinson, Doane, *A History of the Dakota or Sioux Indians*. Minneapolis: Ross and Haines, Inc., 1956.

Robinson, Elwyn B., *History of North Dakota*. Lincoln, Nebraska: University of Nebraska Press, 1966.

Rodenbough, Theo. A., and William L. Haskin, *The Army of the United States*. New York: Argonaut Press for University Microfilms, Inc., Ann Arbor, Michigan, 1966.

Rolfsrud, Erling Nicolai, *The Story of North Dakota*. Alexandria, Minnesota: Lantern Books, 1963.

Rothenberg, Robert E., M.D., *The New American Medical Dictionary and Health Manual*. New York: The New American Library, 1962.

Sandoz, Mari, *Crazy Horse: The Strange Man of the Oglalas*. Lincoln, Nebraska: University of Nebraska Press, 1961.

_____, *The Battle of the Little Bighorn*. New York: Modern Library Editions Publishing Company, 1966.

Sarf, Michael Wayne, *The Little Bighorn Campaign: March-September 1876*. Conshohocken, Pennsylvania: Combined Books, Inc., 1993.

Schneider, Mary Jane, *North Dakota's Indian Heritage*. Grand Forks, North Dakota: University of North Dakota Press, 1990.

Schultz, James Willard, *William Jackson, Indian Scout*. Boston and New York: Houghton Mifflin Company, 1926.

Sheridan, Lieutenant General P.H., *Outline Descriptions of the Posts in the Military Division of the Missouri*. Bellevue, Nebraska: The Old Army Press, 1969.

Stewart, Edgar I., *Custer's Luck*. Norman, Oklahoma: University of Oklahoma Press, 1955.

_____, *Penny-An-Acre Empire in the West*. Norman, Oklahoma: University of Oklahoma Press, 1968.

Sully, Langdon, *No Tears For the General: The Life of Alfred Sully, 1821-1879*. Palo Alto, California: American West Publishing Company, 1974.

Sunder, John E., *Bill Sublette, Mountain Man*. Norman, Oklahoma: University of Oklahoma Press, 1959.

_____, *The Fur Trade on the Upper Missouri, 1840-1865*. Norman, Oklahoma: University of Oklahoma Press, 1965.

Taylor, John M., *Garfield of Ohio: The Available Man*. New York: W.W. Norton and Company, Inc., 1970.

Taylor, Joseph Henry, *Frontier and Indian Life and Kaleidoscopic Lives*. Washburn, North Dakota: Washburn's Fiftieth Anniversary Committee, 1932.

Terrell, John Upton, *Black Robe*. Garden City, New York: Doubleday and Company, Inc., 1964.

_____, and Colonel George Walton, *Faint the Trumpet Sounds: The Life and Trial of Major Reno*. New York: David McKay Company, Inc., 1966.

Tilden, Freeman, *Following the Frontier with F. Jay Haynes, Pioneer Photographer of the Old West*. New York: Alfred A. Knopf, Inc., 1964.

Time-Life Books, *The Old West: The Soldiers*. Text by David Nevin. New York: Time, Inc., 1973.

Trobriand, Philippe Regis de, *Military Life in Dakota*, edited by Lucile M. Kane. St. Paul: Alvord Memorial Commission, 1951.

Utley, Robert M., *Frontiersmen in Blue: The United States Army and the Indian, 1848-1865*. Lincoln, Nebraska: University of Nebraska Press, 1967.

_____, *Frontier Regulars: The United States Army and the Indian, 1866-1891*. Bloomington and London: Indiana University Press, 1977.

_____, *The Indian Frontier of the American West, 1846-1890*. Albuquerque: University of New Mexico Press, 1984.

_____, *Cavalier in Buckskin: George Armstrong Custer and the Western Military Frontier*. Norman, Oklahoma: University of Oklahoma Press, 1988.

_____, *The Lance and the Shield: The Life and Times of Sitting Bull*. New York: Henry Holt and Company, Inc., 1993.

Vestal, Stanley, *Sitting Bull: Champion of the Sioux*. Norman, Oklahoma: University of Oklahoma Press, 1957.

_____, *The Missouri*. Lincoln, Nebraska: University of Nebraska Press, 1945.

Weltfish, Gene, *The Last Universe*. New York: Ballantine Books, 1965.

Wemett, William Marks, *The Story of The Flickertail State*. W. M. Wemett: Valley City, North Dakota, 1923.

Wheeler, Colonel Homer W., *Buffalo Days: Forty Years in the Old West*. Indianapolis, Indiana: Bobbs Merrill Company, 1925.

White, Helen McCann, editor, *Ho! For the Gold Fields*. St. Paul: Minnesota Historical Society, 1966.

Williams, Mary Ann Barnes, *Origins of North Dakota Place Names*. Washburn, North Dakota: Mary Ann Barnes Williams, 1966.

Windolph, Charles A., *I Fought with Custer: The Story of Sergeant Windolph, Last Survivor of the Battle of the Little Bighorn*. As told to Frazier and Robert Hunt, Lincoln, Nebraska: University of Nebraska Press, 1987.

III. Diaries and Journals

Canfield, Sarah E., edited by Ray H. Mattison, "An Army Wife on the Upper Missouri." *North Dakota History*, Vol. 20, No. 4 (October 1953), pp. 191-220.

DeWolf, James M., edited by Edward S. Luce, "The Diary and Letters of Dr. James M. DeWolf." *North Dakota History*, Vol. 25, Nos. 2-3 (April-July 1958), pp. 1-52.

Jackson, Donald, editor, "Journey to the Mandans, 1809: The Lost Narrative of Dr. Thomas." *The Bulletin*, Vol. 20, No. 3, Missouri Historical Society (April 1964), pp. 179-192.

Kellogg, Mark, "Notes of the Little Bighorn Expedition Under General Custer, 1876." *Contributions to the Montana Historical Society*, Vol. 9 (1923), pp. 213-225.

Matthews, Washington, edited by Ray H. Mattison, "The Diary of Surgeon Washington Matthews." *North Dakota History*, Vol. 21, Nos. 1-2 (January-April 1954), pp. 5-74.

Maynadier, H.E., edited by Elmer Ellis, "The Journal of H.E. Maynadier: A Boat Trip from Fort Union to Omaha in 1860." *North Dakota Historical Quarterly*, Vol. 1, No. 2 (January 1927), pp. 41-51.

Reid, Russell, and Clell G. Gannon, editors, "Journal of the Atkinson-O'Fallon Expedition." *North Dakota Historical Quarterly*, Vol. 4, No. 1 (October 1929), pp. 5-56.

Rosser, Thomas L., edited by William D. Hoyt, Jr., "Rosser's Journal, Northern Pacific Railroad Survey, September 1871." *North Dakota Historical Quarterly*, Vol. 10, No. 1 (January 1943), pp. 47-51.

Van Ostrand, Ferdinand, edited by Russell Reid, "Diary of Ferdinand Van Ostrand." *North Dakota Historical Quarterly*, Vol. 10, No. 1 (January 1943), pp. 3-46.

_____, edited by Russell Reid, "Diary of Ferdinand Van Ostrand," *North Dakota Historical Quarterly*, Vol. 10, No. 2 (April 1943), pp. 83-124.

IV. Government Documents

Descriptive List ... of scouts Fire Cloud and Bloody Knife, Yellowstone Expedition of 1873, August 26, 1873, National Archives.

Fort Berthold Indian Agency Records, National Archives. Official Correspondence Pertaining to the War of the Outbreak, 1862-1865,

South Dakota Historical Collections, Vol. 31 (1962), pp. 469-563.
Quartermaster Department Report of Persons and Articles Hired, Fort Abraham Lincoln, Dakota Territory, 1876, March-June, National Archives.
Records of the U.S. General Accountant's Office, Miscellaneous Claims, RG 217, National Archives.
Registers of Enlistments of Indian Scouts, General No. M233, National Archives.
War Department Records of Fort Buford, Dakota Territory: Documents, Letters, Indian Scouts, Letters Sent, Medical Records, Post Returns. National Archives.
War Department Records of Fort Lincoln, Dakota Territory: Letters Sent, September 22,1874. National Archives.
WPA Guide to Minnesota, The. Compiled and written by the Federal Writers' Project of the Works Progress Administration, Minnesota Historical Society Press, St. Paul, 1985.

V. Letters

Boller, Henry A., edited by Ray H. Mattison, "The Letters of Henry A. Boller," *North Dakota History*, Vol. 33, No. 2 (April 1966), pp. 106-219.

Gerard, Frederick F., letters to daughters dated March 8, May 1 and July 6, 1876, North Dakota Historical Society files, No. B 147.

Wallace, George D., letter to his mother about activities of the 7th Cavalry in Tennessee and Dakota Territory, North Dakota Historical Society files, No. B 130.

VI. Newspapers

Army and Navy Journal, November 5, 1864. Letter from Brigadier General Alfred Sully to Major General John Pope, August 29, 1864, from Headquarters Northwestern Indian Expedition, Fort Berthold.

Army and Navy Journal, November 19, 1864. Report of Brigadier General Alfred Sully, from Headquarters of the Northwestern Indian Expedition at Camp No. 76, Farm Island, Dakota Territory, October 7, 1864.

Bismarck Tribune, April 29, 1874. Article on Indian scouts at Fort Lincoln, p. 19.

Bismarck Tribune, September 2, 1874. Article, "Black Hills," p. 1.

Bismarck Tribune, June 2, 1875. Article, "Indians," p. 1.

Bismarck Tribune, July 6, 1876. Article, "Massacred. Gen. Custer and 261 Men the Victims," p. 1.

Bismarck Tribune, August 15, 1939. Article. See Section Three, p. 4.

Fargo Record, July 1896. Interview with Frederick F. Gerard.

VII. Pamphlets

DuBois, Charles G., *Kick the Dead Lion*, Charles DuBois, Billings, Montana, (1961).

Dunn, Adrian R., "A History of Old Fort Berthold," report from *North Dakota History*, Vol. 30, No. 4 (October 1963).

Goplen, Arnold O., "The Historical Significance of Fort Lincoln State Park," reprint from *North Dakota History*, Vol. 13, No. 4 (October 1946).

Hammer, Kenneth, *Little Big Horn Biographies*, Revised Edition, (1965), Custer Battlefield Historical and Museums Association.

Hixon, John C., "Custer's Mysterious Mr. Kellogg," *North Dakota History*, Vol. 17, No. 3 (July 1950).

Holmes, Reuben, "The Five Scalps," reprint from *Missouri Historical Society Bulletin*, Vol. 5, Nos. 1-3, (January-March 1938).

Johnson, Roy P., "Jacob Horner of the 7th Cavalry," reprint from *North Dakota History*, Vol. 16, No. 2 (April 1949).

Kuhlman, Charles, *Custer and the Gall Saga*, Bellevue, Nebraska: The Old Army Press, (1969).

Marquis, Thomas B., *Sitting Bull - Gall, the Warrior*, Thomas B. Marquis, (1934).

_____, *Two Days After the Custer Battle*, Thomas B. Marquis, (1933).

_____, *Which Indian Killed Custer? - Custer Soldiers Not Buried*. Thomas B. Marquis, (1933).

Mattison, Ray H., "Fort Union: Its Role in the Upper Missouri Fur Trade," reprint from *North Dakota History*, Vol. 29, Nos. 1-2 (January-April 1962).

_____, "The Indian Frontier On the Upper Missouri to 1865," reprint from *Nebraska History*, Vol. 39, No. 3 (September 1958).

_____, "The Military Frontier On the Upper Missouri," reprint from *Nebraska History*, Vol. 37, No. 3 (September 1956).

_____, "The Upper Missouri Fur Trade: Its Methods of Operation," reprint from *Nebraska History*, Vol. 42, No. 1 (March 1961).

Pfaller, Rev. Louis, *Father DeSmet in Dakota*, Richardton, North Dakota: Assumption Abbey Press (1962).

_____, "The Killdeer Mountain and Badlands Battles," reprint from *North Dakota History*, Vol. 31, No. 1 (January 1964).

Praus, Alexis, *The Sioux, 1798-1922: A Dakota Winter Count*, Cranbrook Institute of Science, Bulletin Number 44 (1962).

Tostevin, Sarah, *Mantani*, Mandan, North Dakota: Mandan Chamber of Commerce (1964).

VIII. Manuscripts

Innis, Ben H., *The Great Buffalo Country Dictionary, Calendar and Atlas of Historical Events from 1670-1971*. Unpublished.

Innis, Ben H., *Elk River Soldier Lodge: Fort Buford*. Unpublished.

IX. Miscellaneous

Collin, Richard E., *The Fetterman Disaster*. Unpublished. April 12, 1977.

Leighton and Jordan, Post Trader's Ledger. Yellowstone Store Charge Account Book, July 1876-March 1877.

Sports Afield, September 1971.

X. Personal Visitations

Black Hills
Custer Battlefield
Fort Abraham Lincoln
Fort Buford
Fort Rice
Fort Seward
Fort Totten
Fort Union Trading Post
Fort Yates
Killdeer Mountain Battlefield
Pompey's Pillar

Index

A

Index 229

Index   **231**

Custer, Thomas W. 126-127, 142-143, 148, 168
"Custer's Luck" 187

D

E

F

K

Kansas 44, 121
Kellogg, Mark 138, 142, 150
Kelly, Luther S. 60-61, 95
Keogh, Myles 193
Ketchum, Hiram H. 105
Key West 95, 96, 98-99
Kimball, James P. 62-63, 66, 69, 77
Kiowa Indians 3, 187
Kipp, James 8, 14
Knife River 8, 14, 115
Kurz, Rudolph Friederich 24

L

La Barge, Harkness and Company 37
La France 54
Lambert, Joseph 76, 112
Lame Deer Fight 168, 195
Larpenteur, Charles 29, 72, 77, 90
Lead, South Dakota 170
Lean Bear 75-76
Leavenworth, Henry 10
Leech Lake, Minnesota 199
Leighton, Alvin C. 77
Leighton and Jordan 77, 85-86, 174-175
Leighton and Jordan Yellowstone Store 174
Leighton, James 86, 88
Lewis and Clark 5-7
Like-A-Fishhook Village 20, 28, 33
Lincoln, Abraham 43, 122, 180
Lisa, Manuel 6-8
Little Bighorn River 132, 142, 149, 152, 170, 191
Little Brave 157, 166
Little Crow 179-180
Little Missouri River 20, 45, 54, 123, 127, 139, 183
Little Muddy River 95 (*see also* Little Missouri River)
Little Sioux 155

Index 239

171, 173, 175-176, 191 (see also Man With the Dark Face)
Republican River 186
Reynolds, Charley 98,118,120-122,124,126,128,137,146-147, 149, 157, 161-162, 190
Reynolds, Joseph J. 189
Rocky Mountains 2
Roman Nose 186
Roosevelt, Franklin D. 170
Rose, Edward 7-8, 10-14
Rosebud River 29,120,140-142,144–145,165,189, 193
Ross, H.N. 118–119
Rosser, Thomas L. 98
Roulette 90 (see also Ba Ki Na)
"Royal Family" 143

S

Sahnish 3 (see also Arikara Indians, Ree Indians)
San Francisco, California 169
Sanborn Commission 185
Sanborn, John 185
Sans Arc Sioux Indians 28, 184, 193
Santa Fe, New Mexico 2, 44
Santee Sioux Indians 28, 36, 63, 117, 122-123, 179-180, 182
Schultz, James Willard 165
Senate, United States 25
Shahaka 7
She Owl 50, 96, 162
Sheridan, Philip H. 187
Sherman, William T. 71, 184-185
Shoshone Indians 85
Sibley, Henry H. 36, 180-182
Sibley, Minnesota 180
Sioux Indians 1, 3-5, 8, 17-19, 25, 28-29, 31-33, 39-41, 45-46, 51, 56, 58, 60-62, 65, 68, 72, 78, 91, 95-96, 97, 99-101, 103, 113-115, 119, 122-123, 125, 127-130, 132, 135, 137-138, 140, 142, 144-148, 151-152, 156, 158-160, 164-169,177-178, 180-186, 188, 189-194, 195, 197, 198
Sitting Bull 19-20, 22, 31, 51-52, 59-62, 66, 85, 91, 96, 123, 129, 163-166, 170, 179, 188, 191, 193-195 (see also Tatanka Iyotanka)
Slaughter, Benjamin F. 82, 97

Index

BLOODY KNIFE:
CUSTER'S FAVORITE SCOUT

To order additional copies,
send $18.95, plus $2 postage
& handling for each book.
(North Dakota residents add sales tax)

Mail to:
Smoky Water Press
P.O. Box 2322
Bismarck, ND 58502-2322
USA

**Also available as a book-on-cassette
from Meyer Creative Productions**

For ordering information call:
**1-800-ND SOUND
(1-800-637-6863)
or 701-223-7316**